Racial Attitudes
in America

SOCIAL
TRENDS
IN THE
UNITED
STATES

Editors

James A. Davis
John Modell

Committee on Social Indicators

Social Science Research Council

Racial Attitudes in America

Trends and Interpretations

Howard Schuman
Charlotte Steeh
Lawrence Bobo

Harvard University Press

Cambridge, Massachusetts
and London, England 1985

Library of Congress Cataloging in Publication Data

Schuman, Howard.
    Racial attitudes in America.

    (Social trends in the United States)
    Bibliography: p.
    Includes index.
    1. United States—Race relations—Public opinion—
History—20th century. 2. Social surveys—United States—
History—20th century. 3. Public opinion—United States—
History—20th century. I. Steeh, Charlotte. II. Bobo,
Lawrence. III. Title. IV. Series.
E185.615.S293 1985   303.3′87′0973   85-5606
ISBN 0-674-74574-4 (alk. paper)

Foreword

$\mathbf{F}$or much of the first half of this century, American social science was actively engaged in overcoming what Walter Lippmann in 1922 identified as "the central difficulty of self-government" in the modern world, namely, the difficulty of creating a public competent to confront complexity and change without retreating into political passivity. Quantitative social scientists set out to devise ways of tracking and analyzing change that would make it comprehensible to the public. Social "reporting," as originally conceived, was integral to the underlying political purpose of social science: the accommodation of a plurality of interests in the context of expanding popular expectations.

The classic monument to this commitment was the two-volume *Recent Social Trends,* prepared by the President's Research Committee on Recent Social Trends and published in 1933. The blending of science and public information characteristic of the day is expressed in the summary of the committee's findings: "in the formulation of . . . new and emergent values, in the construction of the new symbols to thrill men's souls, in the contrivance of the new institutions and adaptations useful in the fulfillment of new aspirations, we trust that this review of recent social trends may prove of value to the American public."

Optimism about the role of empirical social science continued

into the era of the Great Depression, although it came to emphasize the problems introduced by change rather than progressive improvements. This work nonetheless reflected engaged, hopeful
concern, as did the contributions of American social scientists to
the war effort that followed. When social science emerged from
World War II, however, its characteristic posture was far more
ironic than formerly, less confident in the meaning of its indicators,
more hermetic, more specialized. The task of systematic description and analysis of recent social change fell further away from the
ordinary activities of academic social scientists.

As editors of the series Social Trends in the United States, we
contend that social science has a collective responsibility to report
findings about society to the public, in order to contribute to the
informed choices that are necessary in a democracy. If the reports
of social scientists are to be useful to citizens, their authors must
define questions for educational and political relevance and must
translate technical terminology into the language of common dis-
course. Modern statistical methods make it possible to trace change
along a large number of dimensions in which the pattern of change
over time is rarely visible to people directly involved in it, and to
discern how change in one dimension may affect change in others.
Such information, in compact and comprehensible form, can make
a useful contribution to political discussion.

This is the rationale of the series, which is sponsored by the
Committee on Social Indicators of the Social Science Research
Council. The committee invites authoritative scholars to contribute manuscripts on particular topics and has other scholars review
each manuscript with attention to both the scientific and the
broadly educational purposes of the series. Nevertheless, the volumes in the series are the authors' own, and thus far from uniform.
Each is free-standing, but we hope that the effect of the series will
be cumulative. Taken together, these volumes will not constitute
an overall contemporary history: historical accounts evoke context
rather than extract single dimensions of change. The series, however, will provide insights into interconnected aspects of contemporary society that no contemporary history—and no one interested in understanding our present condition—should ignore.

The Social Indicators Committee of the Social Science Research

Council consists of Kenneth C. Land (Chair), University of Texas; Richard A. Berk, University of California, Santa Barbara; Martin H. David, University of Wisconsin; James A. Davis, Harvard University; Graham Kalton, University of Michigan; Kinley Larntz, University of Minnesota; John Modell, Carnegie-Mellon University; John F. Padgett, University of Chicago; and Stephen H. Schneider, National Center for Atmospheric Research, Boulder, Colorado. Richard C. Rockwell, Staff Associate at the Social Science Research Council, made indispensable contributions to the production of this volume.

James A. Davis
John Modell

Preface

Survey organizations began asking Americans about their attitudes toward racial issues in the 1940s. In this book we trace the changes in such attitudes over the past four decades indicated by national survey data, discuss interpretations of these changes that have been offered by various analysts, and present our own conclusions.

Although some of the trends we describe have been reported elsewhere, this is the first attempt to draw on all available trend data for both whites and blacks. We combine findings from the three major survey organizations that have collected such data over time: Gallup, the National Opinion Research Center (NORC), and the Institute for Social Research (ISR). This breadth makes possible comparisons that turn out to be illuminating. We also report several original experiments in supplementary surveys that throw light on issues raised by the main sources of data.

Trends in racial attitudes are a significant part of the larger picture of race in America, but they are obviously not the whole picture. In Chapter 1 we briefly sketch some historical elements that are useful to keep in mind as background, though this book cannot begin to cover the economic, political, legal, and other factors that contribute to the complexity of black-white relations in the United States. We certainly do not believe that American race relations should be studied only in attitudinal terms, but we do think that a knowledge of changes in black and white attitudes (and in the social norms that attitudes reflect) is important to an understanding of the changing meaning of race in this country from the 1940s to the present.

The order of authorship on the title page does not adequately describe contributions to this book. Lawrence Bobo, a graduate student when the study began, took an increasingly important role as the research progressed. He contributed in significant ways to the conceptual framework of the analysis, drafted Chapter 1, designed and drafted Appendix B on statistical testing, and provided crucial help in many other ways. Charlotte Steeh was responsible for locating, obtaining, and organizing most of the data we use; for drafting sections of Chapters 2 and 3 on sampling and cohort effects, as well as Appendix A; and for many other important steps in the design and execution of the study. Howard Schuman initiated the project and drafted most of Chapters 2–6; although drafts of all chapters went through joint revision, he is ultimately responsible for any limitations in the book.

Acknowledgment is due to Ronald Humphrey and Jacqueline Scott for their helpful research assistance; to Margaret Grillot and Nancy Crosbie for careful typing of several versions of the manuscript; and to Camille Smith, whose intelligent and thorough editing improved the book substantially.

The initial review process employed by the Social Science Research Council was extensive and intensive. We benefited greatly from suggestions from James A. Davis and John Modell, the editors of this series, from Robert Pearson of SSRC, and from Troy Duster, Reynolds Farley, Andrew M. Greeley, Paul Sheatsley, D. Garth Taylor, J. Mills Thornton III, Robin M. Williams, Jr., and William L. Yancey. Patrick Bova located and provided early NORC questionnaires, and Tom W. Smith answered numerous questions about recent NORC data.

A Guggenheim Fellowship allowed time for Howard Schuman to begin the project and develop its overall design. The collection and analysis of the data were supported by an NIMH Grant (MH 34116), with some supplementary help from the Social Science Research Council. The experiments on question form, wording, and context were part of methodological research supported by the National Science Foundation (SES-8016136). For all of these sources of support over several years we are most grateful, and of course none of the individuals and organizations that offered support is responsible for the specific conclusions we reach in the pages that follow.

Contents

*Racial Attitudes
in America*

1   Perspectives and Historical Background

"The pervasive gap between our aims and what we actually do," stated President Truman's Committee on Civil Rights in 1947, "is a kind of moral dry rot which eats away at the emotional and rational bases of democratic beliefs" (U.S. President's Committee on Civil Rights 1947:139). With these words and the moral undercurrent they epitomized, the committee's report, entitled *To Secure These Rights*, placed the rights and status of blacks and other American minorities high on the national agenda. Arguing that the treatment accorded blacks contravened the highest principles of American democracy, the committee called for the swift implementation of measures to assure the physical safety of blacks, to protect their right to vote in the South, and to improve their job opportunities, and beyond these specific steps it made a bold call for the desegregation of American life in general.

The committee was cautious in its assessment of the prospects for rapid change in American race relations. At several points the report addressed the difficulty of moving from abstract democratic principles to concrete implementation. Yet the report concluded on an optimistic note: "We would remind ourselves that the future of our nation rests upon the character, the vision, the high principle of our people" (p. 175).

1

This book is in part an assessment of whether that optimism of 1947 has proved to be well-founded. We are concerned with whether and to what extent the American people, in their beliefs and attitudes, have moved toward bridging the "pervasive gap" between our democratic ideals and our racial practices. What were the attitudes of white Americans toward their black fellow citizens during the period from the beginning of American involvement in World War II to the mid-1980s? Have the changes in white attitudes toward racial integration and toward blacks that were recorded in the 1950s and 1960s been reversed by public sentiment against policies such as school busing? Do blacks believe that progress is being made in eliminating discrimination? How different are the attitudes of blacks and whites on these and other racial issues? Although we offer no final answers to these questions, we present and attempt to interpret a remarkable "attitudinal record." This record consists of the replies of national samples of Americans to survey questions on racial issues asked over the span of years between 1942 and 1984. With this record we hope to document and make comprehensible the changing attitudes of the American people toward what W. E. B. DuBois in 1903 termed "the problem of the twentieth century . . . the problem of the color line" (DuBois 1961:23).

Many scholars have made predictions about the fate of attempts to resolve this problem, and racial attitudes have been a central consideration in such discussions. The tension created by the presence of a large and degraded black population in a nation founded on democratic ideals of equality has haunted American dialogue, ideas, and leaders for more than three hundred years. Thomas Jefferson, a preeminent figure in shaping American democracy in the eighteenth century, believed that a harmonious biracial society was inconceivable. "Deep rooted prejudices entertained by the whites," he wrote, and "ten thousand recollections, by the blacks, of the injuries they have sustained," combine to make equal, peaceful coexistence between blacks and whites impossible. Rather, Jefferson thought, the meeting of free blacks and whites would result in a conflict leading to "the extermination of the one or the other race" (1972:138).

Jefferson's apocalyptic outlook was echoed in the nineteenth century by Alexis de Tocqueville. Citing Jefferson to support his claims, Tocqueville argued that "Negroes and ... whites must either wholly part or wholly mingle" (1945:388). The latter outcome, a mixing of the races in common society, both these thinkers considered to be out of the question. Indeed, Tocqueville added, "I do not believe the white and black races will ever live in any country upon an equal footing" (1945:388–389).[1]

As the writings of Jefferson and Tocqueville suggest, racial imagery and beliefs have been influencing Americans since the founding of the first colonial settlements. Winthrop Jordan makes this clear in his book *White Over Black: American Attitudes toward the Negro, 1550–1812.* Jordan's concern with attitudes about race prompted him to write: "If it were possible to poll the inhabitants of Jamestown, Virginia, concerning their reaction to those famous first 'twenty Negars' who arrived in 1619 I would be among the first at the foot of the gangplank, questionnaire in hand" (1968:viii).

Some might question this concern with attitudes, since attitudes often seem to be only distantly related to behavior. These critics might ask: Is not the color line maintained or changed through actions rather than through thoughts or subjective preferences? Although this question must be answered in the affirmative, there are several important qualifications. Attitudes provide useful clues to a person's behavior, even though they are not always direct and powerful determinants of the behavior. For example, verbally expressed white opposition to school busing has been very high, between 80 and 90 percent, for more than ten years (1972–1983). The hard facts of protest movements and violence, seemingly endless litigation and legislation, and significant white flight to suburban areas not touched by desegregation orders all attest to the relevance of these "softer" attitudinal indicators. There is, in fact, growing evidence that attitudes have considerable influence on participation in antibusing movements (Useem 1980; Begley and Alker 1982). (See Chapter 2 for further discussion of the linkage between attitudes and behavior.)

Beyond their importance to a full understanding of past and potential behavior, attitudes are a central element of the larger social climate. The racial beliefs and opinions characteristic of whites in the 1940s surely established an atmosphere in which behavioral racism and discrimination could flourish with little challenge. The social norms of the time did not clearly condemn the relegation of blacks to a subordinate, segregated, and impoverished status. Moreover, race relations involve more than just external and material ingredients like housing patterns, incomes, or educational attainments, though all of these are major determinants of the quality of life. There are also cultural, intrapersonal, and interpersonal aspects that affect the subjective experience of white and black Americans. Although attitudinal expressions gathered through survey questionnaires provide only a partial view of these deeper, inner states, they are a rich source of information on the intrinsic human meaning of race in America.

Contemporary discussions of the state of American thinking about race, and of the course that racial attitudes are likely to follow in the years ahead, reveal no consensus. Assessments range from almost jubilant optimism at one extreme to bleak depictions of stagnation, resistance, and backlash at the other. We will refer to these two outlooks as the Progressive Trend and Underlying Racism schools of thought. (In Chapter 5 we will elaborate this broad division into a more detailed treatment of specific theories of racial attitudes.)

Progressive Trend

The predominant finding of survey research on racial attitudes has been that things have changed greatly for the better. "The mass of white Americans," wrote Paul Sheatsley in 1966, "have shown in many ways that they do not want a racist government and that they will not follow racist leaders." In fact, he continued, most white Americans "are engaged in the painful task of adjusting to an integrated society. It will not be easy for most, but one cannot at this late date doubt the basic commitment" (1966:237). Sheatsley's conclusions were based on a consideration of attitude data, some of it extending back to 1942, collected by several survey organizations, especially the National Opinion Research Center (NORC). In particular, he reported, trends in support for school integration, residential integration, and the desegregation of public transportation had all undergone extraordinary upturns between 1942 and 1963.

The trends on many of these issues showed continued improvement in the late 1960s and into the 1970s (see Chapter 3). A pattern emerged of such consistent liberalization in the attitudes of white Americans toward blacks that some later analysts, investigating the question of whether there had been a backlash, would find no evidence of retrenchment: "The facts do not support the common assumption that the pace of liberalization in racial matters has been slowed by a white backlash"; if anything, "the rate of change toward a more integrationist attitude has been rather constant since 1963, with a short period of faster change in the early 1970s" (Taylor, Sheatsley, and Greeley 1978:45). Thus at least some of the survey data suggest that white attitudes shifted from widespread acceptance of segregation and discrimination in the 1940s to a new and equally widespread commitment to tolerance, racial equality, and integration in the 1970s.

Underlying Racism

Other analysts of racial attitudes are in strong disagreement with the Progressive Trend perspective. They use terms like "resistance," "eroding commitment," and especially "white backlash" to characterize white attitudes. Discussions of white retrenchment and intransigence intensified around the time of the urban riots in the North and the growth of the Black Power Movement, which briefly eclipsed legalistic and nonviolent strategies of black protest. This was also a time when the focus of civil rights attention moved from Southern white recalcitrance to national issues like open housing and school busing.

After reviewing several research reports on racial attitudes and examining the statements of prominent white intellectuals and politically oriented journals, Faustine Jones concluded that, around 1969, "There [was] a changing mood in the dominant society. This changing mood [was] more negative than positive with respect to the aspirations of blacks, other minorities, and the poor" (1977:77–78). Although Jones pointed to many indicators of an "eroding commitment" to racial justice, the main bases for her conclusion were the negative reactions of whites to school busing, affirmative action, and other attempts to *implement* racial integration and equality.

In a somewhat similar vein, David Sears and his colleagues interpret some of the available survey data as evidence that a new expression of prejudice against blacks is now influencing American politics. The segregationist statements and biological racism of the post–Civil War era, they agree, have essentially vanished. But prejudiced attitudes have not vanished; instead they are now expressed in "abstract, moralistic resentments of blacks." The resentments are based in the belief that "blacks violate such traditional American values as individualism and self-reliance, the work ethic, obedience, and discipline" (Kinder and Sears 1981:416). This new, sophisticated prejudice, or as Sears and his colleagues term it, "symbolic racism," is most evident, they claim, in white opposition to busing and in white unwillingness to vote for black political candidates (see also Sears, Hensler, and Speer 1979; McConahay 1982).

A Third Alternative:
Progress and Resistance

It is possible to marshal attitudinal and behavioral evidence to support both the Progressive Trend and the Underlying Racism theses. On the positive side, American society today is characterized by scenes that would have been inconceivable forty, or even twenty, years ago. Blacks and whites work side by side in many settings, with a level of intimacy that produced antiblack strikes and riots in the 1940s. Interracial couples or groups, once rare and controversial in both North and South, seldom draw much attention today. Such instances of greater interpersonal tolerance—instances of white America taking racial change in stride—complement indicators of the improved political and economic status of blacks. But alongside these scenes of a more racially equalitarian America, there are the images of angry mobs stoning school buses and of staunch resistance to affirmative action programs. Moreover, this less optimistic portrait of blacks and whites is reinforced by racial disparities in earnings, occupations, and educational attainment, which though less dramatic than in the past remain large and problematic. Perhaps most important of all, the degree of segregation of blacks and whites into separate neighborhoods seems to change at a glacial pace at best.

Social psychologist Angus Campbell once commented on the complexities of American race relations: "The racial situation in the United States defies understanding. The complexity and variety of the relationships between members of the two major races is so great that both white people and black tend to rely on simple generalities which reduce the problem to manageable terms" (1971:155). In this book we will attempt to make this complex racial situation more comprehensible. The first and foremost guidepost in our efforts to make sense of the attitudinal record is a liberating assumption: signs of progress on one aspect of racial attitudes, for instance willingness to accept integrated schools, do not invalidate evidence of lack of progress on another aspect, such as unwillingness to accept school busing. Similarly, evidence of resistance in one domain, such as affirmative action, does not render meaningless improvements in attitudes in another domain, such as open housing legislation. The race question, the problem of the color line, is now composed of many different issue domains, such as schooling, politics, and jobs, economic assistance and affirmative action, housing and interpersonal contact. Historical and other complexities in the development of attitudes make each of these domains unique, though each is related to the other areas. It is therefore unlikely that any "simple and sovereign" interpretation of the data on racial attitudes will do justice to the underlying complexities. Acknowledging the implausibility of simple or categorical interpretations, however, does not rule out the prospect of arriving at meaningful conclusions. (Others have also argued that racial progress and resistance to change can be seen as parts of a meaningful whole; see, for example, Levine 1971; Rothbart 1976; Pettigrew 1979.)

A genuine grasp of the changing character of American racial attitudes can be attained if we are sensitive to the history behind changes in attitudes, the limitations of survey data, and the need to weigh all of the data before drawing conclusions.

In the remainder of this chapter we summarize the historical events pertinent to racial change over the past forty years. We do not attempt an original or detailed history of the period. But a review of some of the significant events will make more understandable our later consideration of trends in attitudes. As important as the inner thoughts and preferences of blacks and whites are, historian Ronald Takaki is right to chastise researchers for tending "to isolate racism as a history of attitudes" (1979:xiii). Other economic, political, intellectual, and legal matters must also rank as significant concerns. Six interrelated aspects of recent history are especially pertinent here: (1) a period of prelude to civil rights politics, which involved the discrediting of theories of biological racism, massive black out-migration from the South, and substantial black involvement in World War II; (2) the growing importance of "black ballots" in American electoral politics; (3) the establishment of effective civil rights organizations and protest movements; (4) crucial Supreme Court rulings; (5) the passage of landmark legislation pledging the federal government to protect the rights of black Americans; and (6) a more recent period of disputes over the unfinished civil rights agenda.

Historical Background

Through the late nineteenth and early twentieth centuries, most whites, North and South, considered blacks to be their biological and social inferiors (Fredrickson 1971; Litwack 1961; Takaki 1979). The difference between this period and that of Jefferson and Tocqueville lay in the full development and flourishing of highly intellectualized theories of "biological racism." The proponents of segregation and white supremacy who ushered in the Jim Crow laws of the late 1880s and 1890s pegged their antiblack ideology on notions of social Darwinism that were fashionable at the time. The *Plessy v. Ferguson* ruling of 1896, which proclaimed "separate but equal" facilities to be constitutional, was the political and intellectual capstone of this later era. Justice Brown, writing for the majority, said:

> Legislation is powerless to eradicate racial instincts or to abolish distinctions based upon physical differences, and the attempt to do so can only result in accentuating the difficulties of the present situation. If the civil and political rights of both races be equal one cannot be inferior to the other civilly or politically. If one race be inferior to the other socially, the Constitution of the United States cannot put them on the same plane. (163 U.S. 537, 16 S. Ct. 1138, 41 L. Ed. 256 [1896], pp. 550–551)

It is evident that the ideas and opinions of the day were significant forces in shaping the *Plessy* ruling. As one writer suggests, the ruling was "redolent with [then popular] sociological speculation, permeated with theories of social Darwinism, and carr[ied] overtones of white racial supremacy as scientific truth" (Harris 1960:98).[2]

Prelude to Civil Rights Politics

Despite some erosion of faith in the applicability of "Darwinism" to human groups, in the 1930s and early 1940s many whites still believed that blacks were an inferior people. Data collected by NORC, for example, indicate that more than half of the white population surveyed in 1942 assumed that blacks were less intelligent than whites. At the same time, 54 percent opposed the integration of public transportation, and 64 percent supported racially segregated schools. But a general shift in the thinking of American scientists and scholars had begun in the 1920s and accelerated in reaction to Nazi racism during the 1930s and 1940s. The new intellectual currents were quickly made applicable to the situation of blacks in America. Indeed, the late 1930s have been characterized as a period when

> the research of biologists, psychologists, and social scientists undermined the shibboleths long used to rationalize second-class citizenship for blacks. A new intellectual consensus emerged. It rejected the notion of innate black inferiority; it emphasized the damage done by racism; and it depicted prejudice as a sickness, afflicting both individuals and the very well-being of the nation. (Sitkoff 1978:190)

An example of this change can be found in research by social psychologist Otto Klineberg. Klineberg dealt a serious blow to a key element of the "scientific" case for black inferiority by challenging the results of IQ tests administered by the army in World War I, which showed blacks scoring lower than whites. He demonstrated that such environmental factors as more education, higher socioeconomic status, and exposure to Northern culture improved blacks' scores markedly (see Sitkoff 1978).

The war against Hitler's Germany drove racist doctrines into further disrepute. "American war propaganda stressed above all else," wrote historian C. Vann Woodward, "the abhorrence of the West for Hitler's brand of racism and its utter incompatibility with the democratic faith for which we fought" (1974:131). Thus, both scholarly research and wartime propaganda began to lay a cultural basis for challenging racial discrimination and inequality in America.

One of the most significant pieces of scholarship to come out of this era was Gunnar Myrdal's monumental work *An American Dilemma: The Negro Problem and Modern Democracy* (1944). Myrdal addressed America's treatment of blacks as a significant moral issue and as a major challenge to the national democratic tradition. He pointed out a fundamental contradiction between America's highest values of "liberty, equality, justice, and fair opportunity for everybody," and the degraded position of blacks in society:

> The American Negro problem is a problem in the heart of the American. It is there that the interracial tension has its focus. It is there that the decisive struggle goes on ... The "American Dilemma". . . is the ever raging conflict between, on the one hand, the valuations preserved on the general plane which we shall call the "American Creed," where the American thinks, talks, and acts under the influence of high national and Christian precepts, and, on the other hand, the valuations on specific planes of individual and group living, where personal and local interests; economic, social, and sexual jealousies; considerations of community prestige and conformity; group prejudice against particular persons or types of people; and all sorts of miscellaneous wants, impulses, and habits dominate his outlook. (1944:lxix)

An American Dilemma not only furthered the trend toward racial equalitarianism in American ideas but also documented in remarkable breadth and detail the features of discrimination against blacks. A key facet of discrimination, then as now, was limited black access to jobs. As Myrdal noted, World War II was "of tremendous importance to the Negro in all respects," especially in terms of new job opportunities. The war, he suggested, would create for blacks a new "strategic position strengthened not only because of the desperate scarcity of labor but also because of the revitalization of the democratic Creed" (p. 409). At that time blacks were still excluded from work in many industries and even when hired were generally restricted to unskilled work. Nonetheless, World War II, like World War I before it, drew Southern blacks in record numbers to the industrial centers of the North. It is estimated that 1.5 million blacks left the South between 1940 and 1950 in response to the pull of wartime jobs and the push of growing mechanization in agriculture in the South (Farley 1968).

The wartime upturn in the economy did not, however, provide peaceful entrance into the job market for blacks. By one estimate, during the month of March 1943 alone, "102,000 man-days of war production time" were lost "through hate strikes directed against the employment or upgrading of black workers" (Newman et al. 1978:12). Walter White, then executive secretary of the National Association for the Advancement of Colored People (NAACP), recalled one such striker as saying, "I'd rather see Hitler and Hirohito win the war than work beside a nigger on the assembly line" (see Wilkins 1982:182). The city of Detroit, the destination for many blacks seeking jobs, experienced violent racial disturbances in June 1943. During the rioting more than $2 million in damage was done and 34 people (25 blacks and 9 whites) were killed (U.S. National Advisory Commission on Civil Disorders 1968:104).

Blacks in the 1940s were not without advocates who tried to secure and protect their rights. Under the threat of a massive "March on Washington" organized by black labor leader A. Philip Randolph, in June 1941 President Roosevelt issued Executive Order 8802, which was intended to ban discrimination in all defense plants and branches of the federal government. The order also created the President's Committee on Fair Employment Practices, which later became the Fair Employment Practices Commission. This order, the most important federal effort since Reconstruction, was a great symbolic victory even though it lacked provisions for enforcement.

During the New Deal era and World War II blacks gained access to the ranks of several labor unions, in particular those of the newly formed Congress of Industrial Organizations (CIO). Prior to their acceptance by white labor organizations, blacks seeking jobs often were forced into the role of low-wage strikebreakers.[3] Even after blacks moved into the union rank and file, however, it was rare for them to rise to positions of much influence within unions; segregation of work groups continued and jobs with lower skill levels and limited chances for advancement were often reserved for blacks. Nonetheless, participation in previously all-white labor unions improved blacks' prospects for moving into the economic mainstream. In the words of historians August Meier and Elliot Rudwick, "the CIO's contribution to the changing patterns of race relations has been incalculable. It made interracial trade unionism truly respectable." Moreover, by opening membership to blacks, the CIO began to engender in "black and white workers a sense of common interest, of solidarity, that transcended racial lines" (1976:262).[4]

The changing intellectual currents, shifts in the regional composition of the black population, and improving job prospects were all significant, but they were far from being fundamental transformations in the second-class status of black Americans. World War II was basically a Jim Crow war, with separate units, quarters, and duty assignments for black and white soldiers (see Bogart 1969; Dalfiume 1969). Not until July 1948, when President Truman, under pressure from A. Philip Randolph and the NAACP, issued Executive Order 9981, were segregation and discrimination in the military forbidden. Roy Wilkins, who would follow Walter White as NAACP executive secretary, recounts the cruel contradictions of American policies during the war:

> Negroes did not need us at the NAACP to tell them that it sounded pretty foolish to be against park benches marked JUDE in Berlin, but to be *for* park benches marked COLORED in Tallahassee, Florida. It was grim, not foolish, to have a young black man in uniform get an orientation in the morning on wiping out Nazi bigotry and that same evening be told he could buy a soft drink only in the "colored" post exchange. (1982:184–185)

The discriminatory treatment accorded black soldiers was a poignant display of the depth of the "American Dilemma," but the basic contradiction was apparent in many other domains as well. In 1940 black educational attainment was well below that of whites (Newman et al. 1978:70); the average black male had completed about seven years of schooling, as against approximately ten years for white males (Farley 1984:17). In 1947 the median income of black families was only 51 percent of that of white families (Newman et al. 1978:269). The occupational distributions of blacks and whites were also markedly disparate: in 1940, only 3 percent of employed black men worked in professional, managerial, or other technical jobs, as compared with 16 percent of white men; 41 percent of black men were involved in some farm-related occupation, as compared to only 21 percent of white men; fully 59 percent of black women in the labor force were employed as maids and domestics, more than five times the percentage (11 percent) of white women holding such jobs; and fewer than 6 percent of black women held professional or managerial positions, as compared with 19 percent of white women (U.S. Bureau of the Census 1969:116). The weight of these inequalities was, to some extent, reflected in life expectancy figures: black life expectancy at birth in 1942 was 57 years, a full 10 years below that of whites (U.S. Bureau of the Census 1980:96–97).

These economic and other handicaps were supported by the segregation of schools, housing, and public accommodations. Racial segregation was a matter of law and preeminent social concern in the South, and often a matter of custom and social expectations in the North. One indicator of the pervasiveness of racial segregation can be drawn from "segregation indexes" based on Census housing data. A segregation index, used by Karl and Alma Taeuber, indicates the percentage of blacks "that would have to shift from one block to another to effect an unsegregated distribution" of homes (Taeuber and Taeuber 1965:30). In 1940 the average segregation index score for 107 cities in the United States, North and South, was 85.2 percent.[5] On average, a shift of well over four-fifths of the black population in these cities would have been required to eliminate residential segregation. In the Taeubers' words:

> No further analysis is necessary to reach some broad generalizations concerning segregation: In the urban United States, there is a very high degree of segregation of the residences of whites and Negroes. This is true for cities in all regions of the country and for all types of cities—large and small, industrial and commercial, metropolitan and suburban. It is true whether there are hundreds of thousands of Negro residents, or only a few thousand. Residential segregation prevails regardless of the relative economic status of the white and Negro residents. It occurs regardless of the character of local laws

and policies, and regardless of the extent of other forms of segregation or discrimination. (1965:35–36)

The Black Ballot

Even though in the 1940s blacks seemed to be locked into a segregated and inferior social and economic status, several signs of progress were emerging, especially in politics. One of the portentous results of black out-migration from the South was the growing power of black ballots in the North. Each black person "going to the North meant another potential voter pressuring both parties for civil rights legislation" (Sitkoff 1971:605). These voters would come to rank among the most persistent and persuasive forces for black civil rights.

Politics and the ballot box were not entirely new to blacks even in the South. During the Reconstruction period and shortly thereafter, under the protective presence of federal troops, blacks began to participate in politics. In the years between the passage of the Military Reconstruction Acts of 1867 and the removal of all federal troops in 1876–77, around 800 blacks in the South were elected to public office (U.S. Bureau of the Census 1979:155).

By the early 1900s, however, in the absence of federal scrutiny and protection, black disfranchisement had been effectively reinstated by Southern constitutional conventions and legislatures. For example, "two years before Louisiana revised its constitution in 1898, some 130,000 Negroes were registered to vote; in 1900, only 5000 blacks remained on the rolls. In Virginia the effect of the constitutional provisions was to reduce the black electorate from 147,-000 to 21,000" (Lawson 1976:14–15). Such racial discrimination in voting had been prohibited in principle by the Fifteenth Amendment to the U.S. Constitution, but Southern states enacted a number of ostensibly "color blind" voting restrictions that actually kept blacks off the voting rolls. For example, Oklahoma adopted a permanent Grandfather Clause exempting all people eligible to vote prior to the Civil War and their descendants—that is, whites only—from the requirement that they be literate in order to register to vote (ibid.:12, 18–19). Several other states, such as Louisiana and Alabama, adopted similar provisions on a temporary basis. Even when blacks managed to register, the imposition of poll taxes prevented many of them, along with large numbers of poor whites, from exercising their right to vote. Literacy and character tests, complex registration procedures, separate "white primaries" conducted by the state Democratic parties in the South, registrar malfeasance, and direct acts of intimidation were other tools for stifling black suffrage.

These measures were so effective that Ralph Bunche, who had conducted research on black political participation for Myrdal, reported that "of a total Negro adult population of 3,651,256 in the 8 Deep Southern states (excluding Oklahoma) of Alabama, Georgia, Mississippi, Louisiana, Florida, Texas, South Carolina, and Arkansas . . . only 80,000 to 90,000 . . . voted in the general election of 1940" (Myrdal 1944:475). If the higher estimate of 90,000 is taken as accurate, then fewer than 3 percent of Southern black adults participated in electoral politics in 1940, far below what might have been expected in the absence of extensive disfranchisement and intimidation. Myrdal summarized the situation quite accurately: "The concern of the Southern Negroes is not how they shall use their votes but how to get their constitutional right to vote respected at all" (1944:512).

Among the best hopes for securing the right to vote was the growing potency of black ballots in the North. The influence of black votes upon Northern politicians and national politics first became apparent in the election of 1936 and gained even more prominence in the election of 1948. Blacks had voted disproportionately Republican in 1932, when Roosevelt was first elected to the presidency (see Myrdal 1944:493–495; Sitkoff 1978:95–96). By 1936, as New Deal programs began to ease black poverty, civil rights leaders exhorted black people to recall that the party of Lincoln was also the party of Hoover. They served notice to Democrats and Republicans alike that they would encourage the expanding ranks of black voters to support the party that took the strongest stand in favor of civil rights. Both parties responded by courting black votes as never before. The Republicans adopted a platform supporting anti-lynching legislation and opposing discrimination. Democrats, who for the first time had black delegates at their nominating convention, worked closely with civil rights activists to get out the black vote, and generally "emphasized the economic assistance given blacks by the Roosevelt administration" (Sitkoff 1978:94). In the end, blacks "abandoned the party of Lincoln and joined the party of Roosevelt" (Lawson 1976:21), and did so in such substantial numbers as to "persuade many a civil rights leader and white politician that the Negro vote had become a balance of power in national elections" (Sitkoff 1978:97).

By 1948 the influence of white liberals and civil rights activists in the Democratic party was substantial and had begun to rankle the party's Southern members. In February of that year, responding to the demands of black leaders and to the report of his Committee on Civil Rights, President Truman called for legislation "to abolish the poll tax, make lynching a federal crime, curtail discrimination in employment, and prohibit segregation in interstate commerce" (Sitkoff 1971:600). Southern politicians were outraged. They denounced these plans as the work of liberals out to "Harlemize" the nation, threatened to bolt the party, and buttressed their threats by convincing Southern contributors to cancel several hundred thousand dollars in pledges to the Democratic National Committee (ibid.:601–603).

Truman had apparently underestimated the severity of the Southern response. During the next few months he attempted to placate Southern Democrats by distancing himself from his earlier proposals. These efforts were stymied, however, by a coalition of liberals, civil rights leaders, and labor leaders, who succeeded in having the party platform endorse the original proposals. The Democratic convention of 1948 erupted into applause when Mayor Hubert Humphrey of Minneapolis declared: "The time has arrived for the Democratic party to get out of the shadow of states' rights and walk into the bright sunshine of human rights" (quoted in Ashmore 1982:124). Southern discontent was increased further during the campaign when Truman issued Executive Orders 9980 and 9981. The latter order, as mentioned earlier, desegregated the military, while the former created a Fair Employment Practices board within the Civil Service Commission to assure blacks fair treatment in federal employment (Newman et al. 1978:51).

The defiant splinter candidacy of "Dixiecrat" Strom Thurmond notwithstanding, the civil rights platform, both executive orders, and a last-minute appeal to black voters in the North helped to secure a victory for Truman in 1948. "Dewey would have won," according to Harvard Sitkoff, "if Truman had not polled a higher percentage of the Negro vote than Roosevelt had done in any of his four presidential victories"; in fact, "Truman's plurality of Negro votes in California, Illinois, and Ohio provided the margin of victory" (1971:613). Thus, the election of 1948 placed civil rights high on the national agenda and helped force national leaders to address the pervasive gap between the American creed and the position of blacks in society. As Roy Wilkins saw it: "The message was plain: white power in the South could be balanced by black power at the Northern polls. Civil rights were squarely at the heart of national politics—if we could keep them there" (1982:202).

Although the election of 1948 *seemed* to be a civil rights watershed, white public opinion at the time was mixed on the "Negro problem." The Gallup Poll asked a national sample of Americans about their attitudes toward anti-lynching legislation, the segregation of public transportation, federal efforts to end job discrimination, abolition of the poll tax, and the Truman proposals as a whole. The poll, taken in March 1948, indicated that some 56 percent of those surveyed felt that the Truman proposals, taken "as a whole," should *not* be passed (Gallup 1972:722–723). There were marked North-South differences on some of the more specific measures: over 60 percent of Southern respondents but only 38 percent of Northern respondents were against allowing the federal government to intervene in lynchings; 84 percent of Southerners but only 36 percent of Northerners thought blacks should be "required to occupy a separate part of a train or bus when travelling from one state to another." On the question of federal action to end job discrimination, however, 68 percent in the South and 42 percent in the North, a plurality in both regions, thought the federal government "should do nothing." Abolition of the poll tax elicited more substantial support: 65 percent nationally and a plurality, 48 percent, in the South (ibid.:748). In sum, white public opinion was far from unanimous on any aspect of the Truman proposals, even on the poll tax, which kept many whites from voting and constituted one of the most egregious restrictions of the basic rights of citizens in a democracy.

The Civil Rights Movement and the Courts

The struggle to implement the types of changes advocated by Truman's Committee on Civil Rights would be a long one. As journalist Harry Ashmore put it, "no one in Washington believed that there was any chance of getting the package through Congress without drastic revision. Its introduction was [largely] a symbolic gesture" (1982:121). Nonetheless, there were many who tried to capitalize on the gains made in 1948. Most important in these efforts would be several civil rights organizations, especially the NAACP.

After a serious race riot in Springfield, Illinois, in 1908, William Walling called for "a revival of the spirit of the Abolitionists to win liberty and justice for the Negro in America" (Myrdal 1944:819). Walling, along with Mary White Ovington and Henry Moskowitz, then began plans for what would become the NAACP. Founded in 1909 by black leaders like W. E. B. DuBois and progressive whites like Oswald Garrison Villard and Jane Addams (see Meier and Rudwick 1976:227–228; Myrdal 1944:819-822), the NAACP was dedicated from its inception to improving the legal and material status of black Americans, changing the attitudes of whites toward blacks, and furthering the cause of racial equality and integration. These ambitious goals—and they were certainly ambitious in the early 1900s and even in the 1940s—were the embodiment of civil rights militancy to white Americans at the time.

During its early years the militants of the NAACP championed the drive for anti-lynching legislation and fought the appointment of avowed racists to high government office. They also intervened where they could to protect black people from the caprice and malice of "Southern Justice" and all-white juries. These individual cases, however, were but a small part of the NAACP's larger goal of fundamentally altering the legal status of blacks as a group. This goal linked the NAACP to the courts, especially the U.S. Supreme Court.

An example of the significance of the linkage between the NAACP and the courts can be found in efforts to secure the ballot for Southern blacks. The NAACP scored its first victory in voting rights in 1915 when the Grandfather Clause was declared unconstitutional.[6] The NAACP then sought other cases that might be used to test the constitutionality of voting hindrances aimed at blacks. In the 1940s, under the legal stewardship of Thurgood Marshall, the organization set out to eliminate white primaries. On April 3, 1944, in the case of *Smith v. Allwright,* the Supreme Court sided with the NAACP and ruled the white primary to be unconstitutional.

A decade later a similar but far more consequential victory was achieved in the area of school segregation. On May 17, 1954, Chief Justice Earl Warren read the text of the Court's decision in *Brown v. Board of Education of Topeka.* The direction of the ruling became evident when he read: "We come then to the question presented: Does segregation of children in public schools solely on the basis of race, even though the physical facilities and other 'tangible' factors may be equal, deprive the children of the minority group of equal education opportunities? We believe it does." In this short, unencumbered, and unprovocative paragraph, the *Plessy* doctrine of "separate but equal" had been overturned. Several paragraphs later Chief Justice Warren departed from his prepared manuscript with the addition of just one word: "We conclude—*unanimously*—that in the field of public education the doctrine of 'separate but equal' has no place. Separate educational facilities are inherently unequal" (see Kluger 1975:707). Jim Crow was now on the defensive. The largest legal step since Reconstruction had been taken toward closing the pervasive gap between the American creed and the day-to-day lives of black Americans.

Reactions to *Brown* were quick in coming. Herman Talmadge, then governor of Georgia, accused the justices of having "reduced the Constitution to a 'mere scrap of paper.'" Senator James O. Eastland of Mississippi vowed to fight the ruling, declaring that "the South . . . 'will not abide by or obey this legislative decision by a political court'" (see ibid.:710). But those at NAACP headquarters in New York sensed that a new era was beginning. Roy Wilkins described their feeling:

> Later in the day Thurgood came back from Washington. I heard a commotion in the corridors outside my office—laughing and cheering—then the door flew open and Thurgood walked in and kissed me. Later that afternoon we held a press conference, and Walter [White] did the talking while Thurgood sat quietly in the background. I can still see him sitting there, smiling slightly. Plessy-

Ferguson was through. An American Joshua in the person of Thurgood Marshall fit the battle of Jericho and the walls came tumbling. (1982:213)

Thurgood Marshall would later comment on that day: "I was so happy I was numb." He was happy enough, indeed, to venture the prediction that racially segregated schools would be eliminated within five years (Kluger 1975:706).

Marshall's forecast regarding the implementation of school desegregation was as inaccurate as the Court's ruling was historic. The Court knew that making its ruling a part of daily practice would be no simple task. In the final paragraph of the opinion the justices called for more arguments on how a compliance decree should be drafted.

To further the process of adjustment, the Court kept the *Brown* opinion itself short, clear, and understandable by a lay audience. There was an evident need to persuade as well as to adjudicate. "You know," said Justice Clark, "we don't have money at the Court for an army, and we can't take ads in the newspaper, and we don't want to go out on a picket line in our robes. We have to convince the nation by the force of our opinions" (ibid.).

Public opinion on the ruling was sharply divided by region. In 1954 the Gallup Poll asked the following question: "The Supreme Court has ruled that racial segregation in the public schools is illegal. This means that all children, no matter what their race, must be allowed to go to the same school. Do you approve or disapprove of this decision?" Only 24 percent of Southern respondents, in contrast to 60 percent of Northern respondents, approved (A. W. Smith 1981:580).

A favorable climate of opinion in the North was not enough to implement the *Brown* decision. The job of forcing the hand of Southern politicians and citizens fell to black activists and whites sympathetic to their cause. A milestone event presented itself on December 1, 1955, when Mrs. Rosa Parks, a seamstress and secretary of the Montgomery NAACP, refused to give up her seat on a bus to a white passenger. The bus driver threatened to have her arrested for violating the local segregation ordinance, which required her to yield her seat when instructed to do so. Mrs. Parks replied, "Go on and have me arrested" (Sitkoff 1981:42). News of her arrest spread quickly through the black community. E. D. Nixon, a former president of the Alabama NAACP and the president of the Montgomery local of the Brotherhood of Sleeping Car Porters, was certain that the arrest would lead to a crucial test case of forced segregation in Alabama. He also believed that blacks could play a more direct role in winning their rights by boycotting the buses. One of the first men to whom Nixon took his plan was a local minister, Dr. Martin Luther King, Jr.

Nixon, King, and nearly fifty other prominent blacks organized a boycott to begin on December 5. Nearly 100 percent of the black bus ridership found other means of transportation that day. For 381 days thereafter, and in the face of constant intimidation, black citizens of Montgomery shared taxis, carpooled, rode mules, hitchhiked, and walked, in their collective determination to make Jim Crow yield. "Once a car-pool driver chanced on an old woman hobbling along with great difficulty, and he offered her a ride. She waved him on. 'I'm not walking for myself,' she said. 'I'm walking for my children and my grandchildren' " (Oates 1982:76).

In addition to demonstrating the passionate desire of Southern blacks for their full measure of human rights and the extent to which they would engage in mass protest to gain those rights, the Montgomery bus boycott propelled 26-year-old Martin Luther King, Jr., pastor of the small Dexter Avenue Baptist Church, to the forefront of the civil rights crusade. It was during the Montgomery protest that King's image as an American Gandhi began to take shape, as his strategy of nonviolent protest assumed palpable and effective form.

King spoke on December 5, 1955, at the first mass meeting held to dramatize the bus boycott. He opened his largely extemporaneous address by pointing out that democracy was more than an abstract set of values recorded on paper, but rather concerned moral principles that had to be "transformed from thin paper to thick action" (Oates 1982:70). He talked of the human dimension of the pervasive gap between American principles and practices:

> There comes a time when people get tired. We are here this evening to say to those who have mistreated us so long that we are tired—tired of being segregated and humiliated, tired of being kicked about by the brutal feet of oppression. We have no alterna-

tive but to protest. For many years we have shown amazing patience. We have sometimes given our white brothers the feeling that we liked the way we were being treated. But we come here tonight to be saved from that patience that makes us patient with anything less than freedom and justice (Sitkoff 1981:50).

And he discussed how the struggle to close the gap must be carried out: "In our protest, there will be no cross burnings. No white person will be taken from his home by a hooded Negro mob and brutally murdered. There will be no threats and intimidation. We will be guided by the highest principles of law and order" (Oates 1982:71). When King finished, the massive crowd of listeners were clapping, yelling, and crying for joy. The struggle for black freedom had been elevated to a new stage, and a leader with a voice to move people to action had stepped forward.

Less than a year after the end of the successful bus boycott, a major civil rights confrontation occurred in Little Rock, Arkansas. In defiance of a federal court order and the plans of the local school board, Governor Orval Faubus ordered the National Guard to prevent nine black students from entering all-white Central High School. Faubus's actions precipitated a direct clash with federal authority and prompted President Eisenhower to federalize the Arkansas National Guard. The President dispatched a thousand troops to protect the handful of black students from angry white mobs and to ensure compliance with the court order. Before the troops arrived, crowds of whites milled outside the high school shouting slogans like "Two, four, six, eight, we ain't gonna integrate," and "Niggers keep away from our school. Go back to the jungle." In Eisenhower's words, failure to uphold the court order in the face of such incipient mob violence would have been "tantamount to acquiescence in anarchy and the dissolution of the union" (Sitkoff 1981:32).

Another situation in which an American President was forced to use federal troops to bring Southern whites into compliance with the law of the land took place in Oxford, Mississippi, when James Meredith attempted to become the first black student at the University of Mississippi. Meredith applied for admission to Ole Miss in January 1961, just days after John F. Kennedy was inaugurated as President. Meredith was initially refused admission, but with the assistance of attorneys from the NAACP won a federal court ruling that he had the legal right to enroll and attend classes. Mississippi Governor Ross Barnett called for resistance and "asked a statewide television audience to join in opposing the federal government's policy of racial genocide" (Brauer 1977:181). Again there were large white crowds chanting racial epithets. Violence broke out on September 30, 1962, the day before Meredith was to enroll; two people were killed and many others injured. Despite the efforts of U.S. Attorney General Robert Kennedy and President Kennedy himself, Governor Barnett continued to refuse to uphold the law and protect Meredith. Compliance in the end required several hundred federal marshals and troops.

Just hours before the violence in Oxford, President Kennedy addressed the nation about the developing crisis. He emphasized the need to uphold the law: "Americans are free to disagree with the law, but not to disobey it. For in a government of laws and not of men, no man, however prominent and powerful, and no mob, however unruly or boisterous, is entitled to defy a court of law." He pointed out that he had exhausted all means of upholding the law short of the use of federal troops:

> The enforcement of [the Court's order] had become an obligation of the United States Government. Even though this government had not originally been a party to the case, my responsibility as President was therefore inescapable. I accept it. My obligation under the constitution and statutes of the United States was and is to implement the orders of the court with whatever means are necessary, and with as little force and civil disorder as the circumstances permit. (*New York Times*, Oct. 1, 1962, p. 22)

Kennedy had earlier used federal marshals to suppress the "Freedom Rider" riots in Montgomery in 1961. He would be forced to consider the use of troops again in 1963 when two black students attempted to enroll at the University of Alabama.

New Legislation: A Second Reconstruction

The efforts of James Meredith and of the nine black students in Little Rock to desegregate historically white school campuses are noteworthy because federal troops were used to enforce the rights of blacks. There were other incidents in which the federal government could not intervene to protect blacks because no explicit federal statute or court order had been violated. Two protests that eventually led to the passage of major legislation took place in Alabama: in Birmingham in 1963 and in Selma in 1965.

In April 1963, King and the Southern Christian Leadership Conference (SCLC) determined again to challenge openly white supremacy and segregation in the South. This time they chose Birmingham, which was often labeled the most segregated city in America. The segregation of public facilities such as restaurants and hotels, a key target of the Birmingham protest, did not violate federal law: that is, a hesitant but sympathetic Kennedy White House had no clear legal basis for intervention (Brauer 1977). Moreover, local authorities, under the leadership of Eugene T. "Bull" Connor, were absolutely committed to "keeping the niggers in their place."

The protest began officially on April 2. King and his associates called for an economic boycott of local businesses and began sit-ins at segregated lunch counters. After several days of nonviolent demonstrations and hundreds of arrests, on April 10 local officials secured a court injunction banning the demonstrations. King, having backed down in the face of such an injunction during the abortive "Albany Movement" in Georgia the year before, chose to defy the court order and continue the protests. On April 12 he was arrested while leading a march on the Birmingham city hall. During this incarceration King wrote his famous "Letter from Birmingham Jail," an eloquent statement of why blacks had justifiably lost their patience with Southern unwillingness to end segregation and discrimination.[7]

Shortly after King was released from jail the protests rose to a new level. More than a thousand black children, some as young as six years of age, joined the demonstrations on May 2. Scenes of black youngsters chanting "Freedom Now" as they were arrested by Bull Connor and his men were carried on the national television news. When another thousand children prepared to demonstrate the next day, Bull Connor responded with brute force. Before national and international television audiences, black children and women were attacked by police dogs, beaten by police officers, and blasted with water from high-pressure fire hoses. The viciousness of the attacks on the peaceful demonstrators horrified many whites, including President Kennedy. On May 4 Kennedy said that the scenes in Birmingham had made him "sick." He went on to say, "I can understand why the Negroes in Birmingham are tired of being asked to be patient" (Brauer 1977:238).

Kennedy faced growing political pressure to act. Not all of the pressure involved internal and domestic sources. America's international image as the world's leading democracy was tarnished by the events in Birmingham and other parts of the South. Such pressures forced Kennedy to reexamine his own thinking on the role that the federal government should play in changing race relations. At about the same time, the Kennedy Administration was trying to persuade Alabama Governor George Wallace to allow blacks to enroll at the University of Alabama. Kennedy hoped to be better prepared to prevent violence than he had been in Mississippi the year before, and perhaps to avert another showdown altogether. However, the prospects for peaceful desegregation of the university campus were not bright. In his inaugural address Wallace had pledged to "draw the line in the dust and toss the gauntlet before the feet of tyranny ... Segregation now! Segregation tomorrow! Segregation forever!" (Sitkoff 1981:156).

Although Wallace ultimately settled for a symbolic act of defiance—standing in the schoolhouse door while actually capitulating to National Guardsmen sent to ensure the peaceful enrollment of the black students—the incidents at Ole Miss, at the University of Alabama, and in Birmingham combined to convince Kennedy that new federal legislation was needed. Just a few hours after the two black students enrolled at the University of Alabama, Kennedy made a major address to the nation. It carried the message that gaining full civil rights for blacks was a moral issue requiring new legislation. In the words of Carl Brauer, the speech "marked the beginning of what can truly be called the Second Reconstruction, a coherent effort by all three branches of government to secure blacks their full rights" (1977:259–260). The issues, Kennedy said, were "as old as the scriptures and ... as clear as the American Constitution."

> The heart of the question is whether all Americans are to be afforded equal rights and equal opportunities, whether we are going

to treat our fellow Americans as we want to be treated. If an American, because his skin is dark, cannot eat lunch in a restaurant open to the public, if he cannot send his children to the best public school available, if he cannot vote for the public officials who represent him, if, in short, he cannot enjoy the full and free life which all of us want, then who among us would be content to have the color of his skin changed and stand in his place? Who among us would be content with the counsels of patience and delay? (Quoted in ibid., p. 260)

The Kennedy Administration began work on what would become the landmark Civil Rights Act of 1964. The legislation addressed segregation in public facilities, discrimination in jobs, and school desegregation, and, most important, it set up mechanisms, including the withdrawal of federal funding, for direct federal action to ensure compliance.

The changes in Kennedy's thoughts and attitudes were probably indicative of the thoughts of many Northern whites who witnessed, through television and other media, the brutality of Bull Connor and other white supremacists. Many historical accounts of the period speak of the rethinking and searching of conscience that were prompted by the events of 1963. Public opinion data also suggest that such a rethinking was taking place. The data show that support for the 1964 Civil Rights Act grew substantially between the summer of 1963 and the time of its actual passage in July 1964. The Gallup Poll asked a national sample of whites how they would "feel about a law which would give all persons—Negroes as well as whites—the right to be served in public places such as hotels, restaurants, theaters, and similar establishments." In June 1963, 55 percent of Northern whites supported such legislation, as opposed to only 12 percent of Southern whites. By January 1964, after the peaceful and biracial March on Washington at which King delivered his "I have a dream" speech, and in the wake of continued civil rights protests and the assassination of President Kennedy, white support had risen to 71 percent in the North and to 20 percent in the South (Gallup 1972:1827, 1863).

The growing concern with civil rights could be seen in other ways as well. Figure 1.1 shows the number of civil rights demonstrations and the percentage of respondents in Gallup surveys mentioning civil rights as the nation's "most important problem."

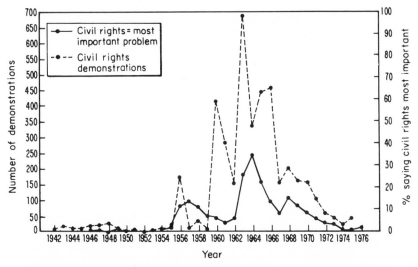

Figure 1.1. Number of civil rights demonstrations in the nation and percentage of respondents naming civil rights as the nation's most important problem. (Data on demonstrations, based on reports in the *New York Times*, made available by Paul Burstein; see Burstein 1979b. Data on perceptions of the most important problem provided by Tom W. Smith.)

As is evident, the two lines move together. In the words of survey analyst Tom Smith, from 1963 "through early 1965, civil rights remained at or near the top of the problem list" (1980:171).

In 1965 King and the SCLC targeted Selma, Alabama, as the place to force a confrontation on voting restrictions aimed at blacks. Again mass marches and demonstrations met with brutal response from local officials. Scenes of police charging and beating a column of peaceful demonstrators brought cries of outrage from across the political spectrum. The *Washington Post* described the events of March 7, 1965, as follows:

> State troopers and mounted deputies bombarded 600 praying Negroes with tear gas today and then waded into them with clubs, whips and ropes, injuring scores.
>
> The troopers and possemen, under Gov. George C. Wallace's orders to stop the Negroes' "Walk for Freedom" from Selma to Montgomery, chased the screaming, bleeding marchers nearly a

mile back to their church, clubbing them as they ran (see Garrow 1978:80).

Leaders ranging from Michigan Congressman Gerald Ford to Minnesota Senator Walter Mondale denounced the actions and called for federal legislation to protect the rights of blacks to vote. King and other black leaders had succeeded in creating the sense of national emergency needed to obtain the desired federal legislation.

The Johnson Administration had wanted to delay new legislation until 1966 in order to give the 1964 act some time to be implemented and tested. But King, along with other more militant figures in the civil rights movement, refused to yield, and the sense of urgency grew. In 1965 the Administration began to draft voting rights legislation that it hoped would attract bipartisan support in both houses of Congress.

President Johnson signed the Voting Rights Act into law on August 6, 1965, and the Department of Justice made good Johnson's promise of swift implementation. Historian Stephen Lawson reported: "On the first anniversary of the passage of the Voting Rights Act, an average of 46 percent of adult blacks in the five Deep South states to which examiners had been assigned could vote, thereby doubling the percentage from the year before" (1976:330). Mississippi underwent perhaps the most dramatic change. In 1964 only 7 percent of adult blacks in Mississippi were registered to vote; by 1969 that figure had risen to a remarkable 67 percent. As one older black woman put it, "I'm going to vote now. I'm going to vote because I haven't been able to vote in my sixty-seven years" (ibid.:331, 339). The Voting Rights Act has since been heralded as the most effective piece of legislation in American history. The act "succeeded so well because it automatically suspended discriminatory voting qualifications and gave the president the authority to send examiners to register Negroes directly" (ibid.:342).

The Civil Rights Act and the Voting Rights Act were, without question, tremendous achievements. But both pieces of legislation, as well as earlier breakthroughs like the *Brown* decision and the Montgomery bus boycott, had come at a price. The cost in human suffering and lives lost was not small. In June 1963, Medgar Evers, field secretary of the Mississippi NAACP, was assassinated. Later that year four black children were killed in the bombing of a church in Birmingham. In the summer of 1964 three young men—Michael Schwerner, James Chaney, and Andrew Goodman—who had been working on a black voter registration program in Mississippi were found buried in shallow graves. All three had been severely beaten and then shot. Others also lost their lives in the struggle for black rights, including Jimmy Lee Jackson, the Reverend James Reeb, Jonathan Daniels, and Viola Liuzzo. And these were but the highly publicized instances. The activities of Klansmen and other racists willing to use violence inflicted a higher, though less visible, toll.[8]

There were other blemishes on what from one standpoint was a remarkable record of progress and achievement. The day-to-day lives of ordinary black Americans, especially in terms of educational and economic opportunities, had not been affected by the great gains of the late 1950s and early 1960s. The level of school segregation in the deep South in 1964, for example, remained virtually identical to what it had been in 1954 (Rodgers 1975). The median family income of blacks fluctuated between 51 percent and 57 percent of that of whites throughout the entire 18-year period from 1947 to 1965 (Newman et al. 1978:269). Moreover, the immediate efforts to enforce the Civil Rights Act of 1964, at least in the areas of school desegregation and job discrimination, were weak and ineffectual (Rodgers 1975; Zashin 1978). All too often, it seemed, new principles and laws would be adopted with great ceremony, only to fall short in enforcement and results.

Change in the daily lives and experiences of most black Americans remained a remote goal. This fact would be given sudden and dramatic emphasis in places like Watts, Newark, and Detroit, and in the growing militance of younger blacks across the nation. With the *Brown* decision fading into the past and landmark legislation on the books, the tortuous and complex task of real implementation and meaningful change had, paradoxically, just begun. In fact, disputes over the nature and extent of the racial change called for in these early civil rights milestones are still active and divisive issues.

The Unfinished Civil Rights Agenda

On August 11, 1965, less than a week after President Johnson signed the Voting Rights Act into law, the Los Angeles community of Watts exploded with the worst racial disturbance since the Detroit riot of 1943. In more than six days of looting, fires, and violence, approximately four thousand people were arrested, 34 people (mostly black civilians) were killed, and an estimated $35 million in damage was done (U.S. National Advisory Commission on Civil Disorders 1968:38). The deep alienation, bitterness, and potential for violence seen in Watts would appear again and again across the country. More than 170 cities experienced racial disturbances between 1961 and 1968 (Spilerman 1976). The sense of national emergency became especially acute during the "long, hot summer" of 1967. In the first nine months of that year there were well over one hundred civil disorders, 41 of them serious disorders involving fires, looting, violence, and the need for significant numbers of police, National Guardsmen, and even army troops to quell the disturbances (U.S. National Advisory Commission on Civil Disorders 1968). Again in April 1968, following the assassination of Martin Luther King, more than one hundred cities experienced violent outbreaks, adding further to the toll of lives lost and the damage to homes and other property.

These events both heralded and spurred a change in the tenor of the campaign for black rights. Most blacks viewed the riots as spontaneous outbursts brought on by years of discrimination and mistreatment (Campbell and Schuman 1968: ch. 5). They also thought the riots had helped the racial situation by focusing attention on the longstanding economic and social grievances of urban blacks (Sears and McConahay 1973). Some analysts concluded that, in fact, a "riot ideology" had emerged and was attractive to many blacks (Tomlinson 1968; Sears and McConahay 1973; Caplan 1970). For instance, Nathan S. Caplan, after an extensive review of the literature on blacks' riot-related attitudes, concluded, "Militancy in the pursuit of civil rights objectives represents a considerable force within the ghetto. Its support approaches normative proportions and is by no means limited to a deviant and irresponsible minority" (1970:71). In particular, there was mounting evidence that the participants in the riots were not deviants, criminals, or other socially marginal "riffraff." Study after study showed riot participants to have been young black males, born in the North, who felt strong group pride and identity, were more likely than most to be involved in the community, and were deeply distrustful of and dissatisfied with white institutions (Tomlinson 1968; Caplan and Paige 1968; Paige 1970; Sears and McConahay 1973).

White reaction to the riots was divided and ambivalent. Many whites viewed the riots as intolerable lawlessness worthy only of severe punishment. Campbell and Schuman, in a survey of 15 Northern cities in 1968, found that, of the whites interviewed, "about a third [saw] the riots as largely unjustified but conspiratorial assaults on law and order led by criminal, demagogic, or other undesirable elements, assaults that should be met first of all by firm police action" (1968:50). Another third, however, viewed the riots in much the same way as did blacks: as protests stemming from legitimate grievances. The remaining third held ambivalent views combining both interpretations.

The ghetto rebellions and the increasing militancy of black protest prompted a deeper examination of the race problem in America. As the National Advisory Commission on Civil Disorders stated: "Our nation is moving toward two societies, one black, one white—separate and unequal." As the commission members saw it, the only way to shrink the rift between blacks and whites was through "new attitudes, new understanding, and above all, [a] new will" to address the racial divisions in America (1968:1–2).

Blacks and whites were especially divided in their interpretations of the increasingly popular political slogan "Black Power." In 1967 Joel D. Aberbach and Jack L. Walker asked Detroit residents what the phrase "Black Power" meant to them. The overwhelming majority of whites, 81 percent, interpreted the phrase negatively, usually taking it to mean black rule over whites. Blacks were more wide-ranging in their interpretations, approximately 50 percent offering unfavorable interpretations and 42 percent favorable ones. Despite this split, very few blacks understood Black Power to mean the sort of radical and violent change envisioned by whites. Instead, for them Black Power aroused debates over tactics and strategies in the struggle for equality and integration. In contrast to more extreme advocates of Black Power who favored black separatism, most blacks who were favorably disposed to the slogan took it "as another call for a fair share for blacks or as a rallying cry for black unity" (Aberbach and Walker 1970:373).

The new militant and sometimes separatist thrust of the civil rights struggle split black leaders. The Black Power Movement, fueled by the stormy rhetoric of Stokely Carmichael, Hubert "Rap" Brown, and groups like the Black Panthers, dramatically altered the character and perceptions of the struggle for racial change. Integration, racial harmony, and coalition politics, primary goals of organizations like the NAACP and SCLC, were challenged as accommodationist, weak, and inadequate. Major and increasingly public disputes ensued among black leaders and between black leaders and their white allies.

The nature of these disputes was clearly revealed in two books published in 1967. Martin Luther King's *Where Do We Go from Here: Chaos or Community?* called for a reaffirmation of the values, goals, and strategies of earlier civil rights efforts. King advocated pressing for full implementation of recent court rulings and legislation. Otherwise, he cautioned, black frustration would continue to grow: "The gap between promise and fulfillment is distressingly wide" (1967:40). King characterized the slogan "Black Power," despite a component that emphasized cultural pride and positive change, as mainly a cry of the despairing. He deplored both the increasingly separatist leanings of those calling for Black Power and their willingness to embrace violence as a strategy of protest.

On the other side of the dispute, *Black Power: The Politics of Liberation in America*, by Stokely Carmichael and Charles Hamilton, argued that Black Power meant a positive cultural identity for blacks, a repudiation of "go slow" tactics or of any coalition with whites that curbed or compromised the black demand for freedom, a willingness to respond to violence with violence, and a profound questioning of the goal of integration or assimilation to middle-class values.

The differences between moderate civil rights leaders like King and advocates of Black Power like Carmichael and Hamilton were in some respects matters of emphasis. Both sides agreed that the early victories had mainly established a new framework and new principles, not an entirely new social order in which genuine racial equality reigned. They also agreed that further change would meet more resistance and be even more divisive because it would require upsetting national, not merely Southern, patterns of economic and social inequality between the races. There was consensus over the value of black cultural pride and identity. The great rift between the two camps was over protest strategies and rhetorical emphasis, though there was also some division with regard to the issue of separatism.

The riots and the Black Power Movement had profound effects. They altered black Americans' sense of themselves as a people, and they altered many white perceptions of the struggle for change. More than anything else, however, these developments spoke to the slow pace at which, in the eyes of many blacks, concrete change had been implemented. The Black Power Movement and "the riots crystallized the belief among many blacks that progress was too slight and their status in American society still basically frustrating" (Schuman and Hatchett 1974:125). And in so doing, the riots and black militancy increased the pressure on the nation to address urban economic poverty more generally.

Some concrete steps on these issues were being taken. In particular, President Johnson's War on Poverty and call to move toward a Great Society had a significant impact on the economic position of blacks (Levitan and Taggart 1976). The Economic Opportunity Act of 1964 created programs like VISTA, Head Start, and the Job Corps, which provided blacks with greater educational and job-training opportunities. In 1965 the Medicaid and Medicare programs were created to improve health care for the poor and the elderly, and the Elementary and Secondary Education Act, which would greatly increase federal support for poor school districts, was passed. Thus, important actions were under way to reduce the effects of economic disadvantage in America. Blacks would benefit greatly from some of these programs, since they were disproportionately represented among the ranks of the ill-housed, the poorly educated, and the recipients of inferior health care. In short, blacks were especially likely to benefit from a broad attack on poverty. Urban and economic problems were all too often black problems.

Johnson's vision of a Great Society began to falter, however. In good part, this occurred as a result of the drain of moral and economic resources caused by the war in Vietnam and by the related difficulties with the domestic economy. In part also, the problems of the cities were not as easy to solve as some of the Great Society rhetoric implied. During the presidential campaign of 1968 one of

Richard Nixon's key themes was that the Great Society and the black protests had gone too far and needed to be scaled down. Nixon said: "For the past five years we have been deluged by government programs for the unemployed, programs for cities, programs for the poor, and we have reaped from these programs an ugly harvest of frustration, violence and failure across the land" (Levitan and Taggart 1976:3–4). Once elected, Nixon did apply pressure to curb and in some cases to eliminate the social programs started by Johnson, and he deemphasized concern with civil rights.

From the beginning, Nixon had been viewed with suspicion by many advocates of civil rights. Besides being against welfare, Nixon was perceived as developing a "Southern strategy" that promised Southern politicians narrowly construed enforcement of civil rights legislation. His emphasis on "law and order" also appeared to many as a veiled antiblack appeal.

Nixon's actions in office seemed to lend credence to many of these apprehensions. Early in his first term, his adviser Daniel Patrick Moynihan wrote in a memorandum: "The time may have come when the issue of race could benefit from a period of 'benign neglect.' The subject has been too much talked about" (*Congressional Quarterly* 1970:24). Nixon, moreover, had great difficulty in retaining high-level appointees to civil rights posts (Newman et al. 1978:119–120), and there was mounting criticism of his record on civil rights. He also declared himself opposed to school busing (*Congressional Quarterly* 1972) at a time when many courts were turning to busing as the only means to achieve meaningful desegregation of schools. And he initially opposed an extension of the Voting Rights Act, though eventually he endorsed the extension in the face of clear congressional resolve.

By mid-1965 public concern over foreign policy (primarily the war in Vietnam) had eclipsed civil rights as "the nation's most important problem" (T. W. Smith 1980). The decrease in the number of civil rights demonstrations and racial disturbances after 1968 contributed much to the declining concern with the black struggle.

During the early 1970s there was a growing belief that the momentum of the civil rights movement had disappeared. *Newsweek* ran an article in 1973 entitled "Whatever Happened to Black America?": "The great surge that carried racial justice briefly to

the top of the nation's agenda in the 1960's has been stalemated—
by war, economics, the flame-out of the old civil rights coalition
and the rise to power of a New American Majority. Blacks and
their special problems have gone out of fashion in government, politics and civil concern" (*Newsweek* 1973:29). Not all civil rights
issues had vanished, for school busing and affirmative action would
get increasing public attention. Both these issues were the legacies
of earlier initiatives, and both concerned the concrete aspects of
implementing racial change. The pressure these policies exerted to
close the pervasive gap, however, drew its impetus not from massive social protests but from the courts and the federal civil rights
bureaucracy.

Two related factors increased the pressure for school desegregation. First, a series of Supreme Court rulings forcefully mandated
compliance with the *Brown* decision and expanded its scope. Second, the Civil Rights Act of 1964 increased desegregation efforts on
the part of the Department of Health, Education, and Welfare
(HEW) and the Department of Justice. HEW could terminate the
flow of federal funds to school systems maintaining segregated
schools, and Justice could enter school desegregation cases on the
side of the plaintiffs.

The original *Brown* decision had been rendered in two parts: the
first ruling, in 1954, *Brown I*, articulated the principle that racially
separate schooling was inherently unequal and was an unconstitutional infringement on the rights of blacks. The second ruling, in
1955, *Brown II*, called for the implementation of *Brown I* with "all
deliberate speed." The phrase "all deliberate speed" was construed
very liberally by the affected Southern school systems, especially
those in the deep South, where little noticeable progress toward desegregation was made in the ensuing ten years.

Three crucial Supreme Court rulings attempted to reverse this
lethargy. In *Green v. County School Board of New Kent County*
(391 U.S. 430 [1968]), the court ruled that a program that was formally "neutral" with regard to race did not constitute *abolition* of a
dual and segregated system, the remedy called for in *Brown II*.
Thus, the voluntary desegregation plan that the school board had
adopted was held to be insufficient because it achieved no noteworthy progress toward desegregation. The Court took the *Green* rul-

ing a step further in *Swann v. Charlotte-Mecklenburg* (402 U.S. 1 [1971]). Here the Court held that, where necessary, racial composition quotas might be used as guides to designing desegregation plans and that busing might be used toward implementing such plans. These two decisions, along with threats of funding cutoffs, led to significant increases in the amount of integrated schooling in the South (Rodgers 1975).

These rulings, however, continued the pattern established in *Brown* of applying mainly to Southern states that had previously had legally sanctioned segregation. With *Keyes v. School District No. 1, Denver, Colorado* (413 U.S. 189 [1973]), court-ordered desegregation moved to the North. The Court held that although the Denver school system had not had legally mandated segregation, the school board, as an agent of the state, had intentionally created a segregated school system. The ruling referred to a District Court opinion in the case: "between 1960 and 1969 the Board's policies with respect to these northeast Denver schools show an undeviating purpose to isolate Negro students in segregated schools 'while preserving the Anglo character of [other] schools' " (pp. 197–198). Such policies, the court held, were a constitutional violation warranting relief.

Busing became an explosive controversy in both North and South. Cities like Pontiac, Michigan, experienced bus burnings and other violence, as district courts ordered desegregation. Boston witnessed large and hostile demonstrations against busing. Several schools required the presence of policemen to retain order. In Boston, Pontiac, Los Angeles, and many other cities vigorous anti-busing protest groups were formed. Many cities facing desegregation orders also experienced significant white flight to unaffected suburban areas (see Farley, Richards, and Wurdock 1980).

School desegregation shared the civil rights limelight during the 1970s with disputes over affirmative action policies. The phrase "affirmative action" had been used originally by President Kennedy; the reasoning behind the phrase and later policies was articulated by President Johnson in a speech delivered at Howard University in 1965:

> You do not take a person who for years has been hobbled by chains and liberate him, bring him up to the starting line of a race, and say,

"you are free to compete with all the others," and still justly believe that you have been completely fair. Thus it is not enough to open the gates of opportunity. All our citizens must have the ability to walk through those gates. (Johnson 1965)

Guidelines promulgated in 1968 by the Office of Federal Contract Compliance in relation to Title VII of the Civil Rights Act were the serious beginning of the controversy over affirmative action. The guidelines called for employers receiving federal funds of $50,000 or more and firms with 50 or more employees to submit affirmative action compliance programs. In particular, the regulations called for "specific steps to guarantee equal employment opportunity keyed to the problems and needs of members of minority groups, including, when there are deficiencies, the development of specific goals and time tables for the prompt achievement of full and equal employment opportunity" (Glazer 1975:46). Stronger and more specific guidelines were issued in 1970 and again in 1971. The 1971 guidelines called for employer affirmative action programs to analyze the reasons behind "deficient" utilization of minorities and women, and to develop specific plans "to increase materially the utilization of minorities and women" (ibid.:48). Underutilization was said to exist if a particular job category had a lower percentage of minorities or women than would have been expected on the basis of their "availability" in the population. These guidelines in particular have been interpreted by some as requiring "not . . . opportunity, but result[s]" (ibid.:48).[9]

After President Reagan was elected in 1980, his administration launched a major effort to change federal policies on busing and affirmative action. Reagan's election, coupled with newly won Republican control of the Senate, was received as distressing news by many blacks and other minorities. Reagan had campaigned against the excesses of "big government," which to him included affirmative action quotas and mandatory busing as well as the growing Great Society bureaucracy.

The apprehensions of civil rights activists seemed confirmed by a number of Reagan initiatives. The Department of Justice began to enter school desegregation cases on the side of school districts facing desegregation orders. Virtually all pressure to use busing as a means of achieving desegregation was suspended. There was even an attempt to restore the tax-exempt status of the Bob Jones University, a private school that forbade interracial dating. Reagan also was silent on extension of the Voting Rights Act, though once it became clear that congressional support for it was solid, he agreed to sign the bill. Similarly, Reagan initially opposed a national holiday honoring the birthday of Martin Luther King, Jr., but relented when faced with a united Congress.

All these actions, along with cuts in social programs of special significance to blacks and a bitterly contested restaffing of the Civil Rights Commission, earned Reagan the enmity of many civil rights organizations. One group went so far as to denounce Reagan for unleashing a full-scale assault on the legislative advances of the 1960s. "The Leadership Conference on Civil Rights," reported the *New York Times,* "has charged that under the Reagan Administration 'there [have] been no significant civil rights enforcement activities anywhere in the government'" (June 26, 1984, p. B7). Moreover, polls conducted by several organizations showed blacks, in sharp contrast to whites, to be extremely pessimistic about their future under Reagan (*New York Times,* August 24, 1981).

Debates on civil rights issues frequently focus on the presence or absence—and, if present, the amount of—concrete change in the economic and social position of black Americans. Some argue that blacks have made much progress during the past several decades (see Scammon and Wattenberg 1973; Sowell 1984). In some respects this is surely true. In the 1980s, blacks are completing high school and entering college at about the same rate as whites, and black college graduates now earn very nearly as much as their white counterparts. And although the overall racial gap in median family incomes is still large, highly educated black husband-wife families have narrowed the earnings gap between themselves and comparable whites (Farley 1984). More than five thousand blacks now hold public office (Clark 1984), among them the mayors of Chicago, Philadelphia, and Los Angeles. Los Angeles Mayor Tom Bradley lost by less than one percent of the vote in his bid to become the nation's first black governor.

Others point to indicators suggesting that the progress made so far is incomplete and vulnerable (Hill 1978; National Urban League 1983). The percentage of black children raised in single-parent female-headed households rose drastically between 1960 and 1980 (Farley 1984), and such families are likely to be poor. The unemployment rate for black adults has been roughly twice that of whites since 1954 (Bonacich 1976). Black teenage unemployment approaches 50 percent (Swinton 1983), twice the rate for white teenagers. Blacks entering college are less likely than whites to finish (Farley 1980), and they usually attend less prestigious institutions. School integration in the North has largely ground to a halt, and despite some positive change between 1970 and 1980 residential segregation of blacks and whites is still the national norm (Taeuber 1983a, 1983b). And although blacks now play a much more visible role in conventional politics, they hold fewer than 2 percent of all public offices (Joint Center for Political Studies 1982:vii).

Race relations in the United States have a long, complex history of conflict and change. With a sense of the larger history in mind, we now shift our attention to racial change as measured by attitude surveys over the past four decades. Public opinion surveys employing reasonably representative, although by no means ideal, samples of the American public began in the mid-1930s. The first questions on racial issues for which trend data later became available were asked in 1942. This was about the time when the first effective actions against racial discrimination were also occurring—Randolph's threat of a March on Washington had forced Roosevelt's Executive Order against discrimination in federal hiring in the previous year—but de jure segregation and de facto discrimination were still largely unchallenged. Several relevant survey questions were also asked in 1946, but then not again until 1956, two years after the Supreme Court overturned the "separate but equal" doctrine. Another gap in the time series occurred between 1956 and the mid-1960s, when a sizable number of questions began to be repeated on a fairly regular basis.

From 1942 on, then, we have occasional snapshots of American public opinion on racial issues. The trend results allow us to trace changes in white, and to some extent in black, public attitudes from the low-activity years of the 1940s and early 1950s; through the late 1950s and 1960s that saw major court and legislative actions, the rise of powerful nonviolent protests against segregation, and the appearance of more radical black movements and of urban riots; and then during the period of decreasing civil rights activities in the 1970s and early 1980s.

In the chapters that follow we describe and interpret these broad trends in public attitudes as reflected in surveys conducted since the early 1940s. As we proceed, the reader may find it useful to refer back to the dates of the more important events in the struggle for civil rights; table 1.1 provides a chronology. Chapter 2 provides the necessary background information for making use of the attitudinal record, including examples of pitfalls to be avoided in this type of trend analysis. Chapter 3 presents the main substantive results over time for the white population, and Chapter 4 details the more limited but nevertheless important parallel results for blacks. We are certainly not the first to attempt to understand racial trend data; in Chapter 5 we consider theoretical interpretations offered by others. Finally, Chapter 6 gives a brief summary and a set of conclusions concerning what we have learned.

Table 1.1 Selected chronology of civil rights events.

1896	– *Plessy v. Ferguson* "separate but equal" ruling.
1909	– Founding of the National Association for the Advancement of Colored People (NAACP).
1910	– Founding of the National Urban League (NUL).
1941	– A. Philip Randolph threatens a March on Washington. President Roosevelt issues Executive Order 8802, banning discrimination in defense industries.
1942	– Founding of the Congress of Racial Equality (CORE).
1943	– Major race riot in Detroit.
1947	– President Truman's Committee on Civil Rights issues its report.
1948	– President Truman introduces civil rights legislation and issues Executive Orders 9980 and 9981 concerning fair treatment in federal employment and desegregating of the military.
	– Blacks play a critical role in Truman's reelection.
1954	– *Brown v. Board of Education* ruling declares separate but equal schooling unconstitutional.
1955–56	– Montgomery, Alabama, bus boycott lasts 381 days, draws national and international media attention, and propels

Table 1.1 (continued)

	Dr. Martin Luther King, Jr., to the forefront of the civil rights crusade.
1957	– Founding of the Southern Christian Leadership Conference (SCLC).
	– Clash in Little Rock, Arkansas, over the desegregation of Central High School. President Eisenhower dispatches federal troops to keep order and enforce desegregation.
	– Passage of the first civil rights legislation since Reconstruction (the Civil Rights Act of 1957).
1960	– Lunchcounter sit-ins by black college students in Greensboro, North Carolina.
	– Founding of the Student Nonviolent Coordinating Committee (SNCC).
1961	– Freedom Rides. President Kennedy dispatches federal marshals to protect demonstrators.
1962	– James Meredith's attempt to enroll at the University of Mississippi meets violent resistance. President Kennedy dispatches army troops to maintain order and allow Meredith to enroll.
1963	– Mass demonstrations in Birmingham, Alabama, protesting segregation of public accommodations and job discrimination.
	– Black students attempt to enroll at the University of Alabama. Governor Wallace engages in symbolic defiance, standing "in the schoolhouse door."
	– March on Washington. More than 250,000 people gather at the steps of the Lincoln Memorial, where King delivers his "I have a dream" speech.
1964	– Murders of James Chaney, Andrew Goodman, and Michael Schwerner.
	– Passage of the Civil Rights Act of 1964.
	– King receives Nobel Peace Prize.
	– President Johnson reelected in landslide over Senator Barry Goldwater.
1965	– Mass demonstrations in Selma, Alabama, protesting voting hindrances against blacks.
	– Passage of the Voting Rights Act of 1965.
	– Rioting in Watts, the worst racial outburst since 1943.
1966	– Stokely Carmichael first uses "Black Power" slogan.
	– Founding of the Black Panther Party.

Table 1.1 (continued)

1967	– Rioting in Newark, Detroit, Milwaukee, and other major urban areas.
	– Carl Stokes elected mayor of Cleveland, first black mayor of major city.
1968	– Kerner Commission releases its report on riots, identifying deeply embedded racism as main cause.
	– Martin Luther King, Jr., assassinated by James Earl Ray.
	– Rioting in many cities.
	– Passage of the Civil Rights Act of 1968, prohibiting discrimination in the sale or rental of housing.
	– Poor People's March on Washington.
	– Richard Nixon elected president over Hubert Humphrey.
1970	– Extension of the Voting Rights Act.
1971	– *Swann v. Charlotte–Mecklenburg* ruling allows busing for desegregation.
1972	– President Nixon calls for a moratorium on court-ordered busing.
1973	– *Keyes v. Denver* ruling opens the way for court-ordered busing in the North.
	– Tom Bradley elected mayor of Los Angeles.
1978	– *Bakke* ruling disallows quota at U.C. Davis Medical School but affirms potential for preferential treatment.
1980	– Ronald Reagan elected president.
1982	– Twenty-five year extension of the Voting Rights Act.
1983	– Anniversary March on Washington.
	– Harold Washington elected mayor of Chicago.
	– Wilson Goode elected mayor of Philadelphia.
	– Martin Luther King's birthday declared a national holiday.
1984	– Rev. Jesse Jackson wages the first major campaign by a black candidate for the Democratic presidential nomination.

2 Problems in Studying Changes in Attitudes

The survey data available for tracing trends in racial attitudes come from answers to questions about attitudes asked of cross-sectional samples of the American population. In the first section of this chapter we discuss the relation between answers to attitude questions and behavior outside the interview situation. Next we describe the relevant questions that have been posed on a repeated basis to national samples, noting some evident gaps in question content and time intervals. The third section concerns the nature of the samples of Americans to which these questions have been put. The final section illustrates some important problems that arise when attempting to interpret answers to survey questions, especially answers that are used to chart change.

Attitudes and Behavior

Virtually all of the data we present in this volume concern individual attitudes, where attitudes can be thought of as consisting of positive or negative responses toward some object, whether that object be another individual, a group, a policy, or whatever. More precisely, the attitudes are assumed to *underlie* the responses expressed in actual surveys, rather than to be the responses themselves. It is important to recognize that attitudes are only one determinant of actual behavior. Even within the survey interview itself, the respondent's assumptions about the interviewer can sometimes influence answers. Outside the interview, it would be altogether naive to expect a rigid one-to-one correspondence between attitude responses in a survey and the ordinary behavior of the same individuals.

The looseness of the relation between attitude data and behavior does not mean that the attitude data are not useful. A moment's reflection will bring to mind examples of attitudes that are quite real and useful to know about, yet which for good reason do not manifest themselves in overt behavior. At the simplest individual level, one person may dislike another yet behave in a polite and even friendly manner toward the other person, whether out of natural courtesy, convention, or a need to please someone more powerful. At a societal level, people living in a police state (or, in earlier times, in slavery), in order to survive, may have to behave in ways quite different from their own inclinations. In such examples it would not make sense to disregard either the attitudes, assuming they could be identified, or the behavior in attempting to understand the present or to have some sense of what the future will be like.

If attitudes and behaviors existed in entirely separate spheres, learning about attitudes would be of little practical value, whatever their interest from the standpoint of total intellectual understanding. But careful reviews of a wide range of past studies (Ajzen and Fishbein 1977; Schuman and Johnson 1976), as well as recent experimental research (e.g., Brannon et al. 1973; Weigel and Newman 1976; Fazio and Zanna 1981), make it clear that this is not the case. Attitudes and behavior at the individual level are usually correlated to some extent, from small to fairly large, and there is increasing knowledge about the conditions under which the correlations will be higher or lower. Once the naive notion that there should be a rigid identity between expressed attitudes and behavior is rejected, then the degree of relation in any particular area of life becomes itself an important fact to understand.

In this book we concentrate on national patterns of attitude change on the assumption that these patterns are relevant to understanding past, present, and potential behavior. Beyond that, our analysis is geared to understanding as well as we can the various levels at which attitudes are held and some of the complexities that affect their expression. We consider at several points the issue of whether respondents are "merely" giving socially desirable responses and what that means, and we use experimentation to test some of the effects of particular survey contexts. Furthermore, we compare answers to different questions in the interest of making sense not only of apparent inconsistencies in attitudes but also of the relation of the attitude data to larger social and political happenings. Finally, in Chapter 6 we consider briefly the parallels between the kinds of national attitude trends we are reporting and other evidence of racial trends over the same period.[1]

The Survey Questions

Our first step in producing an attitudinal record based on surveys was to identify all survey questions dealing with racial attitudes or beliefs that had been asked of cross-sectional samples of the white American population at two or more different times. We were primarily interested in questions for which answers could be conceptualized along a dimension that had at one extreme (here labeled "positive") views favorable to integration, to equal treatment, or to blacks as a group, and at the other extreme (labeled "negative") views supporting segregation or discrimination or unfavorable to blacks.

Only questions asked by nationally recognized organizations and for which trend data could be obtained for at least some reanalysis were useful for our purpose. This limited us to data collected and archived primarily by three organizations. Two of these are the leading academic survey research organizations in the United States; the third is the oldest continuous commercial survey organization producing trend data.

The National Opinion Research Center (NORC) at the University of Chicago is the source of the largest number of questions available for trend analysis and also of those with the earliest baseline date (1942). Before 1972, NORC data on racial attitudes were collected as part of a variety of different surveys, but since 1972 a standard set of items has been included in NORC's General Social Survey (GSS). Although these data constitute our major source for both early and recent years, unfortunately none of the NORC questions were asked between 1946 and 1956.

The Institute for Social Research (ISR) at the University of Michigan is the source of almost as many of our questions as NORC. Since 1964 these questions have been asked on a fairly regular basis until quite recently. Most of the surveys were done as part of studies of national elections, first through ISR's Survey Research Center and from 1970 on through ISR's Center for Political Studies.

The Gallup organization (AIPO: The American Institute of Public Opinion) has repeated fewer racial questions than NORC and ISR, but they constitute a valuable source of data on several important issues. We did not have direct access to data tapes for the Gallup data, but obtained specific cross-tabulations from the Roper Center for Public Opinion Research. (This was also true for most NORC data prior to 1972.)

The Harris organization has also carried out a number of racial studies, but changes in question wording and difficulties in locating and documenting data prevented our use of this source except for brief mention in Chapter 3. We also refer at certain points to trend data based on more limited populations, in particular to results from the Detroit Area Study and from a national panel study of high school seniors and their parents (Jennings and Niemi 1981).

Finally, we report a number of new experimental studies that we ourselves carried out in recent Survey Research Center national surveys in order to clarify issues of question wording, context, and mode of administration relevant to the past trend data.

The Questions

The primary set of positive/negative attitude questions that we will examine is identified in table 2.1 by mnemonic label, survey organization, and time period. Full question wordings follow each of the four main tables in Chapter 3 (tables 3.1, 3.2, 3.3, and 3.4), where the questions are divided into four types: questions concerned with general principles, questions about the implementation of such

Table 2.1 The 32 positive/negative racial trend questions.[a]

Gallup questions	ISR questions	NORC questions
Black Candidate (3.1)[b] 1958 $\underline{10}$ 1983	Residential Choice: 2 alts. (3.1)[d] 1964 $\underline{6}$ 1976	Same Schools (3.1) 1942 $\underline{12}$ 1982
Intermarriage (3.1) 1958 $\underline{4}$ 1983	General Segregation (3.1) 1964 $\underline{7}$ 1978	Equal Jobs (3.1) 1944 $\underline{5}$ 1972
Few (3.3)[c] 1958 $\underline{11}$ 1980	Federal Job Intervention (3.2) 1964 $\underline{4}$ 1974	Segregated Transportation (3.1) 1942 $\underline{4}$ 1970
Half (3.3)[c] 1958 $\underline{11}$ 1980	Federal School Intervention (3.2) 1964 $\underline{8}$ 1978	Same Accommodations (3.1) 1963 $\underline{3}$ 1970
Most (3.3)[c] 1958 $\underline{11}$ 1980	Busing (3.2)[e] 1972 $\underline{4}$ 1980	Residential Choice: 1 alt. (3.1)[d] 1963 $\underline{8}$ 1982
Next Door (3.3) 1958 $\underline{6}$ 1978	Accommodations Intervention (3.2) 1964 $\underline{5}$ 1974	Black Candidate (3.1)[b] 1972 $\underline{7}$ 1983
Great Numbers (3.3) 1958 $\underline{6}$ 1978	Aid to Minorities (3.2) 1970 $\underline{6}$ 1982	Laws against Intermarriage (3.1) 1963 $\underline{12}$ 1982
Ku Klux Klan Rating (3.4) 1965 $\underline{4}$ 1979	Riots (3.2) 1972 $\underline{3}$ 1976	Open Housing (3.2) 1973 $\underline{6}$ 1983
	Neighborhood Preference (3.3) (1972 $\underline{3}$ 1976; 1976 $\underline{2}$ 1981)[f]	Busing (3.2)[e] 1972 $\underline{8}$ 1983
	Thermometer Rating of Blacks (3.4) 1964 $\underline{9}$ 1982	Spending on Blacks (3.2) 1973 $\underline{9}$ 1983
	Civil Rights Push (3.4) 1964 $\underline{8}$ 1980	Few (3.3)[c] 1972 $\underline{7}$ 1983
		Half (3.3)[c] 1972 $\underline{7}$ 1983

Table 2.1 (continued)

Gallup questions	ISR questions	NORC questions
		Most (3.3)[c]
		1972[7]–1983
		Same Block (3.3)
		1942[8]–1972
		Black Dinner Guest (3.3)
		1963[10]–1982
		Intelligence (3.4)
		1942[8]–1968
		Black Push (3.4)
		1963[11]–1982

a. Numbers in parentheses indicate tables in Chapter 3 that give full question wordings and results for national cross-section white samples. Numbers below question labels indicate the earliest and the most recent time points available for that question, plus the total number of time points. For example, 1958[9]1978 indicates that the question was first asked in 1958, most recently asked in 1978, and asked at nine time points altogether. (A question asked more than once within a single year is counted as only one time point here, and such "replications" are averaged for our analysis. Separate discussion of such replications appears at the end of Chapter 2.)

b. Both NORC and Gallup ask a question about white willingness to vote for a qualified black presidential candidate. The wordings of the two questions are not identical, but the meanings seem so close that we have considered the two as one unit. However, we comment at a later point on differences in results, and readers are of course free to try to link differences to wording.

c. Few, Half, and Most refer to three questions concerning degrees of school integration, asked by both Gallup and NORC. The wording of the questions across organizations is almost exactly the same, and we therefore treat these as three rather than six questions, although there are differences in survey dates and in sample definitions that will be noted.

d. The two Residential Choice questions differ sufficiently to be counted twice. "Alts." stands for "alternatives," i.e., the number of alternatives offered to respondents.

e. The two Busing questions differ sufficiently to be counted twice.

f. Neighborhood Preference refers to two different question versions, one asked in face-to-face surveys and one in telephone surveys. They are counted and shown as a single question here, but are presented separately in table 3.3.

principles, questions concerning social distance between whites and blacks, and a residual miscellaneous set of questions.

It is useful to think of a total sample of racial attitude trend questions, and for this purpose we have adopted the number of 32 question units. This number is necessarily somewhat arbitrary. There are actually 36 entries in table 2.1, but as the table notes indicate, some of the entries can be treated for analytic purposes as essentially identical. There are also a few other items, not shown here, that will figure in our later analysis for special purposes.

The 32 questions are themselves the end result of a careful search of all sources we could locate that indexed racial questions of any kind. All questions asked at two or more time points were placed in an initial pool. We then eliminated those questions for which the time span was too limited (for example, if the available time points were very close rather than spread over at least a few years), or where there were other serious problems with the questions. Appendix A provides a detailed account of our search procedure.

Coverage over Time and Issues

Our primary goals in this book are to trace and interpret change over time as fully and adequately as we can. Cross-sectional attitude surveys began in the United States in the mid-1930s—as indicated by the title of Hadley Cantril's huge compendium, *Public Opinion: 1935–1946* (1951). But as Paul Sheatsley (1966) has noted, the major fact about the study of racial attitudes in the 1930s was the absence of any real interest in that subject on the part of leading polling organizations. Gallup asked three questions about a "lynching bill" that was before Congress in 1937, though race was not mentioned, and in 1939 a question was asked about Eleanor Roosevelt's resignation from the Daughters of the American Revolution to protest their refusal to allow a "well-known Negro singer to give a concert in a DAR hall" (two-thirds of the public approved of the resignation). But no other questions about racial issues were asked in those first years of survey research, and none at all were asked that became part of long-term trend series until 1942—the earliest point at which our analysis can begin.[2]

The reason for the late start is not hard to find. "The polls, for obvious reasons, tend to ask questions about the issues that are hot, and it is clear that, during the decade preceding World War II, race relations did not qualify on this basis" (Sheatsley 1966:217). Indeed, our good fortune in having any questions from the 1940s seems to be due largely to the federal government's concern at the beginning of World War II about the effect of racial tension on the war effort. Gallup did not begin a regular series of questions until 1954, when race was becoming a focal issue in the United States, first because of Supreme Court decisions, then later because of the confrontation over school integration in Little Rock, the Montgomery bus boycott, and so on. Nobody carried out a substantial national survey of the racial attitudes of blacks until 1963 (Brink and Harris 1964), but in this case there was the additional complication of the need for special sampling, since black respondents are too few in a typical cross-sectional national survey to allow for detailed analysis.

An equally serious problem is the different and uneven periods available for different questions. For one question (whether black and white students should go to the same or different schools), we have data from both 1942 and 1982, as well as from numerous points in between. For all others, the record is truncated at one or both ends. This not only makes for general noncomparability across questions but also can be seriously misleading: a question asked over one time period (say, 1942 to 1968) may show much more dramatic change than another question asked over a different time period (1964 to 1980), yet it may be impossible to tell whether this difference is due to question content or to variations in the pace of change in different periods. In other words, question content and time period are often confounded, sometimes because questions fit only a particular period (for example, busing is an issue that appeared only at the beginning of the 1970s), but sometimes for reasons that seem more a matter of chance.

Regardless of when a question was first and last asked, there is an additional problem whenever the distance between two time points is substantial. For example, because the question about equal access to jobs was not asked between 1946 and 1963, a graph of responses to this question (figure 2.1) encourages us to think of change in attitudes toward this issue between 1946 and 1963 as constant (as indicated by the solid line in the figure). But this is by no means certain. As the dotted lines suggest, many other trajectories were possible; some are perhaps as plausible as the solid straight line. In the absence of other information, we generally connect time points by straight lines, but the larger the time gap, the more uncertain this becomes, and only the points themselves can be thought of as at all firmly established. Figure 2.1 also notes another "problem": a ceiling effect as responses approach 100 percent within a single category. Not only does the item cease to register change, but ordinary percentage differences may not adequately represent what change is occurring when the distribution is so skewed.

A further point about our set of 32 questions should be emphasized. Just as virtually no racial questions were asked before 1942, so there are important issues for which no trend data at all seem to exist. We could find no questions on voting rights asked on more

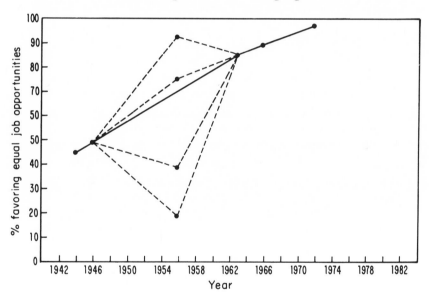

Figure 2.1. Attitudes toward equal job opportunities for blacks and whites: various possible trends for years in which the question was not asked.

Equal Jobs: "Do you think Negroes should have as good a chance as white people to get any kind of job, or do you think white people should have the first chance at any kind of job?"

than one occasion; nor are there repeated questions directly about affirmative action extending far enough into the past to be useful for our purpose. Our analysis throughout is limited to what the polls inquired into, and in this sense the polls influence our account of recent history in much the same way that newspapers play an important role in defining news and available documents shape our knowledge of earlier eras.

Moreover, even for topics on which questions were asked, the relative coverage is uneven. Table 2.2 provides one topical way of organizing our pool of questions. As can be seen, there is fairly good coverage of residential issues, but coverage of employment issues is weaker and coverage of interpersonal relations is disproportionately weighted by questions on intermarriage as against, for example, questions on friendship or membership in social clubs. We will discuss later the extent to which trends differ according to the content areas that are fairly well represented.

The Primary Variables

Researchers working within a single set of survey data can readily investigate many relations among variables. We are working, however, with a different data set for every year for every organization. Thus a decision to look at one single type of relation—for example, trends separately for Northerners and Southerners—entailed more than three hundred cross-tabulations.[3] If one additional variable is added (say, education), the number of relationships doubles again. Moreover, even a small change in the definition of the original items (for example, repercentaging without "don't know" responses) again doubles the total number of relationships, moving it well beyond a thousand. For this reason, the number of demographic or background variables that we could examine is much more limited than in reports of simple cross-sectional surveys.

In addition to race and the various attitude questions themselves, our most important variable is "time." We also routinely employ "region" because of its historic importance for racial attitudes and behavior in the United States, and almost all graphs in this book separate trends according to a South/non-South distinction. (For convenience, we usually refer to the non-South as "North.") In addition, we use "education" because of its importance as both

Table 2.2 Trend questions by issue content.

Residential integration	Next Door (3.3)
	Great Numbers (3.3)
	Residential Choice (1 alternative) (3.1)
	Residential Choice (2 alternatives) (3.1)
	Same Block (3.3)
	Neighborhood Preference (3.3)
	Open Housing (3.2)
School integration	Busing (ISR) (3.2)
	Busing (NORC) (3.2)
	Federal School Intervention (3.2)
	Same Schools (3.1)
	Few (Gallup, NORC) (3.3)
	Half (Gallup, NORC) (3.3)
	Most (Gallup, NORC) (3.3)
Job treatment	Equal Jobs (3.1)
	Federal Job Intervention (3.2)
Public facilities	Same Accommodations (3.1)
	Segregated Transportation (3.1)
	Accommodations Intervention (3.2)
Political arena	Black Candidate (Gallup, NORC) (3.1)
Economic aid	Aid to Minorities (3.2)
	Riots (3.2)
	Spending on Blacks (3.2)
Personal relations	Intermarriage (3.1)
	Laws against Intermarriage (3.1)
	Black Dinner Guest (3.3)
Other	General Segregation (3.1)
	Thermometer Rating of Blacks (3.4)
	Ku Klux Klan Rating (3.4)
	Intelligence (3.4)
	Black Push (3.4)
	Civil Rights Push (3.4)

Note: Numbers in parentheses refer to tables in Chapter 3 that give question wording and national trend results.

a social and a psychological indicator, always controlling simultaneously for region in preliminary analysis. Where education has different effects within the two regions, this is noted. We note age effects less regularly, but a special section at the end of Chapter 3 deals with age as an indicator of cohort experiences for a number of questions. Finally, in some cases, attitude questions are cross-tabulated with one another, though of course we are limited by what questions were asked within the same survey.

Brief definitions of our major analytic variables, along with the typical distribution of cases across categories, are as follows:

Race. Our most basic variable, of course, is race, which we treat as a social rather than a biological category. Except where specifically indicated, all results in this chapter and in Chapter 3 are for the "white population" only, which is ordinarily defined as those remaining after the exclusion of "nonwhites." Chapter 4 deals with the black population, and in all instances we have accepted "Negro" or "black" as defined by the survey organization, which is usually based on interviewer judgments. Orientals and a few other persons classified by one or another survey organization as neither white nor black are omitted from all analysis to the extent that survey codes allowed their identification. There is some inconsistency in such classifications across organizations, as well as within organizations across time, but the cases involved are so few that we do not believe they can affect trends to any important degree.[4]

Region of current residence. For NORC, ISR, and Gallup we use the U.S. Census definition of the South: Alabama, Arkansas, Delaware, Florida, Georgia, Kentucky, Louisiana, Maryland, Mississippi, North Carolina, Oklahoma, South Carolina, Tennessee, Texas, Virginia, West Virginia, and the District of Columbia. All other states are defined as North, except for Alaska and Hawaii, which are not included in national sample surveys. (Harris data code Delaware, Maryland, West Virginia, and the District of Columbia as North, and it was not possible to recode these.) The division of the white population by region remains fairly constant over the 1942–1982 time span: Southerners constitute about a quarter of the total sample over most of that period, with a gradual increase to around 30 percent during the past few years.

Education. In general, we separate education into "less than 12 years," "12 years," and "more than 12 years." (However, 1942 NORC data permit separation only into "less than 12" and "12 or more," and in 1944 and 1946 the only separation possible is "12 or less" and "13 or more.")

There has been a substantial change over time in the proportion of the white population in the three main educational categories we use. The percentage of adults with less than a high school education has declined precipitously in both regions, while the percentages graduating from high school and attending college have risen. Survey samples reflect these changes. Between the NORC surveys in the early 1940s and the 1982 General Social Survey, the percentage of Southern respondents 21 years of age or older with less than a high school education dropped from approximately 60 percent to 36 percent, while the percentage for high school graduates increased from a little less than 20 percent to 31 percent and for those with at least one year of college from a little more than 20 percent to 33 percent. In the North the changes have been somewhat greater, with a drop from 57 percent to 26 percent for respondents with less than 12 years of school and increases from approximately 22 percent to 37 percent for high school graduates and from 21 percent to 37 percent for those with at least one year of college. In addition, most national surveys tend to underrepresent lower educational levels somewhat, as determined by Census data, and this was especially true for samples from the 1940s.

Age. In order to maintain comparability over years, we have ordinarily restricted all samples to persons 21 and over, since this was the age range used in most surveys before the change in the voting age to 18. (Results for persons aged 18–20 are noted at certain points where this is useful.) At the end of Chapter 3 we focus on age as a variable, reporting and adding to cohort analyses carried out primarily by others.

The Survey Samples

Sample Sizes

The total sample sizes of the surveys on which we draw are usually between 1,000 and 2,000, the major exceptions being the three NORC surveys from the 1940s, which were 2,500 and up, and several American National Election Studies that exceeded 2,000. The 1970 Election Study used a split-ballot sample design so that most of the racial attitude questions were asked of only half the respondents, reducing the available sample size to approximately

625. With these exceptions, the total sample sizes for the post-1950 surveys ranged from 1224 to 1913 for NORC, from 1291 to 1834 for ISR, and from 1507 to 1665 (unweighted) for Gallup. The Ns on which percentages and other statistics in tables and figures are based are somewhat smaller, because in Chapter 3 we have ordinarily limited our analysis to whites 21 years of age and older and because there are also small amounts of missing data (volunteered "don't know" responses and the like). When we turn to black data in Chapter 4, the sample sizes become much smaller, as we will explain at the beginning of that chapter.

Significant Differences and Other Sampling Issues

In most survey analysis, statistical significance provides a helpful criterion for distinguishing "real differences" in the population from those differences which may be due to sampling error.[5] Since the samples we work with are almost all clustered, we adopted the relatively stringent criterion of a .01 probability level before regarding a difference at the national level as "real." Even so, with samples as large as most of those we work with in Chapter 3, almost any difference in responses between two years that looks real to the eye turns out to be significant. For example, if two simple random samples of 1,000 differ from each other by 6 percent on a response to a dichotomous question, where one is 47 percent and the other is 53 percent, the probability that a difference this large would occur through sampling variation alone is less than one in a hundred (.01).

Thus for comparing national white responses across years, and for responses of subsamples of Northerners as well, there is rarely any uncertainty as to statistical significance. When only Southern samples are involved, and especially when we divide samples by both region and education (or age), statistical significance cannot so readily be taken for granted. Although we do not usually give explicit significance levels in the text, we have used formal tests (or equivalent rules of thumb) in reporting trends or other differences as "real" and in describing the shape of the trend. (Appendix B describes our main statistical testing procedure and gives several examples; tests for specific conclusions are usually included in notes.) At the same time, as examples later in this chapter indicate, statistical significance can only be a starting point in most of our analysis, since there are a number of factors that can create large response differences but do not signify true changes in attitudes for the population.

The definitions of the populations to which samples refer have been generally similar across the survey organizations. Only civilian adults living in households in the coterminous United States are sampled. However, the age specifications for adults have shifted over time, usually from 21 and over before the early 1970s to 18 and over thereafter. The General Social Survey has added the further requirement that its samples refer only to the English-speaking population of the United States, while the ISR National Election Studies sample only citizens of voting age. We have assumed that these minor differences do not create important differences in results by organization, but they probably do cause some minor variations.

Thus far we have been describing full or modified probability sampling methods, which have been employed since the early 1950s to the present by the three organizations that provide most of our data.[6] The three earliest surveys from which we have data were conducted by NORC in the 1940s using quota control sampling—a very different kind of design. Characteristics or control factors upon which the sample distributions were to match the population distributions were defined by NORC: geography (including both region and level of urbanization), sex, race, and "standard-of-living level." Thus, as NORC's Basic Instructions explained to interviewers, "if 7.5 percent of the people in the United States live in the New England states, then 7.5 percent of our sample is drawn from the New England states in a national survey" (NORC 1946). Working in areas that were chosen for their representativeness along several dimensions, interviewers were assigned quotas that enumerated how many persons were to be interviewed for each control factor. Then the interviewer was to select respondents "at random—in the home, on the street, in the office, in a store, etc." While samples drawn in this way are generally believed to be representative with respect to the control factors, they may be seriously unrepresentative on characteristics not subject to controls and on combinations of control variables (male Southerners, for example) that were not specified in the quotas (Glenn 1975). Education and occupation were not control factors in the NORC samples from 1942 to 1946; nor were controls for combinations of factors utilized other than the one for region and level of urbanization. (In addition, the shifting composition of the civilian population as a result of World War II introduced unique sampling problems.) Substantial bias could be introduced as the interviewers were given the responsibility of selecting respondents "at random" within quotas. Usually this meant that interviewers chose people who were accessible, and these may have differed systematically in their attitudes from those harder to contact.[7]

Another source of variation among organizations, and also between time points for the same organization, is the nonresponse rate—the proportion of people who refuse or are unavailable to take part in a survey. With quota or modified probability sampling, no clear nonresponse rate can be calculated. But whether calculated or not, trends and fluctuations in nonresponse rates may well affect inferences about substantive changes in the target population (see Steeh 1981; Farley, Hatchett, and Schuman 1979).

In summary, differences in sampling methods over time and among organizations could easily lead to some variations in results. This is the first of a number of factors that point to the need for caution in interpreting minor fluctuations in trend data across time or across organizations, regardless of their statistical significance. It is important to concentrate on major trends, on the broad picture, and to avoid attempting to interpret every squiggle that catches one's eye.

Interpreting Trend Data

Suppose that in 1942 only 20 percent of a sample of white Americans favored the integration of public schools, but in 1982 the figure was 80 percent. Before taking this dramatic evidence of change at face value, we must consider the nature of the sample and the sampling method used at each time point, as discussed in the previous pages. In addition to sampling considerations, there are a number of other features of surveys that must be taken into account if one is to avoid serious misinterpretation. These involve the exact questions asked and the larger questionnaires in which the questions are embedded, the method of questionnaire administration and the kinds of interviewers employed, and possibly even the organizations that direct the work.

Consistency of Question Wording

There is no more important point in survey research than the need to keep the wording of questions constant for all comparisons. Even variations in wording that seem minor can produce important differences in response and sometimes in relationships as well. For example, both NORC and ISR ask a question on residential integration, and the one question might be thought of as a shorter version of the other:

> *Residential Choice, 1 alternative plus scale (NORC):* "Here are some opinions other people have expressed in connection with black-white relations: White people have a right to keep blacks out of their neighborhoods if they want to, and blacks should respect that right." [Respondents were presented with a card and asked to choose one of four alternatives: strongly agree, slightly agree, slightly disagree, strongly disagree.]
>
> *Residential Choice, 2 alternatives (ISR):* "Which of these choices would you agree with more: 1. White people have a right to keep blacks out of their neighborhoods if they want to. 2. Black people have a right to live wherever they can afford to, just like white people."

Part of the wording of these two questions is identical: "White people have a right to keep blacks out of their neighborhoods if they want to." The other differences might at first seem unimportant, since they do not change the basic issue of whether white people have a right to prevent blacks from moving into white neighborhoods.

However, the NORC one-alternative question is probably easier for respondents to agree to because it does not present the other side of the picture, namely black rights to residential choice. In addition, the one-alternative version places the burden on blacks to "respect" white rights. From past research (Schuman and Presser 1981, ch. 8) we would expect the NORC one-alternative version of the question to elicit less positive responses (that is, a lower degree of support for open residential choice by blacks). If we dichotomize

the NORC 4-point scale in the most natural way (strongly agree +
agree vs. disagree + strongly disagree) in order to create greater
comparability, this is the case for white respondents, as shown in
figure 2.2. Where the same years are involved, on the average
about 25 percent more respondents give a positive response on the
ISR version than on the NORC version. This is a clear example of
why one cannot shift in midstream from one question wording to

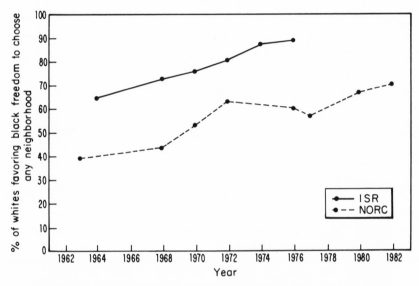

Figure 2.2. Responses to the ISR and NORC questions on residential
choice.
   Residential Choice (ISR): "Which of these statements would you
agree with: White people have a right to keep black people out of their
neighborhoods if they want to, or, black people have a right to live wherever they can afford to, just like anybody else?"
     1. Keep blacks out   2. Blacks have rights
   Residential Choice (NORC): "Here are some opinions other people
have expressed in connection with black-white relations. Which statement on the card comes closest to how you yourself feel? White people
have a right to keep blacks out of their neighborhoods if they want to,
and blacks should respect that right."
     1. & 2. Agree strongly or slightly   3. & 4. Disagree strongly or
     slightly

another. It also indicates why the absolute percentage figures on any particular wording should not be given too much weight: a different wording might have yielded quite different percentages.[8]

Even when two somewhat different questions on the same issue yield different absolute percentage levels, they may nevertheless show much the same trend over time. Indeed, there is evidence that in most cases this is likely to occur, but it definitely cannot be taken for granted. Figure 2.2 provides mixed indications on this point for the two Residential Choice questions. Both versions clearly reveal increased support by whites for free residential choice by blacks. However, the change is quite steady for the ISR version, whereas for the NORC version it seems to level or even dip slightly during the 1970s.[9] We have not been able to determine for certain why this difference occurs, but it warns us that we must look carefully at the trend for every item that is available for study on a given issue, and not take any single trend as definitive. Of course, we could average all trends over all items (for example, by creating a single summary index of all items in table 2.1), which would produce an overall mild positive record of change—but, as will become evident, this would obscure much more than it would clarify.

Organizational Differences

The comparison of Residential Choice questions in figure 2.2 involves a difference in organizations as well as in question wording. It might seem as though surveys carried out by different organizations could present a serious problem, but comparisons of such "house differences" indicate that they are seldom an important source of variation in survey results (T. W. Smith 1984). There is some difference in the way "don't know" and other spontaneous responses are handled by interviewers trained by different organizations, but once substantive alternatives are repercentaged to exclude such responses, even small differences tend to disappear.

We do not have any trend question asked by different organizations to exactly the same type of sample at exactly the same time points, but a valuable approximation is available for three questions on sending white children to schools attended by varying

proportions (a few, half, more than half) of black children. (These
are the questions listed as Few, Half, and Most in tables 2.1 and
2.2.) Gallup asked the three questions to parents with children in
school over the period 1958 to 1980. NORC asked exactly the same
questions to cross-sectional samples from 1972 to 1982. Unfortunately, the NORC questionnaire does not provide information that
would allow reduction of the NORC sample to fit the Gallup sample specifications, but there is no theoretical reason to expect the
differences in the samples to have large effects. Figure 2.3 shows
both sets of data for the time points that are closest together. The
comparisons are instructive in several respects. First, there do not

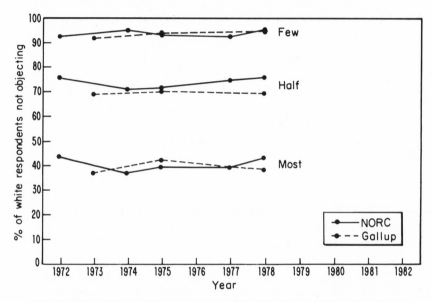

Figure 2.3. Gallup and NORC results for three questions about schools
with different proportions of blacks.

Few: "Would you, yourself, have any objection to sending your children to a school where a few of the children are black?"
    1. Yes   2. No

Half: (If No to Few) "Where half of the children are black?"
    1. Yes   2. No

Most: (If No to Half) "Where more than half of the children are
black?"
    1. Yes   2. No

appear to be important differences by organization either in absolute levels or in trends. Where years are identical the largest absolute difference attributable to the organizations is 7 percent, for one time point there is no difference at all, and for two points the difference is only 1 percent. Because of the large sample sizes, the 7 percent difference for Half in 1978 is significant at the .01 level and even the 5 percent difference for Most in 1978 is significant at the .05 level. But these differences at specific time points are so small and unsystematic that we believe it best to treat them as lacking substantive significance. (It is difficult even to attribute them to sample definitions, since they are too inconsistent for such an explanation.) Furthermore, differences in trends by organization are even less evident for the time period 1972–1978, and a summary statement for both organizations would stress the lack of visible change in either a positive or negative direction on any of the three items.

In comparison with the nonexistent or trivial variation by organization, however, the variations by question content are quite large, averaging 94 percent acceptance of integration for the question about a few blacks in a school, 72 percent for the question about a school that is half black, and only 40 percent for the question about a school with more than half the students black. It obviously makes a great deal of difference which description of integration is used, and it is clear that the distinction is one of substance. The huge difference of 54 percent between the Few and Most questions indicates that a large proportion of the respondents take the exact meaning of the question seriously, rather than answering carelessly or simply in terms of some general "set" such as a desire to appear unprejudiced, although such sets may also occur.

The data presented in figure 2.3 are confined to the period 1972–1978. For Gallup, however, we have data going back to 1958, and as figure 2.4 shows for the Half question, the stability from 1972 to 1978 was reached only after a steep climb during the previous decade. (The Few question shows a very similar trend, and the Most question also shows a similar picture except that the slope for the South is not quite as steep.) Moreover, as one might expect, the climb occurred almost entirely in the South and during the years after the 1954 *Brown* decision. This is clearly a case in which a

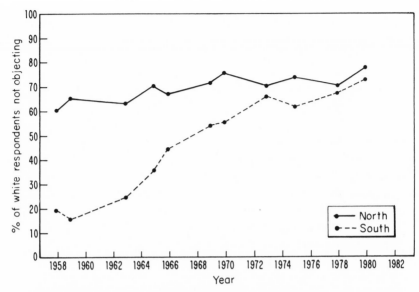

Figure 2.4. Attitudes toward half black, half white school, by region and year ("don't know" responses excluded).

Half: "Would you, yourself, have any objection to sending your children to a school where half of the children are black?"

straight line would not represent well the course of change over the total period 1958–1980. (NORC data are available for 1982 and 1983 as well; see table 3.3.) Thus question wording, time, and region are all important in understanding trends on these items, but survey organization as such plays little or no role in producing variation.

In another way, however, organizational differences have been important in past findings and interpretations of trends in racial attitudes. Virtually all published analyses have been confined to data collected by one organization. One series of articles in *Scientific American* (discussed in Chapter 5) has used only NORC data; other publications have relied only on ISR data; and Gallup compilations have printed only Gallup results. This has tended to limit the view of any single analyst, a narrowing accentuated by the fact that the *types* of questions asked tend to differ from one organization to another. Questions about broad principles of racial integration, for example, are found especially in NORC surveys, and this means that analysts of NORC data are more affected by such content—and analysts of ISR data less affected—insofar as question content produces distinctive trends over time. As in the story of the blind men and the elephant, each analyst perceives only a part of the creature. A primary aim of this book is to draw on all available sources of racial trend data and therefore to obtain a fuller view of the complexity of change. At the same time, we must acknowledge that our own views are largely limited to the 32 questions available, and that we also almost certainly miss or misinterpret some trends that have not been measured well or not measured at all. This is merely to acknowledge that a full understanding of social change even in a single area is a goal to move toward, not one likely to be attained completely.

Race of Interviewer

There is substantial evidence that responses to many racial items are influenced by whether interviewers and respondents are of the same or different races. In the case of white respondents, in one controlled study the responses to a question on intermarriage varied by 46 percent depending upon whether the interviewers were white or black (Hatchett and Schuman 1975–76). None of the organizations that we use provides information on whether interviewers and respondents are matched by race, but we have good reason to doubt that this is done on a systematic basis. However, since all ISR, NORC, and Gallup interviewing staffs are heavily white and since most interviewers are assigned to respondents who live near their own neighborhoods, it is reasonable to assume that the proportion of whites interviewed by blacks is very small. Nevertheless, this probably does occur occasionally, especially in more integrated neighborhoods, and it constitutes a minor disturbance in comparing different organizations and different years within organizations. The problem is potentially more severe when we later consider black samples, since the proportion of blacks interviewed by whites is probably greater and also more variable over time; fortunately the types of questions we focus on in this book are not those on which blacks seem to be most susceptible to race-of-interviewer effects (Schuman and Converse 1971).

Mode of Administration

Almost all of our trend data come from face-to-face interviewing. In the last several years there has been a major shift to telephone interviewing, primarily for reasons of cost. If we had been able to include data from telephone interviewing, we might have been able to obtain data for 1982 or later time points for all our questions. Unfortunately, a shift from face-to-face to telephone interviewing poses very serious problems for questions concerning race. As noted, race of interviewer is an important influence on responses, and whereas respondents can be fairly sure of the race of the interviewer in a face-to-face situation, a telephone survey creates ambiguity in this regard. Moreover, interviewers in face-to-face surveys normally work in the regions in which they live, so that, for example, Southern whites are normally interviewed by Southern whites. In national telephone surveys, interviewing is usually centralized, so that a respondent in Mississippi is typically interviewed by a person calling from Ann Arbor or New York. For these reasons, we cannot assume that data on racial attitudes obtained from telephone surveys can be considered equivalent to data obtained in face-to-face surveys. In addition, there are other differences between the two modes of administration of the surveys having to do with sampling, with the inability to use "show cards" on the telephone, and possibly with subtle factors of pace and related variations (see Groves and Kahn 1979).

The inadvisability of treating telephone and face-to-face data as equivalent is illustrated in table 2.3. The Neighborhood Preference question we use was included in a large-scale experimentally controlled comparison of telephone and face-to-face surveys in 1976 (Groves and Kahn 1979). The comparison is shown in table 2.3 separately for white Northern and white Southern respondents because the regional variation is particularly important in this case. For those living in the South, responses on preferred racial composition of neighborhood are significantly more positive (that is, more in favor of residential integration) from those who were interviewed by telephone than from those who were interviewed face-to-face. A much weaker and nonsignificant trend in the same direction appears for those living in the North.[10] A plausible interpretation of the results for the Southern sample is that Southern

Table 2.3 Responses to Neighborhood Preference question, by mode of administration and region.

	North					South				
	All white	Mostly white	Mixed[a]	Total	N	All white	Mostly white	Mixed[a]	Total	N
Telephone	22%	31%	46%	100%	(927)	38%	29%	33%	100%	(370)
Face-to-face[b]	23	36	42	100	(874)	51	27	22	100	(368)
Difference	−1	−5	+4			−13	+2	+11		

Question (ISR): "Would you personally prefer to live in a neighborhood with mostly whites, mostly blacks, or a neighborhood that is mixed half and half?"

[IF MOSTLY WHITE] "Would you prefer a *mostly* white neighborhood or an all-white neighborhood?"

a. "No difference" was accepted if offered spontaneously, but is combined here with mixed half and half. DK responses are omitted; they were almost identical for both modes in both regions. Only two persons gave the response "mostly blacks" and these are included here under "mixed."

b. Restricted to households owning telephones.

whites are more likely to express preferences for residential segregation when talking face-to-face with Southern white interviewers than when talking by telephone to voices they perceive as Northern (and conceivably black). Whether the weaker and less reliable trend for Northerners also points to an effect by mode of administration is uncertain. Indeed, both results for both regions require replication before being regarded as conclusive, but certainly for the present it would be unwise to treat face-to-face and telephone data as equivalent when studying trends in racial attitudes. This methodological problem will pose serious difficulties for our ability to study future changes in racial attitudes if surveys move entirely to a telephone mode of administration.

Effects of Context

There is increasing awareness among survey investigators of the effects of question order or context on responses (Schuman and Presser 1981). Such effects do not appear to be frequent, but when they occur they can be fairly large. This means that the same question in different surveys may yield different results not because of true change but because its placement within the surveys differed. Even in the NORC General Social Survey, where there is considerable emphasis on keeping items constant, there are variations in context because of the rotation of items into and out of the questionnaire on an annual basis.

We carried out two important context experiments as part of our efforts to understand unexpected trends for certain questions. One of these experiments, which dealt with a general question on attitudes toward segregation (table 3.1, the General Segregation item), produced dramatic results that help to explain a curvilinear trend that is radically out of line with findings on closely related items. These results are discussed in Chapter 3, since they bear heavily on substantive conclusions in that chapter. The second experiment concerned the Few, Half, and Most school-integration items. In this case (also discussed in detail in Chapter 3), the experiment did not confirm a suspected context effect and therefore supported a more substantive interpretation of the trend in question. In both of these instances, the experimental results contribute significantly to our understanding, and we wish it had been possible to carry out similar experiments with all of the items that figure importantly in this book, though none of the others seemed so obviously open to contextual influence.[11]

The main implication of the possibility of context effects is to emphasize the importance of looking for evidence of systematic change, or lack of change, over as many time points as possible. A single outlier, even if significantly different from other points, does not deserve too much effort at substantive interpretation in terms of change, since it may result from questionnaire context rather than from events in the external social or political environment.

Missing Data

All the questions available for our analysis are "closed" in the sense that respondents are offered two or more explicit alternatives to choose from. However, respondents sometimes reject such choices and insist on another response, most often (or at least most often recorded as) "don't know." Moreover, survey organizations seem to differ in how readily they accept and report such nonsubstantive responses. For racial questions, nonsubstantive responses are not very common, seldom over 5 percent of all responses to a given question. However, they complicate the analysis and presentation of data: for example, by transforming a simple dichotomous question into a three-alternative item.

In all of our analysis we initially included "don't know" and similar nonsubstantive responses in figures and tables in order to determine whether they affected conclusions about substantive trends. In most cases they had virtually no effect at all; that is, percentaging data with and without nonsubstantive responses did not appreciably alter trend lines or other results and conclusions. One such example is shown in figure 2.5, which repeats figure 2.4 but this time including "don't know" responses when calculating substantive percentages. Conclusions about substantive trends do not differ appreciably for the two figures. There are a few other cases where spontaneous "don't know" or other "missing data" responses throw some light on a trend, usually because a change in "don't know" level reflects a change more in one than in another substantive response, and we will note these cases when they seem to be of importance. However, all tables and figures in this book omit spontaneous "don't know" and similar responses, except as specifically noted.

Our procedure is different when a nonsubstantive or similar re-

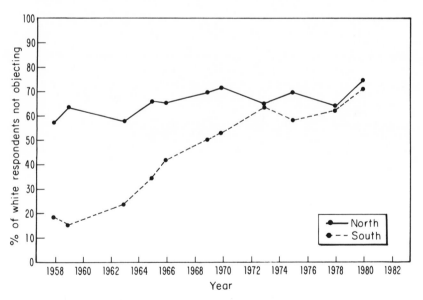

Figure 2.5. Attitudes toward half black, half white school, by region and year ("don't know" responses included).
Note: Compare with figure 2.4.

sponse such as "no interest" or "in-between" is included as an explicit alternative to a question. The proportions of respondents who choose these alternatives cannot be regarded as trivial, and of course the alternatives are also intrinsic parts of the questions as asked. Therefore they are included in all our tables and figures except where stated otherwise.

As the preceding examples indicate, analyzing trend data on racial attitudes (and on most other attitudes as well) is more than a matter of simply stringing together results from whatever surveys are at hand. Great care must be exercised to make certain the data sets are as comparable as possible and to take account of noncomparability when it occurs. Despite all feasible precautions, however, it is evident that not every variation, nor even every statistically significant variation, necessarily represents real change over time in the attitudes of the population.

For 12 of the 32 main questions we worked with there were two or more sets of results from different surveys taken by the same organization *in the same year.* These "replications" give us some idea of the variation that occurs in these data even when there is considerable comparability (same organization, same mode of administration, and same year, but not necessarily the same questionnaire context). For these 12 replicated questions, the variation within a year averages just under 3 percent, and all but one of the replications were within 6 percent of each other, the single exception differing by 9.8 percent. Most of the differences are not significant, but about one-third reach the .05 level.

The figure of 3 percent provides a rough guide of likely variation due to factors other than temporal change, but since it does not take fully into account some other possible sources of variation (such as long-term changes in sampling designs, response rates, or racial composition of staffs), it is more a minimum than a maximum. Throughout our analysis we have tried to exercise both caution and judgment in inferring change in the underlying racial attitudes of the white American population over the past forty years.

3   Trends in
White Racial Attitudes

What can we learn about changes in white racial attitudes from the results for 32 questions asked of white Americans two or more times between 1942 and 1983? One possibility—certainly the simplest—would be to discover that all questions show much the same trend. This is not the case: although there is a dominant pattern to which the majority of questions conform, the exceptions are too many, too striking, and we think too important to be treated as incidental deviates that prove the rule.

A second possibility would be to classify the questions in terms of the kinds of trends they show, and then to infer from the questions common to each pattern the nature of their commonality. Promising as this purely inductive approach might at first seem, it does not work well: some questions with different patterns turn out to have common content (for example, see figure 3.5 on two questions dealing with school integration), and questions that seem similar in pattern sometimes have quite different content. No simple trend-to-content inferences appear to organize all of the important data adequately.

After exploring carefully both of these possibilities, we settled on a third approach, which begins by organizing the questions themselves in a theoretically meaningful way and then looks at the trends produced by each type of question. This approach has the advantage of pointing up certain consistencies in pattern that are immediately informative, as well as important inconsistencies that require close attention. The latter can sometimes be resolved to provide insights that are as useful as the more obvious trends.

The organizing scheme that we use is not the only possible one. All of the questions and overall trends are presented in the four main summary tables of this chapter, so that readers are free to consider other schemes as well, as indeed we ourselves do at some points. Whatever organizing scheme is adopted, we should keep in mind that although our focus is necessarily on questions, our ultimate concern is with the people who answered the questions and even more with the changing (or unchanging) attitudes of these people as we infer them from the trend data.

The concepts we use to organize the questions are as follows:

Principles. These are questions that ask respondents whether they endorse broad principles of nondiscrimination and desegregation in important areas of social life. The questions do not deal with problems of enforcement or implementation of principles, which we treat as a separate category. The bulk of the principle questions come from NORC surveys, but fortunately there are some from Gallup and ISR as well, so that the conceptual distinction is not entirely congruent with that of survey organization. The partial congruence of conceptual content and survey organization here and in other categories is an unfortunate factor in the delineation of trends in racial attitudes.

Implementation. These questions deal with steps that the government (usually but not always meaning the federal government) might take either to reduce discrimination or segregation or to improve the economic status of blacks. There are fortunately some close parallels between principle and implementation questions, and these will be particularly critical for interpretation. Most of the implementation questions are from ISR surveys, but fortunately three are from NORC, though none is from Gallup. The importance of the distinction between broad principle and the implementation of principle has been emphasized before by other authors (see Prothro and Grigg 1960; Jackman 1978; Pettigrew 1979).

Social distance. These questions ask how the respondent would react in particular situations that involve some degree of integration at a personal level. Thus the questions deal with the principle of integration, but they do so not in an abstract way or in terms of government enforcement but rather at the level of the individual's behavior or feelings about being personally a part of the change. The questions can be considered abstract in another sense, however, for they ask people to *predict* how they would react in the hypothetical situations described. Both NORC and Gallup questions are well represented here, and there is one question (in two different versions) from ISR. The term "social distance" comes from the name of a classic attitude scale developed long ago by Bogardus (1928), though none of the original items were carried over in an exact way into these national surveys.

Miscellaneous racial questions. This category includes several residual types of questions too few in number to warrant separate treatment. Of particular interest are two simple pro/con attitude questions, one toward blacks and one toward the Ku Klux Klan. There is also one question that deals with what have traditionally been called stereotypes—an NORC item about possible differences in intelligence between blacks and whites; this is the only question about beliefs that any of three major survey organizations repeated over time.

Each of these four types of questions will be presented and discussed in turn. For each type, an initial table shows trends for the white adult population as a whole and includes the exact wording of the questions. (The tables carry the trends through 1983; a note at the end of the chapter adds results for 1984.) Graphs are then used to present selected trends by region and by education, and for comparisons across questions. A separate discussion of age and cohort effects appears near the end of the chapter.

Principles

Table 3.1 presents the questions that we classify as exclusively or primarily concerned with broad principles. Results are given for all available time points for samples intended to represent the total white adult population. Percentages are given only for the more positive or pro-integration responses, but the reader can calculate

Table 3.1 Questions concerning principles.

	Year of survey														
Question	42	43	44	45	46	48	50	56	57	58	59	60	61	62	63
Same Schools (NORC)															
% Same	32	–	–	–	–	–	–	50	–	–	–	–	–	–	65
Equal Jobs (NORC)															
% As good a chance	–	–	45	–	49	–	–	–	–	–	–	–	–	–	85
Segregated Transportation (NORC)															
% No	46	–	–	–	–	–	–	62	–	–	–	–	–	–	79
Residential Choice 1 alt. (NORC)															
% Agree slightly	–	–	–	–	–	–	–	–	–	–	–	–	–	–	21
% Disagree slightly	–	–	–	–	–	–	–	–	–	–	–	–	–	–	20
% Disagree strongly	–	–	–	–	–	–	–	–	–	–	–	–	–	–	19
Residential Choice 2 alts. (ISR)															
% Blacks have rights	–	–	–	–	–	–	–	–	–	–	–	–	–	–	–
Same Accommodations (NORC)															
% Yes	–	–	–	–	–	–	–	–	–	–	–	–	–	–	73
Black Candidate (Gallup)															
% Yes	–	–	–	–	–	–	–	–	–	37	46	–	50	–	45
Black Candidate (NORC)															
% Yes	–	–	–	–	–	–	–	–	–	–	–	–	–	–	–
Laws against Intermarriage (NORC)															
% No	–	–	–	–	–	–	–	–	–	–	–	–	–	–	38
Intermarriage (Gallup)															
% Approve	–	–	–	–	–	–	–	–	–	4	–	–	–	–	–
General Segregation (ISR)															
% Something in between	–	–	–	–	–	–	–	–	–	–	–	–	–	–	–
% Favor desegregation	–	–	–	–	–	–	–	–	–	–	–	–	–	–	–

Question wordings and variants

Same Schools (NORC): "Do you think white students and black students should go to the same schools or to separate schools?"
   1. Same
   2. Separate
(**Variant:** in 1964 added "but equal" after "separate.")

Equal Jobs (NORC): "Do you think Negroes should have as good a chance as white people to get any kind of job, or do you think white people should have the first chance at any kind of job?"
   1. As good a chance
   2. White people first

Segregated Transportation (NORC): "Generally speaking, do you think there should be separate sections for Negroes in streetcars and buses?"
   1. Yes
   2. No

								Year of survey													Last minus first
‹64	65	66	67	68	69	70	71	72	73	74	75	76	77	78	79	80	81	82	83	
‹64	70	–	–	73	–	75	–	84	–	–	–	84	86	–	–	88	–	90	–	+58
–	–	89	–	–	–	–	–	97	–	–	–	–	–	–	–	–	–	–	–	+52
–	–	–	–	–	–	88	–	–	–	–	–	–	–	–	–	–	–	–	–	+42
–	–	–	–	25	–	18	–	15	–	–	–	18	21	–	–	17	–	15	–	–6
–	–	–	–	25	–	19	–	23	–	–	–	26	29	–	–	29	–	32	–	+12
–	–	–	–	19	–	34	–	40	–	–	–	34	28	–	–	38	–	39	–	+20
‹65	–	–	–	73	–	76	–	80	–	87	–	88	–	–	–	–	–	–	–	+23
–	77	–	–	–	–	88	–	–	–	–	–	–	–	–	–	–	–	–	–	+15
–	58	–	52	–	71	–	71	–	–	–	–	–	–	78	–	–	–	–	81	+44
–	–	–	–	–	–	–	–	73	–	81	81	–	77	83	–	–	–	86	85	+12
39	–	–	–	44	–	49	–	60	61	65	60	66	71	–	–	68	–	66	–	+28
–	–	–	–	–	–	–	–	27	–	–	–	–	–	33	–	–	–	–	40	+36
‹48	–	–	–	50	–	46	–	48	–	53	–	53	–	60	–	–	–	–	–	+12
‹27	–	–	–	33	–	37	–	38	–	36	–	36	–	35	–	–	–	–	–	+8

Residential Choice, 1 alternative (NORC): "Here are some opinions other people have expressed in connection with black-white relations. Which statement on the card comes closest to how you yourself feel? White people have a right to keep blacks out of their neighborhoods if they want to, and blacks should respect that right."
1. Agree strongly
2. Agree slightly
3. Disagree slightly
4. Disagree strongly

Residential Choice, 2 alternatives (ISR): "Which of these statements would you agree with: White people have a right to keep black people out of their neighborhoods if they want to, or, black people have a right to live wherever they can afford to, just like anybody else?"
1. Keep blacks out
2. Blacks have rights

(**Variant:** in 1964 replaced "anybody else" with "white people.")

Table 3.1 (continued)

Question wordings and variants

Same Accommodations (NORC): "Do you think Negroes should have the right to use the same parks, restaurants, and hotels as white people?"

1. Yes
2. No

Black Candidate (Gallup):[a] "There's always much discussion about the qualifications of presidential candidates—their education, age, race, religion, and the like—if your party nominated a generally well qualified man for president and he happened to be a black, would you vote for him?"

1. Yes
2. No

Black Candidate (NORC): "If your party nominated a black for President, would you vote for him if he were qualified for the job?"

1. Yes
2. No

Laws against Intermarriage (NORC): "Do you think there should be laws against marriages between blacks and whites?"

1. Yes
2. No

Intermarriage (Gallup): "Do you approve or disapprove of marriage between whites and nonwhites?"

1. Approve
2. Disapprove

General Segregation (ISR): "Are you in favor of desegregation, strict segregation, or something in between?"

1. Desegregation
2. Something in between
3. Strict segregation

a. Introductions to the Gallup Black Candidate question frequently refer to an upcoming election year or convention. This is the case in 1958 (reference to the 1960 election), 1959 (the 1960 conventions), 1961 (the 1964 election), and 1978 (the 1980 conventions). Other groups (most notably Jews, Catholics, and women) have also been offered to respondents as potential presidential candidates. Blacks were the first group mentioned in 1958, 1959, 1961, 1971, and 1978; the last group mentioned in 1963 and 1965; and the third of several groups mentioned in 1967 and 1969.

the figure for any substantive response not shown in the table by subtracting the table figure(s) from 100 percent. For example, in 1942 the principle of having black and white children attend the same schools was supported by 32 percent and opposed by 100 − 32 = 68 percent of a national white sample.[1]

The questions on principles deal with many of the major racial issues of the last four decades: school integration, residential integration, integration of buses and streetcars, and job discrimination. In addition, two more symbolic issues, intermarriage and vote for a black presidential candidate, are represented, and there is one quite general question about segregation as an overall principle. Most of the questions inquire into principles in a fairly neutral way, but in two cases (both dealing with residential choice), arguments for one or both sides of an issue are given in less neutral fashion.

Schools

The predominant trends for most of these items between 1956 and 1983, by region and by educational level, are displayed in figure 3.1, using attitudes toward the principle of school integration as an example. We employ the starting date of 1956 in this figure because full information about respondents' education is not available before that time, but the 1942 to 1956 overall trends are similar, as can be seen in table 3.1 (and also in figure 6.1). We will note later the pre-1956 results by region and broad educational grouping. (As we indicated in Chapter 2, statistical testing in support of statements in the text, using methods described in Appendix B, will be found in notes.) The findings can be summarized as follows:

1. *Overall trend.* There has been a massive and continuing movement of the American public from acceptance of the principle of segregated schooling in the early 1940s to present acceptance of the principle of integrated schooling. The change has been continuous over the entire period. By 1982, 9 out of 10 Americans in the national sample chose the positive or pro-integration response.

2. *Regional trends.* From the start there has been a sizable gap between attitudes in the South and in the North, but both regions have shown essentially the same type of change. Within the past decade the two regions have shown signs of convergence, but this can largely, if not entirely, be attributed to the fact that acceptance

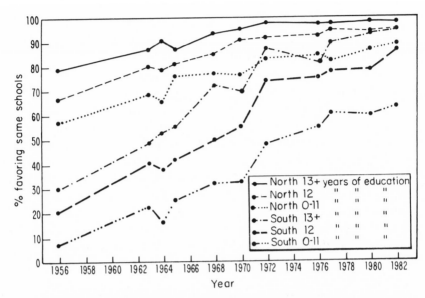

Figure 3.1. Attitudes toward black and white students' attending the same schools, by region and education.
Same Schools (NORC): "Do you think white students and black students should go to the same schools or to separate schools?"
   1. Same   2. Separate

of the principle of integrated schooling in the North is approaching 100 percent, thus creating a ceiling constraint. At the earliest point in 1942 (not shown in figure 3.1 but given in table 3.1), the "same schools" response was given by 42 percent of Northern respondents and only 2 percent of Southern respondents; in 1982 the two figures were 94 percent and 81 percent, respectively.

   3. *Trends by education.* Acceptance of integrated schooling is positively and clearly associated with respondents' education at each point throughout the entire time period, and since the trend over time is much the same for each educational category, there is no substantial shift in the association between education and acceptance. The trends by education are basically similar for the two regions, except that ceiling effects compress the change possible among more-educated Northerners.

   4. *Ceiling effect.* The Same Schools question can no longer show

substantial overall change for the simple reason that part of the sample is already close to unanimity in choosing the positive response. The ceiling effect is not total; less-educated respondents, especially in the South, were still quite divided in their answers in 1982. When we consider black responses in Chapter 4, we will see that it is possible for the entire sample to reach an absolute ceiling, but this never happens with data for whites. Instead, in most cases when a white trend line rises toward 90 percent, disaggregation of the sample by education and region reveals that more-educated Northerners are close to 100 percent in their choice of the pro-integration response, but that other educational and regional categories are less unanimous.

Public Accommodations, Jobs, Transportation

The trends shown in figure 3.1 for attitudes toward the principle of school integration apply almost identically for attitudes toward principles of equal treatment in public accommodations, employment, and seating on public transportation. This is true not only in terms of overall change, as shown in table 3.1, but in terms of trends by region and education as well. There are, to be sure, some small variations in results due to differences in issue content. For example, there was greater divergence between Northern and Southern respondents in the 1940s for the Segregated Transportation and Same Schools questions than for the Equal Jobs question, probably due to the existence of legal segregation of schools and transportation in the South at that time. But such variations are small compared to the great similarity in overall trends for all three questions.

Residential Integration

A fifth important area dealt with at the level of principle is housing integration (Residential Choice). In this case there are two questions available in table 3.1, one from NORC beginning in 1963 and one from ISR beginning in 1964. (Residential integration did not become a continuing issue for surveys until two decades after transportation, schools, and jobs. The 1942 NORC questionnaire did include a principle question on residential segregation, but it was not repeated at later time points.) Both Residential Choice questions in table 3.1 are somewhat "loaded" in the sense that they emphasize individual rights, and this is especially true for the NORC question, which speaks only of white rights. Perhaps for this reason, trends on the two questions are somewhat different. The ISR Residential Choice question reveals both overall trends and regional and educational results that are remarkably similar to those for attitudes toward equal treatment in public accommodations, schools, employment, and transportation. The level of acceptance of black rights that is reached by 1976 is not quite as high as for these other issues, but it approaches 90 percent, and it might well have exceeded that point had the question been asked in the past eight years. (The one other distinctive result for this item is a volunteered "it depends" response, not included in percentaging in table 3.1, which is appreciable in the early years—1 out of every 7 responses given—and decreases regularly over time to 1 out of 14 in 1976. But this has little effect on the substantive trends, and its inclusion in percentaging would hardly alter the results.)

The NORC Residential Choice question presents a somewhat different picture, as noted in Chapter 2 (see figure 2.2). Starting at a much lower level of acceptance of the right of blacks to choose any residential neighborhood they wish, the acceptance—which involves disagreeing with the item—shows signs of leveling off after 1972, though perhaps resuming a small upward slope in the last four years. However, if the break on the four-point scale for this item is made between "strongly agree" and the other three choices, the absolute level and the overall trend are more similar to the ISR version. And regardless of how the scale is divided, regional and educational differences are essentially like those in figure 3.1. We believe that the difference in absolute levels between the ISR and NORC versions is due to the more one-sided wording of the NORC question, a phenomenon noted in other research (Schuman and Presser 1981) and one which indicates that adherence to principles at the abstract level is somewhat a function of how the principles are stated. More puzzling is the partial difference in trends: although this also may be due to the difference in question wording, the provision of a scale of four choices, with two degrees on each side of the issue, may play a role as well. It is possible that attitudes are not moving so clearly toward acceptance of integrated housing as they appear to be when a dichotomized choice is forced, but rather that they are moving away from strong adherence ("strongly agree") to the principle of segregated housing. In any case, with the exception of this puzzling difference in trend in the years 1972 to 1977, the NORC question also shows much the same regional, educational, and broad temporal pattern as all the other questions dealt with thus far, and we are inclined to regard the deviations as less important than the similarities.

Black Presidential Candidate

There are also two different versions of a question about willingness to vote for a black presidential candidate of one's own party. In this case (as table 3.1 shows) the questions are closer to one another in wording. Both questions ask how the respondent would vote in a hypothetical situation, and in this sense they are similar to the social distance questions to be discussed below. But because voting does not involve personal involvement in an integrated living situation, reference to intention in these cases is really a way of measuring attitudes toward nondiscriminatory political choices. Therefore the voting questions are best classified as dealing with basic principles of equal treatment.

The Gallup version of the Black Candidate question provides the longer time series, extending from 1958 through 1983. It shows much the same positive trends that we have seen for other questions. The highest point attained in 1978 for the national sample does not reach a ceiling, but the overall trend in both regions is clearly positive, with the North always more so than the South. The three educational categories are also separated much as in figure 3.1, and each presents an overall movement upward.

NORC measured attitudes toward a black presidential candidate only between 1972 and 1983, providing a much shorter trend. The NORC question is also not quite the same as the Gallup version, speaking of a "qualified" rather than a "well-qualified" person. Regional and educational differences are basically similar to those for Gallup, however, and the overall trend is positive, though as can be seen in table 3.1 the shape is less monotonic than for the Gallup question. We are unable to explain this difference, but we regard the much longer Gallup time series as more indicative of the broad trend on the basic issue of willingness to vote for a black presidential candidate. It should be noted that both the Gallup and NORC questions speak of a black candidate *nominated* by one's party, and thus cannot be directly compared to actual white voting for a black candidate such as Jesse Jackson who attempts to win a party nomination.

Intermarriage

We turn now to two items that deal with a quite different issue, but that still are phrased in a way that can be considered to deal essentially with principles. Both NORC and Gallup have asked questions on racial intermarriage, but the questions have been formulated differently. The NORC question, the one most clearly embodying abstract principle, asks whether there should be laws against intermarriage. In a sense this also involves an inquiry about implementation, but here the real issue is whether government should *stop*

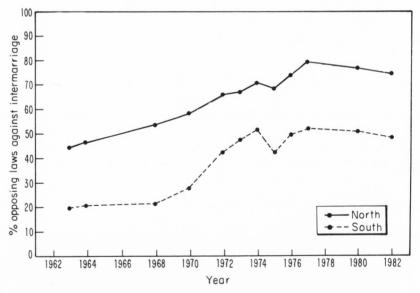

Figure 3.2. Attitudes toward laws against intermarriage.
   Laws against Intermarriage (NORC): "Do you think there should be laws against marriages between blacks and whites?"
   1. Yes   2. No

intervening to prevent a form of integration, rather than whether it should intervene to bring about integration. The overall trend for this question, as shown in figure 3.2, is positive in both regions, but it appears to have leveled off in the past few years in both the North and the South, and there is no sign of convergence. Educational differences (not shown here in the figure) are also large in both regions, with college-educated (13+) respondents most positive (rejecting laws against intermarriage) and the least-educated (0–11) respondents least positive, and again with no sign of convergence. It is not even clear that Northern college-educated respondents have reached a ceiling, since the percentage opposing laws against intermarriage in 1982, 90 percent, is noticeably under the levels reached for questions dealing with school integration (figure 3.1) and equal job opportunities and also represents no change from the 1980 results on the question and a 5 percent decline from 1977. Thus attitudes toward laws against intermarriage, though similar to previously discussed attitudes in terms of overall trend and relations to region and education, differ importantly in having apparently reached a plateau for all regional and educational categories. In the South this plateau is quite low, below the 50 percent mark. Thus in this symbolically more personal area of life, there is not the same consistent movement toward consensus on an ideal principle as in the other areas we have examined.

Gallup's question on intermarriage asks directly about approval versus disapproval, and as might be expected, a lower proportion of the population approves of intermarriage than opposes laws banning intermarriage. There are only four time points for the Gallup question, but the data for the South suggest a pattern similar to that for the NORC question—a rise in approval until the early 1970s, followed by some leveling off in approval—while in the North the change seems to be more monotonic. This difference for the North between approval of intermarriage and disapproval of laws against intermarriage is not easily explicable, but the levels of pro-integration sentiment are so different for the two questions that differences in the two Northern trends (slopes) are not necessarily inconsistent. The educational categories for the Gallup question on intermarriage do show the same differences as the other questions already discussed.[2]

General Segregation/Integration

The final question in table 3.1, labeled General Segregation, appears to embody the principles of racial desegregation at the most abstract level, and thus might be expected to show even more clearly the main trends we have been discussing: continuous positive change over the entire time period, a regional difference but with convergence toward a ceiling, and a clear positive association to educational level.

In fact, however, the results in important ways run counter to these expectations. True enough, few people even in the early 1960s claimed to favor segregation in general, and their number has decreased regularly between 1964 and 1978; there is a clear but decreasing North-South difference in this attitude; and at each time point general segregationist sentiments decline as education increases. But the opposite findings do not hold with regard to the *de*-segregation response. Beginning about 1970 this response shows a tradeoff with the vague middle response "something in between," producing a striking curvilinear effect for both these alternatives. Moreover, this effect occurs almost entirely in the North and is especially pronounced among the college educated. Figure 3.3 presents the three responses separately for college-educated Northern respondents. (No point in this figure is based on fewer than 120 cases, and most points are based on more than 350 cases.) Separate analysis by age indicates that the pattern shown in this figure appears especially among the relatively young age-group (18–29).

One possible interpretation of these trends, so different from all others in table 3.1, is that the provision of an ambiguous middle response ("something in between") allows whites an acceptable way of expressing their anxieties and reservations about integration, and that these anxieties and reservations suddenly took on new life around 1970 and increasingly thereafter. If so, responses on the General Segregation question could be a harbinger of things to come. The fact that it is young, well-educated Northerners who show the reversal most clearly is all the more meaningful, since they are both the best-informed and normally the most liberal part of the population on questions dealing with principle.

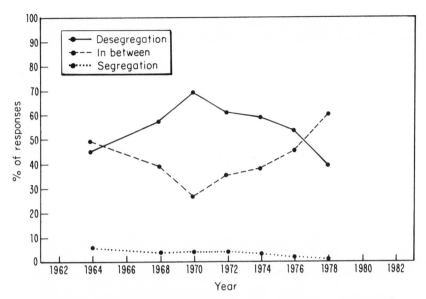

Figure 3.3. Attitudes toward segregation as a principle, among Northern, college-educated whites.
General Segregation (ISR): "Are you in favor of *desegregation*, strict *segregation*, or something in between?"
    1. Desegregation   2. Something in between   3. Strict segregation

If this interpretation is correct, the General Segregation question is very important. We therefore sought other evidence to support the interpretation. However, we found virtually no other such evidence for attitudes that concern principles of integration. Other questions dealing with broad principle do not show a turnabout, even as late as 1983 and even when college-educated or young Northerners are the focus. While no other principle question provides a middle alternative quite like the one in the General Segregation item, other questions do code ambivalent volunteered responses (such as "depends"), yet none shows a pattern much like that in figure 3.3.

For the moment we must leave open the issue of whether the General Segregation question points to a very important feature of change not captured by other items, or whether it indicates an idiosyncratic trend of little general importance. In the following section we will present experimental data involving context effects created by another question, data that point to a narrow interpretation of the curvilinear trend, though one that is of considerable interest. The delay is required because the related question deals not with principles but with the implementation of principles.

Summary

Almost all of the principle questions show strong positive trends over time. If only this set of questions were available to chart white racial attitudes over the past four decades, it would be reasonable to conclude that there has been a remarkably large, wide-ranging, and generally consistent movement toward white acceptance of integration in most important areas of American life; that is, the results for these questions strongly support the Progressive Trend school of thought discussed in Chapter 1. Moreover, clear-cut educational differences support the assertion that more educated respondents are more liberal in their racial outlook, and consistent regional differences indicate a historic North-South difference that tends to disappear only when a complete transformation in attitudes (a ceiling) has been reached. The one jarring note in all this is a peculiar reversal on a single item that deals with general attitudes toward integration—but in the absence of corroboration from other items this remains for the time being something of an oddity. There is also evidence that a question about laws against intermarriage, which combines elements of both principle and implementation, showed positive trends till the late 1970s, then leveled off over later years. But for the major public areas of life, trends in white racial attitudes in America since 1942 might well seem to integrationists to deserve the triumphant cry in Longfellow's poem: Excelsior! But when we turn to a different kind of inquiry, the picture changes markedly.

Implementation

Questions about implementation deal with approval or disapproval of steps the government might take to combat discrimination or segregation or to reduce racial inequalities in income or status. It would be useful if these questions exactly paralleled the principle questions in both content and dates. This is not always the case, but it does occur often enough to provide insight into white support for certain concrete steps that might be taken to put principles into practice. All of the questions classified as dealing with implementation are shown in table 3.2, with results for the white adult population as a whole.

Jobs

Figure 3.4 presents the results, by region, for a question we have labeled Federal Job Intervention. Since the question speaks simply of the government seeing that blacks get "fair treatment in jobs," it provides a close parallel to the principle question we labeled Equal Jobs. The latter is also shown in figure 3.4, with the time period limited as closely as possible to those years when both questions were asked. (See tables 3.1 and 3.2 for data for other years.) Both questions are quite general, and neither explicitly introduces new issues involving affirmative action in hiring. Thus there seems to be no very good reason for white respondents to regard the questions as dealing with substantially different issues. The two questions do differ in format: the intervention question includes a "no interest" filter, which complicates the comparison. Since the filter is built into the question itself, we include this response explicitly in table 3.2 and implicitly in figure 3.4 and similar figures.[3] We will regularly note the effect of removing "no interest" responses both by repercentaging and by excluding them from significance testing.

The results presented in figure 3.4 for the two jobs questions can be summarized as follows:

1. There is essentially no change over time in support for federal job intervention overall or in either region. (The small upward trend for Southerners that appears in the figure reversed in 1974.) This contrasts with the clear upward trend for the principle of equal job opportunities. Unfortunately we have no data for the intervention question before 1964, but the data we do have certainly do not suggest a sharp rise in support from 1944 like the one we found for the Equal Jobs question (table 3.1), and of course the latter question reaches a much higher percentage of positive responses throughout the 1960s than does the former.

2. The inclusion in the intervention question of the filter re-

Table 3.2 Implementation questions.

Question	62	63	64	65	66	67	68	69	70	71	72	73	74	75	76	77	78	79	80	81	82	83	Last minus first
Federal Job Intervention (ISR)																							
% Government should see to it	–	–	38	–	–	–	37	–	–	–	39	–	36	–	–	–	–	–	–	–	–	–	–2
% No interest	–	–	13	–	–	–	12	–	–	–	19	–	24	–	–	–	–	–	–	–	–	–	+11
Open Housing (NORC)																							
% No discrimination	–	–	–	–	–	–	–	–	–	–	–	34	–	34	35	–	37	–	40	–	–	46	+12
Federal School Intervention (ISR)																							
% Government should see to it	a	–	42	–	48	–	36	–	46	–	35	–	31	–	21	–	25	–	–	–	–	–	–17
% No interest	a	–	11	–	11	–	11	–	13	–	12	–	17	–	31	–	24	–	–	–	–	–	+13
Busing (ISR)																							
% Bus (1–4)	–	–	–	–	–	–	–	–	–	–	9	–	9	–	10	–	–	–	9	–	–	–	0
% Haven't thought much about this	–	–	–	–	–	–	–	–	–	–	6	–	8	–	9	–	–	–	5	–	–	–	–1
Busing (NORC)																							
% Favor	–	–	–	–	–	–	–	–	–	–	13	–	15	14	12	12	17	–	–	–	15	21	+8
Accommodations Intervention (ISR)																							
% Government should see to it	–	–	44	–	–	–	50	–	60	–	60	–	66	–	–	–	–	–	–	–	–	–	+22
% No interest	–	–	11	–	–	–	11	–	12	–	11	–	14	–	–	–	–	–	–	–	–	–	+3
Spending on Blacks (NORC)																							
% Too little	–	–	–	–	–	–	–	–	–	–	–	27	26	21	23	20	18	–	20	–	22	26	–1
% About right	–	–	–	–	–	–	–	–	–	–	–	46	48	49	46	49	50	–	51	–	53	51	+5

% Government help (1–3)	22								26	22	24	21	c	18	–4
% Haven't thought much about this	9								9	11	15	9	c	12	+3
Riots (ISR)															
% Solve problems (1–3)	d							d	51	46	41	20			–10
% Haven't thought much about this	d							d	9	14	20	9			+11

Question wordings and variants

Federal Job Intervention (ISR): "Some people feel that if black people are not getting fair treatment in jobs the government in Washington ought to see to it that they do. Others feel that this is not the federal government's business. Have you had enough interest in this question to favor one side over the other? [IF YES] How do you feel? Should the government in Washington see to it that black people get fair treatment in jobs or leave these matters to the states and local communities?"

1. Government should see to it
2. Government should stay out
3. No interest

Open Housing (NORC): "Suppose there is a community-wide vote on the general housing issue. There are two possible laws to vote on. One law says that a homeowner can decide for himself who to sell his house to, even if he prefers not to sell to blacks. The second law says that a homeowner cannot refuse to sell to someone because of their race or color. Which law would you vote for?"

1. Homeowner can decide
2. No discrimination

Federal School Intervention (ISR):[a] "Some people say that the government in Washington should see to it that white and black children are allowed to go to the same schools. Others claim that this is not the government's business. Have you been concerned enough about this question to favor one side over the other? [IF YES] Do you think the government in Washington should see to it that white and black children go to the same schools, or stay out of this matter as it is not its business?"

1. Government should see to it
2. Government should stay out
3. No interest

(Variant: in 1966 and 1970 replaced "white and black children go to the same schools" with "white and black children are allowed to go to the same schools.")

Busing (ISR): "There is much discussion about the best way to deal with racial problems. Some people think achieving racial integration of schools is so important that it justifies busing children to schools out of their own neighborhoods. Others think letting children go to their neighborhood schools is so important that they oppose busing. Where would you place yourself on this scale, or haven't you thought much about this?"

1. Bus to achieve integration (1–4)
2. Keep children in neighborhood schools (5–7)
3. Haven't thought much about this

Busing (NORC): "In general, do you favor or oppose the busing of black and white school children from one school district to another?"

1. Favor
2. Oppose

Accommodations Intervention (ISR): "As you may know, Congress passed a bill that says that black people should have the right to go to any hotel or restaurant they can afford, just like anybody else.

Table 3.2 (continued)

Question wordings and variants

Some people feel that this is something the government in Washington should support. Others feel that the government should stay out of this matter. Have you been interested enough in this to favor one side over another? [IF YES] Should the government support the right of black people to go to any hotel or restaurant they can afford, or should it stay out of this matter?"

1. Government should see to it
2. Government should stay out
3. No interest

(**Variant:** in 1964 replaced "anybody else" with "white people.")

Spending on Blacks (NORC):[b] "We are faced with many problems in this country, none of which can be solved easily or inexpensively. I'm going to name some of these problems, and for each one I'd like you to tell me whether you think we're spending too much money on it, or about the right amount. Improving the conditions of blacks. Are we spending too much, too little, or about the right amount on improving the conditions of blacks?"

1. Too little
2. About the right amount
3. Too much

Aid to Minorities (ISR):[c] "Some people feel that the government in Washington should make every possible effort to improve the social and economic position of blacks and other minority groups. Others feel that the government should not make any special effort to help minorities because they should help themselves. Where would you place yourself on this scale, or haven't you thought much about this?"

1. Government help (1-3)
2. Minority groups help themselves (4-7)
3. Haven't thought much about this

Riots (ISR):[d] "There is much discussion about the best way to deal with the problem of urban unrest and rioting. Some say it is more important to use all available force to maintain law and order—no matter what results. Others say it is more important to correct the problems of poverty and unemployment that give rise to the disturbances. Where would you place yourself on this scale, or haven't you thought much about this?"

1. Solve problems (1–3)
2. Use force (4–7)
3. Haven't thought much about this

a. An earlier version of the Federal School Intervention question was asked in 1962, but wording changes were too great for inclusion in trend analysis. The question read: "The government in Washington should see to it that white and colored children are allowed to go to the same schools. Do you have an opinion on this or not? [IF YES] Do you agree that the government should do this or do you think the government should not do it?" Of the respondents, 49 percent supported government action, 30 percent opposed it, and 15 percent said they had no opinion. Versions of this question involving even more substantial changes in wording were asked in 1956, 1958, and 1960.

b. Improving the conditions of blacks is eighth in the list of problems, following such things as improving and protecting the environment, halting the rising crime rate, and improving the nation's education system.

c. In 1980 the phrase "even if it means giving them preferential treatment in jobs" was added to the first sentence. It is quite probable that this change in wording altered the meaning of this question for respondents, and therefore we do not include the 1980 data in our trend analysis. For interested readers, however, 16 percent supported government aid to minorities, 73 percent thought minorities should help themselves, and 11 percent said they hadn't thought much about the issue.

d. In 1968 and 1970 the Riots question was asked *without* the interest filter, and for that reason we have not included those time points in our trend analysis. For interested readers, however, 37 percent of the white respondents in 1968 and 1970 said that we should solve poverty and unemployment and 63 percent supported the use of all available force to maintain law and order.

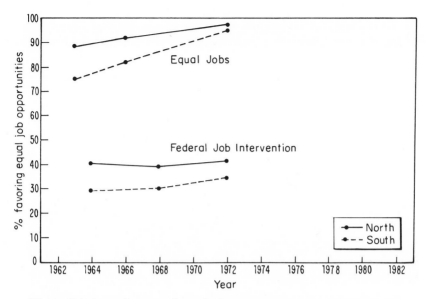

Figure 3.4. Attitudes toward equal job opportunities and toward federal intervention to ensure equal job opportunities.

Equal Jobs (*NORC*): "Do you think Negroes should have as good a chance as white people to get any kind of job, or do you think white people should have the first chance at any kind of job?"

    1. As good a chance   2. White people first

Federal Job Intervention (*ISR*): "Some people feel that if black people are not getting fair treatment in jobs the government in Washington ought to see to it that they do. Others feel that this is not the federal government's business. Have you had enough interest in this question to favor one side over the other?" (If Yes) "How do you feel? Should the government in Washington see to it that black people get fair treatment in jobs or leave these matters to the states and local communities?"

    1. Government should see to it   2. Government should stay out
    3. No interest

---

sponse "no interest" needs to be taken into account, for as table 3.2 shows, the proportion of whites who said they had "no interest" in federal job intervention doubled between 1964 and 1974, entirely at the expense of the response that government should not intervene. In other words, there was some movement in responses over the ten-year period, but the shift was entirely from the negative position on government intervention to the "no interest" position. Substantively, this bears some resemblance to the trend for the General Segregation question, but here it is the negative responses rather than the positive ones that move to the middle. Methodologically, there is no sure way to handle such a complex pattern, but one approach would be to omit "no interest" responses and to re-percentage the responses including only the positive and negative alternatives. If we do that for the data in table 3.2, the percentage favoring government intervention reveals a small but statistically significant rise, from 44 percent to 47 percent between 1964 and 1974 (linear trend: $p < .01$). This small increase, however, is overshadowed by the rise of 12 percent in support for the principle of equal job opportunities over approximately the same period (1963–1972), and the differences between the two slopes treated linearly is highly significant ($p < .001$). Thus, whether or not we include the "no interest" filter, support for federal intervention to promote equal job opportunities does not show the same degree of positive upward trend as does support for the principle of equal jobs over the comparable time period.[4]

3. There is a regional difference in the two trends in figure 3.4, but the recent convergence for the principle of equal job opportunities as support approaches a ceiling does not occur for federal intervention. Furthermore, although college-educated respondents show from 10 to 15 percent more acceptance of federal job intervention than do those with less education, there is virtually no difference in acceptance between the two lower educational levels (0–11 and 12 years). Thus the resemblance to the Equal Jobs principle question is only partial with respect to education.

In sum, in the period 1964–1974 white respondents showed much less support for having the federal government implement the principle of nondiscrimination in jobs than for the principle itself. Perhaps even more important, the levels of support for implementation showed little change during a time when adherence to the principle increased substantially, reaching nearly 100 percent. Trends by educational level are more ambiguous: college-educated respondents do tend to show greater support than other groups for both the principle and its implementation, but the difference is not as great on implementation as on principle, and the association with education disappears below the college level.

Schools

A second issue for which we have both principle and implementation questions is that of school integration. As we saw in table 3.1, there has been a steady increase in support for the principle of having black and white children attend the same schools. The implementation question in this case asks whether the federal government should "see to it" that this occurs, or should "stay out of this area." The contrast in results for the two questions is striking, as shown in figure 3.5. During the period for which data are available for both items, from 1964 to 1977–78, attitudes favoring the principle of school integration rose by 22 percentage points, but support for federal intervention to further school integration showed a *drop* of some 17 points. (If "no interest" responses are omitted from the percentages, the drop is 14 points.) The decline takes place entirely in the North, there being little long-term change in the South. The two regions therefore converge (in 1978), but the convergence is downward rather than upward as in previous regional comparisons. Moreover, although at the beginning of the time period support for federal school intervention is higher among the more educated, differences by education tend to disappear after 1970. There is also, after 1972, a sharp rise in "no interest" responses; these seem to be mainly shifts from the positive, "government see to it" response (see table 3.2)—a finding bearing some resemblance to that for the General Segregation item.

The interpretation of the unusual trends for attitudes toward federal school intervention seems clear. In the South the modest but stable support for federal intervention probably represents limited acceptance, however reluctant, of the federal role in ending legalized school segregation. (If "no interest" responses are omitted, there is a clear increase in Southern support for intervention.) It is likely that, if we had data going back to the 1950s when federal court desegregation began, we would find the level of opposition to federal intervention close to 100 percent in the South. In the North, support for federal desegregation efforts may have been as high in the late 1950s as in the early 1960s, since attention was then focused only on ending *de jure* segregation in the South. Northern support began to erode by the mid-1960s, when efforts were begun to alter *de facto* segregation in the North, and slipped even more

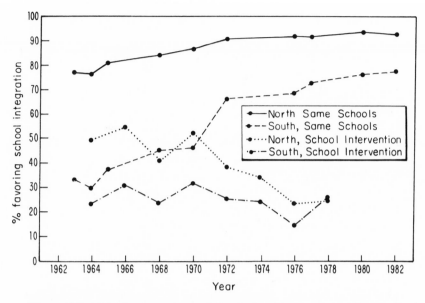

Figure 3.5. Attitudes toward principle of school integration and toward federal intervention to ensure school integration.

Same Schools (NORC): "Do you think white students and black students should go to the same schools or to separate schools?"
   1. Same   2. Separate

Federal School Intervention (ISR): "Some people say that the government in Washington should see to it that white and black children are allowed to go to the same schools. Others claim that this is not the government's business. Have you been concerned enough about this question to favor one side over the other?" (If Yes) "Do you think the government in Washington should see to it that white and black children go to the same schools, or stay out of this matter as it is not its business?"
   1. Government should see to it   2. Government should stay out
      3. No interest

rapidly in the 1970s as the controversy over busing began to heat up. The decline in support for federal school intervention was not entirely a white phenomenon; data to be presented in Chapter 4 show a somewhat similar trend among blacks. In any case, with respect to white attitudes toward school integration, trends in support of principle and of implementation have proceeded in opposite directions.

At least part of the reason for the loss of support for federal intervention was doubtless due to, and symbolized by, the school busing issue. Attitudes toward busing are shown in table 3.2 for both an NORC question and an ISR question. Although the precise trends for the limited period available (1972–1983) are not entirely clear, what is evident is the overwhelming white opposition to busing at *all* time points. The opposition is a little stronger in the South than in the North, and slightly stronger among high school graduates than among other educational categories (data not shown), but these are minor variations in an overall pattern of nearly unanimous sentiment against busing as a means of desegregating schools. The findings fit well with and help to explain the decline in the North in support for federal school intervention during the 1970s, as such intervention increasingly became identified with busing. (Shifts in sentiment in the South concerning federal intervention cannot be similarly explained, but the whole history of school desegregation in the South provided a different context when busing was first introduced, primarily in the North, in the 1970s.)

The nearly unanimous opposition of whites to busing may well have an impact that extends beyond questions on the implementation of school integration. Recall the puzzling reversal in trends of responses to the very general question dealing with the broad principle of desegregation versus segregation or "something in between" (figure 3.3). That reversal occurred in 1970, exactly when the decline in support for federal implementation of school desegregation revealed in figure 3.5 begins. This suggests that from 1970 on the two trends may be linked in some way. Furthermore, there is evidence from other studies that very general items like the General Segregation question (figure 3.3) are especially subject to context effects, presumably because their meaning is vague and therefore tends to be interpreted in terms of the more specific questions that precede them (Schuman and Presser 1981). And, in fact, in all of the ISR surveys in which the General Segregation question appeared, it came soon after the School Intervention item.[5] Thus we hypothesize that the downturn after 1970 in support for the general principle of desegregation was due to the change in attitudes toward the specific issue of federal intervention to promote school integration, which in turn was due largely to the sudden prominence of the busing issue.

This hypothesis cannot be tested directly, but it is possible to determine whether responses to the General Segregation question can be affected by its placement after the School Intervention question. We carried out such a split-ballot experiment in January 1983: half of a national telephone sample were asked the General Segregation item after the Federal School Intervention item; the other half were asked the General Segregation item after the Equal Jobs item (the latter a principle question with nearly 100 percent agreement to the pro-integration response; see table 3.1). The findings from this experiment lend striking support to our hypothesis:

Response to General Segregation item	When preceded by Equal Jobs item	When preceded by School Intervention item
Desegregation	61.4%	38.9%
Something in between	36.1	57.1
Segregation	2.5	4.0
Total	100	100
N	(158)	(149)

These figures show a 23 percent difference in the choice of the "desegregation" response between the two contexts, with most of the shift involving the "something in between" response ($X^2 = 15.6$, d.f. = 2, p < .001). Such results strongly suggest that the pattern presented in Figure 3.3 may be an artifact resulting from a combination of the vagueness of the General Segregation question, its regular placement after the Federal School Intervention item in the standard ISR surveys, and the fact that the Federal School Intervention item itself showed an important decline during the same period. In sum, what appeared to be a decrease in support for the broad *principle* of desegregation—a decrease wholly inconsistent with trends on other principle items—may have been a reflection of a much more specific decrease in support for the *implementation* of school desegregation through busing or other federal action.

Open Housing Laws

There is not quite as close a parallel between principle and implementation questions for residential choice as for jobs and schools,

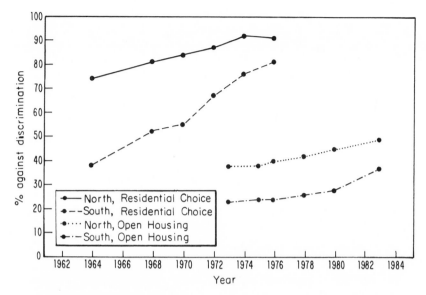

Figure 3.6. Attitudes toward the principle of free residential choice and toward open housing laws.

Residential Choice, two alternatives (*ISR*): "Which of these statements would you agree with: White people have a right to keep black people out of their neighborhoods if they want to, or, black people have a right to live wherever they can afford to, just like anybody else?"

   1. Keep blacks out   2. Blacks have rights

Open Housing (*NORC*): "Suppose there is a community-wide vote on the general housing issue. There are two possible laws to vote on. One law says that a homeowner can decide for himself who to sell his house to, even if he prefers not to sell to blacks. The second law says that a homeowner cannot refuse to sell to someone because of their race or color. Which law would you vote for?"

   1. Homeowner can decide   2. No discrimination

---

but the question on open housing laws (table 3.2) does give a clear indication of willingness to have the government enforce free choice for black homeseekers. The question has the advantage of referring to a "community-wide vote" to prevent housing discrimination, so that concern over federal intrusion into local affairs is not relevant to the results.

Table 3.2, figure 3.6, and other analysis show, first, that support for open housing legislation is not strong, reaching only 46 percent in 1983. This is in contrast to the levels reached in support of the *principle* that blacks have a right to live in white neighborhoods if they wish: 88 percent on the ISR version of the question (shown in figure 3.6) and 71 percent on the NORC version. (The ISR Residential Choice question seems the more appropriate one for comparison, since it, like the Open Housing question, presents a dichotomous choice between two alternatives that are balanced in that each offers an appealing rationale.) Although we do not place heavy emphasis on isolated instances of differences in marginal percentages, we cannot disregard them when they occur repeatedly and consistently in these comparisons of principle and implementation questions. Second, there is a significant positive trend (p < .01) overall between 1973 and 1983 on the Open Housing question, although during the comparable time period when both were asked (1972–73 to 1976), the Residential Choice question showed a clear positive change (+8 percent), whereas the Open Housing question showed virtually none at all (+1 percent).[6] Third, there are regional differences with regard to open housing, as there are for residential choice. Finally, there are clear monotonic differences by educational category: the more education, the more support for open housing. The differences are somewhat smaller, however, than for the principle of residential choice.[7]

In sum, the results for the implementation question on Open Housing appear to resemble, though on a reduced scale, the results for the Residential Choice question. There is some support for open housing legislation, but it is more limited than support for the principle of residential choice; some definite increase in that support, but it is less sharp; and some difference by educational level, but not quite as much. It is important to note, however, that support for an open housing law has continued to grow in the recent past; it is possible that in this area of life attitudes toward implementation will parallel, with some lag, attitudes toward principle. Future time points are going to be especially important to follow for this trend.

Public Accommodations

We have now seen trends in attitudes toward implementation that are variously level, negative, and moderately positive. It might be argued that the lack of clearly increasing support for implementation in some areas is due to the unwillingness of whites to endorse federal interference and coercion to solve problems. Such an interpretation fits the fact that the most positive trend we have discovered occurs on a question that specifies local rather than federal implementation of desegregation. But this interpretation fails when we consider attitudes toward the implementation of black rights to the use of public accommodations. As table 3.2 shows, there was a 16 percent increase between 1964 and 1970 in willingness to support federal enforcement of the desegregation of hotels and restaurants, a rise of the same magnitude as the rise of 15 percent for the closely parallel question on attitudes toward the *principle* of equal access to accommodations (table 3.1). Both these questions show a monotonic increase over three nearly identical time points, and the implementation item has two additional time points that maintain the rise.

As figure 3.7 shows, in both North and South the positive trends for federal intervention to enforce desegregation in this sphere of life have been fairly strong and steady, though the trend for the *total* sample did not reach by 1974 (the most recent time point available) the level attained in 1963 by the parallel principle question. Attitudes toward federal intervention in the sphere of public accommodations also show clear educational and regional differences—attitudes being more positive in the North and among those with more education—throughout the time period. In these respects, as in overall trend, the results fit quite well the dominant model we found to hold for principle items. However, the lower level for implementation throughout the whole time period does suggest that the implementation component to the question is having *some* effect different from principle items, though not an effect on the trend itself.

Why should trends in attitudes toward federal intervention in public accommodations be so different from those for what are basically similar intervention questions regarding jobs and schools? There are probably several reasons, although they are difficult to disentangle without experimentation. First, unlike all the other questions about federal intervention, this one begins by stating that "Congress has passed a bill that says that black people have a right to go to any hotel or restaurant . . ." Thus the basic intervention it-

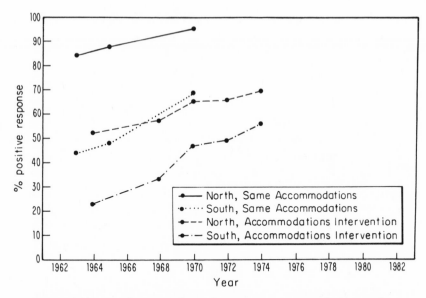

Figure 3.7. Attitudes toward equal access to accommodations and toward federal intervention to ensure equal access.

Same Accommodations (NORC): "Do you think Negroes should have the right to use the same parks, restaurants, and hotels as white people?"
    1. Yes 2. No

Accommodations Intervention (ISR): "As you may know, Congress passed a bill that says that black people should have the right to go to any hotel or restaurant they can afford, just like anybody else. Some people feel that this is something the government in Washington should support. Others feel that the government should stay out of this matter. Have you been interested enough in this to favor one side over another?" (If Yes) "Should the government support the right of black people to go to any hotel or restaurant they can afford, or should it stay out of this matter?"
    1. Government should see to it 2. Government should stay out
      3. No interest

self is already said to be legitimized, and it only remains to ask whether "the government in Washington" should support this legislation. (Moreover, the phrasing of this question differs subtly from that of the jobs and school intervention questions; it speaks of government "supporting," rather than "seeing to," a right. These kinds of variation in wording make comparisons across questions very difficult.) Second, as already noted, at least token desegregation in most hotels and restaurants is no longer a live issue. Endorsement of government action may be easier when it is no longer much needed. A third explanation may be that the kind of interracial interaction implied by hotel and restaurant integration is so superficial that it poses little threat to whites, unlike the more profound interaction involved when jobs, schools, and neighborhoods are integrated. In this sense, federal enforcement in this area might be seen as more symbolic than practical, closer to the level of principle than to the implementation of change.

Whatever the explanation, the 22 percent increase over the ten-year period in support for federal intervention to guarantee blacks access to public accommodations is of the same order of magnitude as the increase for comparable periods in support for principles (table 3.1). This indicates that opposition to federal intervention per se is not an adequate explanation for the quite different trends in the spheres of employment and school integration.

Economic Intervention

We turn finally to three questions concerning a problem that is not dealt with at all by the questions on principle in table 3.1. This is the issue of direct government intervention to improve the economic status of blacks as a group. The absence of parallel principle items is a disadvantage, but nevertheless these economically oriented questions provide valuable data on an important type of government intervention. It seems possible that white respondents who are reluctant to approve coercive intervention to end segregation may be more willing to favor constructive economic intervention to improve the condition of blacks in America.

The clearest of the three economic questions in table 3.2, which we have labeled Spending on Blacks, asks whether the amount of money "we" are spending on "improving the conditions of blacks" is too much, too little, or about right. The main result during the 1973–1983 period when NORC asked this question was a *drop* in support for such expenditure, represented by a decrease in the response "too little" and a nearly comparable increase in the response "about right." Most of the decline in "too little" occurs among college-educated respondents, as shown in figure 3.8. (There

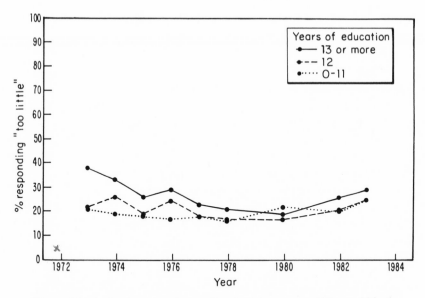

Figure 3.8. Attitudes toward spending to improve conditions of blacks, by education.

Spending on Blacks (NORC): "We are faced with many problems in this country, none of which can be solved easily or inexpensively. I'm going to name some of these problems, and for each one I'd like you to tell me whether you think we're spending too much money on it, too little money, or about the right amount. Improving the conditions of blacks. Are we spending too much, too little, or about the right amount on improving the conditions of blacks?"

1. Too little   2. About right   3. Too much

---

is also a small regional difference in the 1970s, but it disappears in recent years.) However, in 1982 and 1983 there is evidence of an upswing, with the college educated again taking the lead.[8] Overall, the responses to this question reveal a relatively low level of support for government action in the economic area, with a further dip during the mid-1970s, followed by a partial recovery in the most recent years. The volatility in the trend is due largely to the college-educated segments of the population.

An ISR question on government efforts "to improve the social and economic position of blacks and other minority groups" (labeled Aid to Minorities) is somewhat more vague in content, but seems fairly close in implication to the NORC Spending on Blacks item. Breaking the 7-point scale into two parts (1–3, support for such government efforts; 4–7, opposition), we find little noticeable change over the six-year period (table 3.2). College-educated respondents indicate greater support for government economic intervention than do others, but a decline for this educational category is noticeable for Northern respondents after 1972. Support for such efforts is greater in the North than in the South for the entire time period.[9]

The third question on economic intervention, the question we have labeled Riots, was initiated by ISR in 1968 after the riots of 1967 in Newark, Detroit, and other American cities. The question offers respondents a 7-point scale on which to indicate the best way to deal with urban unrest—with "force" at one extreme and correcting problems of poverty and unemployment at the other. There is evidence that during the four-year period in which the same wording was used—1972–1976—there was some movement away from an emphasis on dealing with the economic sources of the riots, and an increase in the "haven't thought much about this" response. A North-South difference is clear throughout, white Southerners being more willing to recommend force. There is also a slight tendency for less-educated respondents to approve of force. The overall results on this question do not substantially alter the picture provided by the more general economic questions.

In sum, during the 1970s support for government economic intervention to aid blacks showed none of the rise manifested by support for equalitarian principles. Rather, there is some decline in support, most noticeably among college-educated Northerners, although the dominant note is lack of change over this time span. Unfortunately, only data from the 1970s and early 1980s are available. We therefore have no way of knowing what the picture would look like if trends on these economic questions were available for the 1940s, 1950s, or 1960s.

Summary

The results for questions dealing with implementation present a different picture from those dealing with principle. Whereas the latter almost invariably show steady progress by whites toward complete acceptance of racial integration in each sphere examined, the implementation questions present a picture of relatively low levels of support for translating principles into practice, and only partial signs of that support increasing over time. Whether the implementation is at the federal or local level, whether it is legal or economic, white Americans are much less enthusiastic about modes of implementation than about abstract principles. The clearest exception concerns a transient and relatively impersonal sphere of life: desegregation of hotels and restaurants. In this single area, where efforts at desegregation have achieved probably their greatest success, whites do increasingly endorse federal enforcement of equal treatment. A second important positive sign is the statistically significant and continuing, though still modest, increase in support for local open housing laws during the 1970s and into the 1980s. These are the exceptions to levels and trends that otherwise appear to provide support for the Underlying Racism thesis we described in Chapter 1.

The recurrent differences in level and trend between questions dealing with principles and questions dealing with the implementation of these principles warn against drawing broad conclusions about change in racial attitudes from only one of these two types of items. Differences by educational level are also usually weaker for implementation questions than for principle questions, and tend to disappear altogether on some items because of declining support for implementation among the college educated. In general, where there is abrupt change upward or downward in attitudes toward implementing integration, the college educated appear to take the lead.

Social Distance

The third substantial set of questions that are available at various time points ask white respondents how they personally would feel or act with regard to particular situations involving racial integration. These questions, shown in table 3.3, focus not on government or other political forms of implementation, but on predicting one's own individual behavior in certain practical situations. For most respondents, of course, the situations are hypothetical, and we are not here directly concerned with whether the predictions would turn out to be valid. Instead, we take the predictions as informative in their own right. They are especially useful because they differentiate rather clearly among several degrees of integration and indicate which are more acceptable to whites at a personal level.

School Integration

All but one of the social distance questions concern either school integration or residential integration, the exception being an item on interracial dining in one's home. The three questions on varying degrees of school integration were asked by both Gallup and NORC. We concentrate on the Gallup series for overall trends, since it offers a much longer time span (1958–1980, as against 1972–1983 for NORC). Although the Gallup sample was restricted to parents of children in school, as compared to the full adult sample used by NORC, the two organizations show essentially the same overall levels of support for comparable years. (See figure 2.3 for a comparison of the Gallup and NORC data.) We use the NORC data for internal analysis by region and education because the NORC samples are larger and provide better representation of the total population.

The three school integration questions, which we have labeled Few, Half, and Most, ask whether respondents would object to sending their own children to a school with different proportions of black children: "a few," "half," "more than half." The basic results are rather different from those reported for either principle or implementation questions. Over the 1958–1980 period, there is a slight rise among Northerners in the "no objection" (that is, the pro-integration) response, and a sharp rise among Southerners in the same response, so that by the end of the 1970s the South is close to the North in level of personal acceptance of school integration (see figure 2.4). Almost exactly the same pattern is manifested for each of the three questions, although the overall levels of "no objection" are quite different for the three degrees of integration.

The differential trends by region no doubt reflect the special history of legal segregation of schools in the South, and it is striking to note the speed and completeness with which Southern responses reached nearly Northern levels in about a decade and a half. At the

Table 3.3 Social distance questions.

Question	Year of survey														
	42	43	44	45	46	48	50	56	57	58	59	60	61	62	63
Few (Gallup)															
% No objection	–	–	–	–	–	–	–	–	–	75	81	–	–	–	7
Half (Gallup)															
% No objection	–	–	–	–	–	–	–	–	–	50	55	–	–	–	5
Most (Gallup)															
% No objection	–	–	–	–	–	–	–	–	–	33	31	–	–	–	2
Few (NORC)															
% No objection	–	–	–	–	–	–	–	–	–	–	–	–	–	–	–
Half (NORC)															
% No objection	–	–	–	–	–	–	–	–	–	–	–	–	–	–	–
Most (NORC)															
% No objection	–	–	–	–	–	–	–	–	–	–	–	–	–	–	–
Next Door (Gallup)															
% Might	–	–	–	–	–	–	–	–	–	23	–	–	–	–	2
% No	–	–	–	–	–	–	–	–	–	56	–	–	–	–	5
Great Numbers (Gallup)															
% Might	–	–	–	–	–	–	–	–	–	29	–	–	–	–	2
% No	–	–	–	–	–	–	–	–	–	20	–	–	–	–	2
Same Block (NORC)															
% No	36	–	–	–	–	–	–	53	–	–	–	–	–	–	6
Black Dinner Guest (NORC)															
% Mildly	–	–	–	–	–	–	–	–	–	–	–	–	–	–	1
% Not at all	–	–	–	–	–	–	–	–	–	–	–	–	–	–	5
Neighborhood Preference A (ISR-Personal)															
% Mostly white	–	–	–	–	–	–	–	–	–	–	–	–	–	–	
% Mixed/Makes no difference[a]	–	–	–	–	–	–	–	–	–	–	–	–	–	–	
Neighborhood Preference B (ISR-Telephone)															
% Mostly white	–	–	–	–	–	–	–	–	–	–	–	–	–	–	
% Mixed/Makes no difference[a]	–	–	–	–	–	–	–	–	–	–	–	–	–	–	

Question wordings and variants

Few (Gallup): "Would you, yourself, have any objection to sending your children to a school where few of the children are black?"

  1. Yes
  2. No

Half (Gallup): [If No to FEW] "Where half of the children are black?"

  1. Yes
  2. No

	65	66	67	68	69	70	71	72	73	74	75	76	77	78	79	80	81	82	83	Last minus first
	Year of survey																			
–	84	90	–	–	89	92	–	–	92	–	94	–	–	95	–	95	–	–	–	+20
–	60	60	–	–	67	70	–	–	69	–	70	–	–	69	–	76	–	–	–	+26
–	35	35	–	–	39	39	–	–	37	–	42	–	–	38	–	42	–	–	–	+9
–	–	–	–	–	–	–	–	93	–	95	93	–	93	95	–	–	–	94	95	+2
–	–	–	–	–	–	–	–	76	–	71	71	–	75	76	–	–	–	76	76	0
–	–	–	–	–	–	–	–	43	–	37	39	–	39	43	–	–	–	43	37	–6
–	23	21	24	–	–	–	–	–	–	–	–	–	–	10	–	–	–	–	–	–13
–	63	66	63	–	–	–	–	–	–	–	–	–	–	86	–	–	–	–	–	+30
–	30	31	32	–	–	–	–	–	–	–	–	–	–	33	–	–	–	–	–	+4
–	28	30	28	–	–	–	–	–	–	–	–	–	–	46	–	–	–	–	–	+26
4	69	71	–	77	_	–	–	85	–	–	–	–	–	–	–	–	–	–	–	+49
–	–	21	–	–	–	17	–	15	15	16	–	15	17	–	–	15	–	12	–	–5
–	–	55	–	–	–	65	–	70	69	73	–	72	71	–	–	74	–	78	–	+26
–	–	–	–	–	–	–	–	23	–	34	–	32	–	–	–	–	–	–	–	+9
–	–	–	–	–	–	–	–	31	–	27	–	28	–	–	–	–	–	–	–	–3
–	–	–	–	–	–	–	–	–	–	–	–	29	–	–	–	–	34	–	–	+5
–	–	–	–	–	–	–	–	–	–	–	–	43	–	–	–	–	42	–	–	–1

Most (Gallup): [If No to HALF] "Where more than half of the children are black?"
 1. Yes
 2. No

Few (NORC): "Would you, yourself, have any objection to sending your children to a school where a w of the children are blacks?"
 1. Yes
 2. No

Table 3.3 (continued)

Question Wordings and Variants

Half (NORC): [If No or DK to FEW] "Where half of the children are blacks?"
1. Yes
2. No

Most (NORC): [If No or DK to HALF] "Where more than half of the children are blacks?"
1. Yes
2. No

Next Door (Gallup): "If black people came to live next door, would you move?"
1. Yes, definitely
2. Might
3. No

Great Numbers (Gallup): "Would you move if black people came to live in great numbers in you neighborhood?"
1. Yes, definitely
2. Might
3. No

Same Block (NORC): "If a Negro with the same income and education as you have moved into you block, would it make any difference to you?"
1. Yes
2. No

Black Dinner Guest (NORC): "How strongly would you object if a member of your family wanted bring a black friend home to dinner? Would you object strongly, mildly, or not at all?"
1. Strongly
2. Mildly
3. Not at all
(Variant: in 1966 used "Negro" instead of "Negro friend"; "black" introduced in 1977.)

Neighborhood Preference (ISR-Personal): "Would you personally prefer to live in a neighborho with all white people, mostly white people, mostly blacks, or a neighborhood that's mixed half and half
1. All white
2. Mostly white
3. Mostly blacks
4. Mixed
5. No difference (volunteered)
(Variant: in 1976, the question read, "Would you personally prefer to live in a neighborhood that is white, mostly white, about half white and half black, or mostly black?")

Neighborhood Preference (ISR-Telephone): "Would you personally prefer to live in a neighborho with mostly whites, mostly blacks, or a neighborhood that is mixed half and half? [If Mostly white Would you prefer a mostly white neighborhood or an all white neighborhood? [If Mostly blacks] Wou you prefer a mostly black neighborhood or an all black neighborhood?"
1. All whites
2. Mostly whites
3. Mostly blacks
4. Mixed
5. No difference (volunteered)
6. All black

a. Almost all of these responses are in the "mixed" or the volunteered "no difference" categories. All the categories are collapsed in tables and reported under the category labeled "Mixed/Makes no difference."

same time, responses to the Half question resemble some of the implementation items in that they show little change once the regions converge. In another sense, however, the comparison is misleading, for the level of "no objection" responses on the Half question is quite high (over 70 percent), much higher than approval for government intervention to bring about school or residential integration. It can also be argued that few racial or ethnic groups will voluntarily choose to be in a fifty-fifty, let alone minority, situation vis-à-vis some other group.

Indeed, the level of acceptance of full-scale school integration is so high that it seemed to us possible that there might be artifactual inflation here because of the order of the items. Some white respondents who genuinely feel and report "no objection" to having their children in a school with a *few* black children might feel constrained to answer "no objection" to the next question about a fifty-fifty situation and even to the third question about a mostly black school. This would create a spuriously high acceptance of situations where white students would not be in the majority. In order to test this possibility we carried out an experiment that varied the order of the Few and Half questions. To our surprise, there was no evidence at all that responses to the Half question are inflated by a context effect.[10]

Turning to internal analysis within both regions, education shows some positive association with acceptance of schools with few or equal numbers of black students, but not of schools where more than half the students are black. Figure 3.9 presents the trends by education for Northern respondents since 1972, when the three questions were first asked in NORC's General Social Survey. The differences by education on the Few and Half questions are not large, but their general consistency leaves the basic relation, modest though it is, in little doubt.

A useful feature of all the findings for these three school integration questions is the sharp difference in response that the words "few," "half," and "more than half" evoke. Analysts who claim that most white respondents do not reveal anti-integration sentiments in survey interviews must contend with the willingness of a considerable number of respondents to give different answers to questions that differ only in the degree of integration posed. This

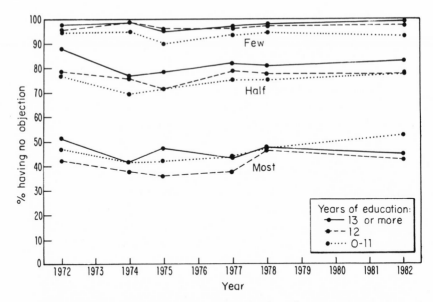

Figure 3.9. Attitudes toward attending schools with various proportions of blacks, by education (North only).

Few (NORC): "Would you, yourself, have any objections to sending your children to a school where a few of the children are blacks?"

　　1. Yes　2. No

Half (NORC): (If No or DK to Few) "Where half of the children are blacks?"

　　1. Yes　2. No

Most (NORC): (If No or DK to Half) "Where more than half of the children are blacks?"

　　1. Yes　2. No

does not imply that concealment in answers to racial questions is entirely absent—our earlier discussion of telephone versus face-to-face differences indicates otherwise—but simply to note that within these data on racial attitudes a *major* determinant of response is the substance of the question itself, and that many white respondents are quite willing to distinguish between degrees of integration they find acceptable and unacceptable. If there is little reason to doubt the relatively high rejection by white parents of having their children attend predominantly black schools, there should also be little reason to doubt their willingness to have their children in schools where a few of the children are black.[11]

Residential Integration

We have no graded set of questions on residential integration to match the three school integration items, but there are two that come close to the extremes of "few" and "most," and a third differently worded item that provides additional data relevant to the "few" pole. The first two questions ask whether respondents would themselves move if, at the one extreme, blacks came to live "next door," and at the other extreme, "great numbers" of blacks came into the neighborhood. (Although the "next door" question is not wholly unambiguous, respondents probably take it to refer to a single black family considered in isolation from other changes.) These two questions were always asked together (by Gallup) in that sequence at different points between 1958 and 1978. The third question, by NORC, more clearly involves a single black person or black family, specifies that income and education are the same as the respondent's, and speaks of the same block rather than next door—all of which might elicit more white acceptance; on the other hand, the question asks whether this would "make any difference" to the respondent (rather than whether the respondent would actually move), which might more easily allow a negative answer. The time period for this item is also different (1942–1972) from the Gallup period, but there is enough overlap to allow close comparison. Such a comparison, presented graphically for the total population in figure 3.10, indicates that the "same block" and "next door" questions yield quite similar results, despite their several differences in wording, and that both show much higher support than the "great numbers" question. All of the questions show a clear upward trend in acceptance of integration. By the end of the time periods (late 1970s in one case, mid-1970s in the other) Northern respondents approach 90 percent positive answers with regard to a black family moving next door or onto the same block, and 48 percent for great numbers of black people moving into the neighborhood. Separate regional analysis shows that Southern respondents are definitely less positive; the trends for the South parallel those for the North at a lower level over the entire time period, with some convergence in more recent years.

On the two questions about single black families, college-educated respondents in the North give more positive responses

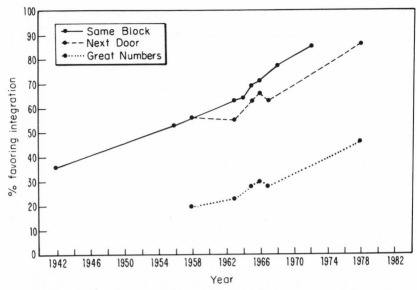

Figure 3.10. Attitudes toward various levels of neighborhood integration.

Same Block (NORC): "If a Negro with the same income and education as you have moved into your block, would it make any difference to you?"

    1. Yes 2. No

Next Door (Gallup): "If black people came to live next door, would you move?"

    1. Yes, definitely 2. Might 3. No

Great Numbers (Gallup): "Would you move if black people came to live in great numbers in your neighborhood?"

    1. Yes, definitely 2. Might 3. No

than do other educational groups, but the difference is not large and does not hold as clearly for Southern respondents. In the case of the Great Numbers question, there are no clear educational differences in either region, just as there were none for the "more than half" school integration question. In other words, education is positively associated with personal acceptance of a small number of blacks, but this effect of education disappears when the degree of integration posed by a question is so great as to put whites in the minority.

A fourth question, Neighborhood Preference, approaches personal involvement in residential integration from a different standpoint—not degree of personal objection, but rather degree of positive personal preference. The data are somewhat complex, for there are two different versions of the question. Version A was asked at three time points in face-to-face surveys, version B at two time points in telephone surveys. Thus the two different trends, neither of which extends very long in time, must be kept separate, since either question wording or mode of administration might have created differences in the patterns of response. Both versions are shown in table 3.3.

The responses are indeed different for the two questions, with more positive responses given to version B than to version A. Much of this difference can be attributed to mode of administration, as discussed in Chapter 2.[12] Other than this constant difference in level, however, the two time series lead to similar results. There is little evidence of change over the two periods, though there seems to be some shift from a preference for "all white" to one for "mostly white." (The lack of change for the limited periods covered by these two questions is not unusual; there is no change over comparable short periods for the other residential questions.) Examination of the trends by region indicates that Northern respondents are regularly more positive about living in integrated neighborhoods than are Southern respondents, but that most of the positive change occurs within the Southern sample, especially between 1976 and 1981. Educational differences are fairly large and similar to those found for the principle questions: college-educated respondents are more likely to prefer some degree of integration than are those with a high school education, who in turn are more likely to favor integration than are those with less than a high school education.

Social Interaction

One other question asks respondents to predict their personal behavior, namely, whether they would object "strongly, mildly, or not at all" if a family member "wanted to bring a black friend home to dinner." The question deals with a more directly interpersonal situation than we have been considering thus far and allows for even "mild" objection, but the context makes the interaction transient and defines the black guest as already a friend of a family member. For some respondents there may be overtones beyond a casual meeting (in the film *Guess Who's Coming to Dinner* a white woman invited her black fiancé home to meet her parents), but there is no way of telling how common such overtones are.

As figure 3.11 shows, there were large regional differences on this item in the early 1960s, but these have tended to decrease in the ensuing decade. In the North the response of objecting "not at all" has reached 80 percent, but there is some evidence of leveling off at this point rather than of moving rapidly toward a ceiling; this pattern is reminiscent of attitudes toward laws against intermarriage (table 3.1). There are also clear educational differences within both regions: the more educated the respondent, the less objection to a black dinner guest.

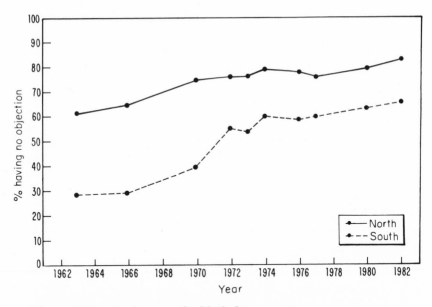

Figure 3.11. Attitudes toward a black dinner guest.
  Black Dinner Guest (NORC): "How strongly would you object if a member of your family wanted to bring a black friend home to dinner? Would you object strongly, mildly, or not at all?"
  1. Strongly   2. Mildly   3. Not at all

It is interesting to note that the choice of the middle response "mildly" is always low (around 15 percent) and shows little sign of changing over the period. The visible shift in answers over time is from one extreme ("object strongly") to the other ("not at all"), rather than via the middle alternative of "mildly." More important, there is no sign of the phenomenon observed for the question on general attitudes toward segregation, in which a middle response seemed to offer respondents a way to backtrack in recent years from an earlier acceptance of desegregation.

Summary

Despite some puzzles, the social distance questions form a generally meaningful pattern both internally and in relation to the principle and implementation questions. First, it is important to note that Northern white acceptance of (lack of objection to) "a few" black children in a school has been quite high, essentially at a ceiling, almost from the earliest time the question was asked by Gallup (1958). Acceptance of a single black family moving into one's immediate neighborhood, on the other hand, starts at a much lower level, but shows a sharp climb over the time period for which data are available. This difference between the two types of questions probably reflects the fact that a school defines a neighborhood setting as a good deal wider and less personal than a person's own block—and in fact throughout the North some small amount of integration of schools has long been more common than integration within blocks. The upward slope for the housing questions thus represents the increasing acceptance in the past four decades of such small-scale neighborhood residential integration. The question about a black dinner guest shows much the same upward trend, though the more clearly personal and voluntary nature of the situation may account for the leveling off that occurs at around 80 percent for this question but not for the others.

Most of these questions reveal a relation to education that is similar to that for questions dealing with abstract principle: the more education, the more personal acceptance of one or a few blacks into a school, on a block, or as an invited guest. The relation to education is strongest for the most voluntary and individualized action, namely inviting a black dinner guest, and for the Neighborhood Preference item that deals with *wishing* to live in a somewhat integrated neighborhood. The relation to education is weaker where more realistic and less voluntary everyday situations are involved, as in the case of a few black children in school or blacks moving in next door.

Acceptance of larger numbers of blacks into previously white schools or neighborhoods is clearly more limited, though it is surprisingly high. We thought at first that questionnaire order might play a role here, since the questions about integration involving a single black family or a few black children always precede questions about higher proportions of blacks. But at least in the case of the sequence of questions on schools, our new experimental evidence indicates that the order of questions is not important. We are also not certain why acceptance of "great numbers" of blacks moving into a neighborhood shows a sharp upward trend over time, while acceptance of "more than half" black children in a school shows only a slight rise, but the wordings are too different to be completely comparable. Easier to interpret is the disappearance of educational differences for questions about "more than half" blacks in a school or "great numbers" of blacks in a neighborhood: when the degree of integration proposed would make whites into a minority, highly educated respondents are no longer in the vanguard.

Southern respondents generally show less acceptance of personal involvement in desegregated situations, but the regional difference has tended to decrease in recent years. This decrease occurs most strikingly for acceptance of school integration; a large regional difference in earlier decades—no doubt due to the heritage of legal segregation of schools in the South—virtually disappeared by the 1970s.

The results for the social distance questions can be connected to those for the principle and implementation questions by the following reasoning. The major change in the past four decades has involved rejection of absolute racial segregation and acceptance of the principle of movement by blacks into previously all-white spheres of life. This is supported by the claim by most whites that they personally would not mind if a particular black adult, family, or child moved into their neighborhood, school, or other area of life. Moreover, this acceptance of integration goes beyond the single black individual, and similar answers would probably be given if the questions involved almost any number of blacks, so long as the number represented a clear minority. But as soon as questions indicate that blacks might constitute a majority of the neighborhood, school, or other sphere, open white objection becomes more pronounced. Moreover, a large proportion of whites object to any governmental action that might facilitate such a change from a white to a black majority, and, so far as we can tell, this opposition has decreased very little since the 1940s. Most whites also do not support economic steps that would give special advantage to blacks, even if this is in compensation for, or as a way of removing, past disadvantage. In sum, the change over the past four decades has been away from both the principle and, to an extent, the practice of absolute segregation—and in this sense it has been a genuine and large change—but it has not been clearly toward full integration of blacks into white society. And thus the results seem most consistent with the Progress and Resistance hypothesis we outlined in Chapter 1.

Miscellaneous Questions

The final set of five questions presented in table 3.4 is more miscellaneous in character. One provides the only direct measure of white affect toward blacks, while a second provides a measure of white affect toward a traditional antiblack organization, the Ku Klux Klan. The third question offers the only available indicator of white stereotypes of blacks. The last two questions have been used by other writers to measure white reactions to black activism; while these questions are somewhat ambiguous for the purpose of assessing trends, we include the results here briefly for the sake of completeness.

Attitudes toward Blacks

In the standard ISR "thermometer" series, respondents are asked to indicate on a 100-point scale how "warm" or "cold" they feel toward various groups. Toward "blacks," white respondents average about 60 on this scale, with essentially no change over the entire time period (1964–1982) for which data are available. (A score of 60

Table 3.4 Miscellaneous questions.

Question	Year of survey													
	42	43	44	45	46	48	50	56	57	58	59	60	61	62
Thermometer Rating of Blacks (ISR)														
Mean 100-point scale	–	–	–	–	–	–	–	–	–	–	–	–	–	–
Ku Klux Klan Rating (Gallup)														
% Unfavorable (−1, −2, −3)	–	–	–	–	–	–	–	–	–	–	–	–	–	–
% Highly unfavorable (−4, −5)	–	–	–	–	–	–	–	–	–	–	–	–	–	–
Intelligence (NORC)														
% Yes	47	–	48	–	57	–	–	80	–	–	–	–	–	–
Civil Rights Push (ISR)														
% About right	–	–	–	–	–	–	–	–	–	–	–	–	–	–
% Too slowly	–	–	–	–	–	–	–	–	–	–	–	–	–	–
Black Push (NORC)														
% Agree slightly	–	–	–	–	–	–	–	–	–	–	–	–	–	
% Disagree slightly	–	–	–	–	–	–	–	–	–	–	–	–	–	
% Disagree strongly	–	–	–	–	–	–	–	–	–	–	–	–	–	

Question Wordings and Variants

Thermometer Rating of Blacks (ISR):[a] "There are many groups in America that try to get the government or the American people to see things more their way. We would like to get your feelings toward some of these groups. Blacks. Where would you put them on the thermometer?"

Response: Mean of a 100-point scale

Rating of KKK (Gallup):[b] "How far up the scale or how far down the scale would you rate the following organizations: Ku Klux Klan?"

1. Highly favorable (4, 5)
2. Favorable (1, 2, 3)
3. Unfavorable (−1, −2, −3)
4. Highly unfavorable (−4, −5)

Intelligence (NORC): "In general, do you think Negroes are as intelligent as white people—that is, can they learn things just as well if they are given the same education and training?"

1. Yes
2. No

(Variant: in 1944, 1946, and 1956, "things" and "and training" were omitted.)

Civil Rights Push (ISR): "Some say that the civil rights people have been trying to push too fast. Others feel they haven't pushed fast enough. How about you: Do you think that civil rights leaders are trying to push *too fast*, are going *too slowly*, or are they moving at *about* the *right* speed?"

1. Too fast
2. About right
3. Too slowly

							Year of survey												Last minus first
65	66	67	68	69	70	71	72	73	74	75	76	77	78	79	80	81	82	83	
–	60	–	61	–	58	–	61	–	63	–	58	–	–	–	60	–	61	–	+1
9	–	–	–	–	12	–	–	16	–	–	–	–	–	17	–	–	–	–	+8
84	–	–	–	–	79	–	–	75	–	–	–	–	–	71	–	–	–	–	−13
–	80	–	77	–	–	–	–	–	–	–	–	–	–	–	–	–	–	–	+30
–	18	–	24	–	32	–	41	–	50	–	49	–	–	–	51	–	–	–	+29
–	3	–	4	–	6	–	5	–	5	–	5	–	–	–	9	–	–	–	+6
–	26	–	31	–	24	–	26	30	–	28	29	29	–	–	32	–	32	–	+5
–	16	–	13	–	8	–	16	15	–	15	16	18	–	–	19	–	23	–	+10
–	7	–	8	–	8	–	17	11	–	10	12	9	–	–	12	–	16	–	+8

Black Push (NORC): "Here are some opinions other people have expressed in connection with black-white relations. Which statement on the card comes closest to how you yourself feel? Blacks shouldn't push themselves where they're not wanted."

1. Agree strongly
2. Agree slightly
3. Disagree slightly
4. Disagree strongly

a. The wording of the introduction is as shown here for 1964, 1966, and 1968. A small change occurred in 1970: the second sentence was replaced with "Please use the thermometer again—this time to indicate your feelings toward these groups or persons." More changes too cumbersome to report in detail (and unlikely to affect results) were made in the introduction to the thermometer rating at the remaining five time points (1972, 1974, 1976, 1980, 1982). Generally, respondents were asked to express their feelings toward a number of groups (an average of roughly 21 different groups or organizations across the 9 surveys involved), with blacks falling about 12th on average but never earlier than 8th or later than 17th. Other groups asked about most regularly (at least 7 of the 9 time points) were liberals, conservatives, the military, big business, Democrats, Republicans, and whites. For 6 of the 9 time points big business was the first group mentioned. Whites generally preceded blacks in the list of groups to be evaluated, except in 1976 and 1980 when blacks were mentioned earlier. At only one point, 1982, were blacks and whites mentioned contiguously. "Don't know" responses were automatically coded as 50 in 1964, 1966, 1968, and 1970, but were coded separately in later years; for all analyses we have rescored "don't know" to 50.
b. The Ku Klux Klan was the first organization to be rated in 1970 and 1979, the fourth in 1965, and the third in 1973. The YMCA, CORE, and the FBI were first, second, and third in 1965; CORE and the FBI were first and second in 1973.

places blacks slightly below "Jews" in the opinion of white respondents, but slightly above "labor unions"; see Converse et al. 1980). It is not entirely clear what a question like this measures, since it does not deal with any issue and does not seem to vary with external events or show a secular trend. But as figures 3.12 and

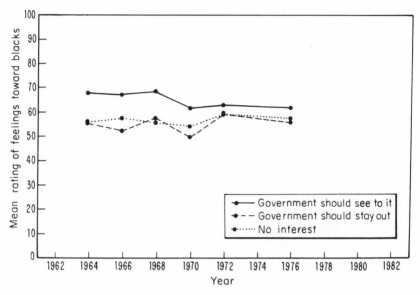

Figure 3.12. Relation between feelings toward blacks and attitudes toward federal intervention to ensure school integration.

Thermometer Rating of Blacks (ISR): "There are many groups in America that try to get the government or the American people to see things more their way. We would like to get your feelings toward some of these groups. Blacks. Where would you put them on the thermometer?"

Response: Mean of a 100-point scale.

Federal School Intervention (ISR): "Some people say that the government in Washington should see to it that white and black children are allowed to go to the same schools. Others claim that this is not the government's business. Have you been concerned enough about this question to favor one side over the other?" (If Yes) "Do you think the government in Washington should see to it that white and black children go to the same schools, or stay out of this matter as it is not its business?"

1. Government should see to it   2. Government should stay out
3. No interest

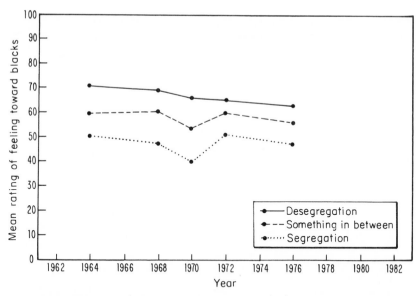

Figure 3.13. Relation between feelings toward blacks and attitudes toward segregation as a principle.

Thermometer Rating of Blacks (**ISR**): "There are many groups in America that try to get the government or the American people to see things more their way. We would like to get your feelings toward some of these groups. Blacks. Where would you put them on the thermometer?"

Response: Mean of a 100-point scale.

General Segregation (**ISR**): "Are you in favor of *desegregation*, strict *segregation*, or something in between?"

1. Desegregation   2. Something in between   3. Strict segregation

3.13 show, the question is related to important issue items we have already discussed. For example, those favoring federal school intervention to hasten school integration are more favorable toward blacks as a group, and those opposed to such intervention or claiming no interest in the issue are more unfavorable. Even sharper contrasts appear for attitudes toward segregation in general: those favoring segregation rate blacks at 47.3 on the average, those favoring desegregation at 66.9, and those wanting "something in between" at 58.0. If whites are answering the thermometer question honestly, the lack of temporal change despite the relation of the question to other volatile issues suggests that people respond to these issues over time in terms of their policy content, but do not generalize them to influence overall feelings toward blacks.[13]

Attitudes toward the Ku Klux Klan

A second rating question, used by Gallup, provides a quite different type of perspective. In this case respondents are asked to rate on a scale of −5 to +5 (with zero omitted) a number of groups, including the Ku Klux Klan. Data are available at four time points from 1965 to 1979. Most respondents—at least 75 percent—place the Klan on the unfavorable side of the scale (−5 to −1) at all four times, but there is a significant *lessening* of *un*favorability in the North at the two most recent time points. This shows up most clearly if we contrast extreme negative scores (−4 and −5 combined) with all others (−3 to +5 combined). As figure 3.14 shows, there was a sharp decrease in extreme disapproval of the Klan in the North between 1970 and 1973, as well as possibly an earlier and less sharp movement in the same direction in the South. A large but lessened gap between the two regions persisted in 1979, the most recent year for which we have data.

This reduction in disapproval of the Ku Klux Klan does not imply that whites positively embrace the organization but rather that fewer whites now regard it as totally objectionable. We should emphasize that the changes involve a fairly small part of the white population, so that a contrast of the earliest and latest time points leads to the following division of the population in the North:

	Favorable (+1 to +5)	Mildly negative (−1 to −3)	Very negative (−4 to −5)
1965	3.5%	7.5%	88.9%
1979	9.8	15.4	74.8

Only a small proportion of Northerners, early or late, are willing to rate the Klan at all favorably, but some 14 percent have shifted from extremely negative to mildly negative or positive. These changes seem to involve all educational levels, with the largest shift occurring among high school graduates in the North.

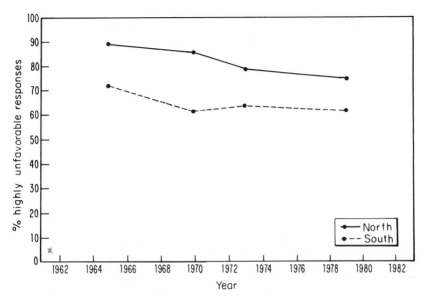

Figure 3.14. Negative attitudes toward the Ku Klux Klan.
Rating of KKK (Gallup):"How far up the scale or how far down the scale would you rate the following organizations: Ku Klux Klan?"
Highly unfavorable (−4, −5) versus all other responses.

One possible explanation is that the Klan is perceived to have changed in character—or that its basic character has become less well known—in the North over the past decade. Alternatively, it may be that a not insignificant element in the white Northern population is finding the Ku Klux Klan and its antiblack philosophy and actions more tolerable today than a dozen years ago. (It is unfortunate that this question has not been asked since 1979, for this is a trend that clearly bears watching.) Data on black attitudes toward the Klan suggest that the first interpretation may be the more plausible one (see Chapter 4).

Beliefs about Intelligence

Those who study ethnic and racial attitudes have traditionally been concerned with the beliefs that one group holds of another. These beliefs are often labeled stereotypes because of the categorical and rigid nature with which they are held (Allport 1954). Some theorists see such beliefs as one factor creating negative attitudes (for example, Fishbein and Ajzen 1975), while others regard the beliefs as either products or rationalizations of existing attitudes (for example, Myrdal 1944). In either case they are an important type of measure to obtain when studying race relations.

Unfortunately, the data available on change over time in white beliefs about blacks are extremely limited. In fact, of our three survey organizations only NORC provides any trend data at all, and this is restricted to a single question on whether blacks and whites are equal in intelligence, asked between 1942 and 1968. Why the question was discontinued after 1968 is not clear, especially since the nature of the trend surely invited further study; there is some informal evidence that survey investigators came to believe that even asking the question carried racist overtones.

For the time period available, responses to the Intelligence question show almost identical trends in the North and the South, but with belief in equal intelligence about 20 percentage points higher in the North (see figure 3.15). There is very little systematic difference along educational lines in either region, though in the South more-educated respondents are a little more likely to be positive than less-educated ones. The most important point about the trend, however, is the sharp rise between 1942 and 1956 in belief in equality of intelligence, followed by a severe leveling off at around 80 percent from 1956 on (see table 3.4). There is even a hint of a decline between 1966 and 1968, especially for the South, though we are reluctant to place much emphasis on this downturn since it is relatively small and based on a single time point. Had further measurements been made we would know whether the downturn continued, or whether leveling off or even positive movement resumed.

The strong positive trend between 1942 and 1956 is similar to that for most of the principle questions discussed earlier, except that for beliefs about intelligence there are only slight and somewhat inconsistent tendencies for more-educated respondents to give more positive responses. The upward trend in figure 3.15 evidently represents part of the general rethinking about race in America that occurred among whites during and after World War II. (Of course, it may have begun earlier than that, but we cannot tell because 1942 is the first point at which any question on race

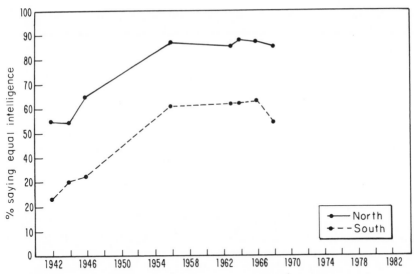

Figure 3.15. Belief in equal intelligence of blacks and whites.
Intelligence (*NORC*): "In general, do you think Negroes are as intelligent as white people—that is, can they learn things just as well if they are given the same education and training?"
    1. Yes   2. No

was asked.) But why the lack of further change between 1956 and 1963? These were the years of Freedom Rides, sit-ins, and other direct but nonviolent actions, but how these could have directly influenced beliefs about intelligence is by no means evident. In these years actual integration did not increase markedly on more than a superficial level (such as desegregation of buses); hence increased black-white contact in, say, neighborhoods or schools can hardly have been an important cause of the leveling off on this item. Overall, the trends for this question are unlike those for any other question we have considered, and we find no adequate interpretation of the pattern.[14]

Civil Rights Push

The last two miscellaneous questions are of more limited value for our purposes, but we include them here for completeness and because they are used in other analyses of racial attitudes that we consider in Chapter 4. The question on whether "civil rights people" are pushing at the right speed (table 3.4) falls broadly within the implementation area, but since it does not concern government action, we deal with it separately here. Moreover, responses to this item are somewhat ambiguous, since they depend to some extent on what the respondent perceives as the "speed" of change attempted by civil rights leaders.

The trends for this question are clear: whites have decreasingly seen civil rights leaders as pushing too fast and increasingly seen them as moving at the right speed. Only a tiny proportion of whites have ever rated the push as too slow, though there has been a slight increase in this proportion. Trends in the North and South are similar, with Southerners more likely at all time points to say "too fast." People with less education are also more likely to consider civil rights leaders as moving too fast.

One interpretation of these trends is that whites have increasingly accepted civil rights activism and increasingly seen the current level, whatever it may be, as the right speed. Another is that civil rights leaders have gone more slowly in the last decade. There is probably some truth to both of these interpretations. One point seems clear: there is no increase in rejection of civil rights activism in recent years, as there is an increase, for example, in opposition to federal intervention to ensure integration of schools.

Black Push

The question we have labeled Black Push is also somewhat uncertain in meaning, but NORC continues to ask it regularly. On the one hand, it can be taken as a negative way of asking about the principle of integration: disagreement indicates acceptance of blacks into presumably all-white spheres of life. On the other hand, the question has a ring of implementation in the word "push," though again the implementation is not through government action. In either interpretation, the question is more loaded than most, for a respondent might feel that no one, of any race, should push in where not wanted; the cliché might be accepted without much thought. This assumption is supported by the fact that well over half of the respondents agree strongly or slightly with the statement.

The overall trend for the item is one of decreasing choice of the "strongly agree" response, but its replacement differs somewhat by region. In the South the main replacement is "slightly agree," so that what occurs is some moderation of response, but not a change in direction. In the North the change involves some movement into the "disagree" categories, that is, more positive views of blacks "pushing" into new areas.

Summary

Important in this miscellaneous set of questions is the trend for attitudes toward the Ku Klux Klan. The results suggest decreased rejection (which amounts to increased acceptance) of this extreme antiblack organization. Only a small minority of the white population either supports the Klan or shows movement in this direction, but the shift (portrayed in figure 3.14) is surprising, especially since it occurred primarily in the North, and it represents a cause for concern to those who believe extreme racial hostility to be fading.

Equally important, but more uncertain in meaning and trajectory, are the data on white beliefs about black intelligence. The absence of recent data here and the lack of any completely reliable data on beliefs about other traits leave a major gap in our knowledge. Although concern about the dangers of publicizing such beliefs may be what prompted the survey designers to drop this question, the absence of systematic survey data does not mean that the beliefs are absent or unimportant to race relations in this country.

White attitudes toward blacks as a group (thermometer ratings) show no change at all over the 16 years from 1964 to 1980. The simplest inference from this is that the substantial changes in white attitudes toward racial issues over the period have not influenced or been influenced by white affective orientations toward blacks. These self-reported affects cannot be dismissed as unimportant, however, for at any given time point they are associated in a meaningful way with attitude questions dealing with particular issues.

The Relation of Age to Racial Attitudes

We have reported a number of changes in the racial attitudes of the white adult population of the United States over the past four decades. Such changes in the total population can come about in either of two main ways. First, individuals in the population may change their own attitudes because of events they witness or experience. For example, as described in Chapter 1, the use of violence by segregationist white authorities in Birmingham in 1963 seemed to shock the general public and probably made many whites more sympathetic to the goals of the civil rights movement. Second, attitudes in a population can shift as older persons holding one set of attitudes die and younger persons holding different attitudes enter the adult population. This form of replacement can shift the overall attitudes for the population even if no single individual changes his or her own attitude. For example, Southern children experiencing integrated schooling may grow up with racial attitudes quite different from those of their parental generation, which had experienced only segregated schooling. It is also possible for both of these two types of change to occur simultaneously, so that individuals within the population alter their attitudes while at the same time the newly arriving members of the population bring still greater differences in attitude. The two types of change may be in the same direction or may be opposite in direction and tend to cancel each other out in terms of net effects.[15]

To study the processes of attitude change within a population we can place each member of a sample into a birth cohort—that is, a group of people born at approximately the same time. ("Approximately the same time" is defined as any period of years that is reasonable in terms of the goals of the analysis and convenient in terms of the data that are available.) Where repeated samples of the population are available from different time points, we can track each birth cohort as it moves through time. Even though we do not interview the same individuals each time, we do interview representative samples from each cohort, and these samples can be compared to determine whether and how attitudes have changed for that cohort.

Evidence of change due to the replacement of older cohorts by younger ones is manifest at any time point when we examine the relation of age (or approximate birth date) to the attitude in question. With data from different times, one can determine whether the process is a continuous one: for example, whether each new cohort entering the population is more liberal on racial issues than the one that preceded it. The effects of cohort replacement have often been assessed with multivariate models (Davis 1975, 1980; Condran 1979; Taylor, Sheatsley, and Greeley 1978), but less rigorous procedures can be illustrative (Hyman and Sheatsley 1956, 1964; Greeley and Sheatsley 1971).

We will track both types of change over as long a period as possible for several questions representing our three main theoretical categories of principles, implementation, and social distance. Most of the NORC tabulations by cohort are drawn from Condran (1979), since we did not have cross-tabulations by cohort for early NORC studies, but we have added the 1982 time point. The ISR tabulations by cohort are our own. (No cohort data were obtained for Gallup questions.) Use of Condran's tabulations constrained our definition of cohorts to the ones he employed, and in other respects also this presentation is less complete than our earlier analysis, but not in ways likely to interfere with major conclusions.

Table 3.5 presents the basic results by birth cohort for seven questions. To assess the degree to which individuals in a given cohort may have altered their attitudes toward integration, read down the columns for each question. Even a cursory glance reveals that there has been a great deal of change in the direction of more liberal racial attitudes within cohorts for most questions. Liberalization on issues involving principles or social distance occurred primarily between 1963 and 1972, when the attitude change within cohorts ranged between 10 and 22 percentage points. In the subsequent decade the increases for these same questions were substantially lower, clustering between 4 and 8 percentage points and never exceeding 16 percentage points. Some cohorts showed actual decreases during this period, though only one of these (for the cohort born in 1906–1915 on the question about intermarriage laws) could be considered noteworthy. Only for the Same Schools question does a ceiling effect appear to explain the slow pace of attitude change during the 1970s.

It is interesting to note that the large changes in individual attitudes on principle and social distance questions occurred at a time when national attention was focused on ending legalized segregation in the South. A few scattered bits of data from the 1950s sug-

Table 3.5 Percentage of pro-integration responses by birth cohort for seven questions.[a]

Items by conceptual category and year	Birth cohort							Youngest minus oldest
	Before 1906	1906–1915	1916–1925	1926–1935	1936–1945	1946–1955[b]	1956–1964	
Principles								
Same Schools (% Same)								
1963	51	62	66	70	68	—	—	17
1972	73	84	84	90	87	96	—	23
1982	79	79	83	94	95	96	96	17
1972–1963	22	22	18	20	19	0	—	
1982–1972	6	−5	−1	4	8	0	—	
Residential Choice (NORC) (% Disagree)								
1963	26	36	43	47	46	—	—	20
1972	42	47	55	64	66	78	—	36
1982	58	59	59	72	73	76	79	21
1972–1963	16	11	12	17	20	—	—	
1982–1972	16	12	4	8	7	−2	—	
Laws against Intermarriage (% No)								
1963	22	32	39	46	45	—	—	23
1972	32	53	58	65	67	81	—	49
1982	37	39	51	65	75	82	81	44
1972–1963	10	21	19	19	22	—	—	
1982–1972	5	−14	−7	0	8	1	—	
Social Distance								
Black Dinner Guest (% Not at all)								
1963	43	54	48	51	56	—	—	13
1972	60	72	64	71	71	79		19

1982	67	76	64	82	77	85	85	18
1972–1963	17	18	16	20	15	—	—	
1982–1972	7	4	0	11	6	6	—	

Implementation

Federal School Intervention
(% Government should see to it)

1964	39	38	45	45	45	—	—	6
1972	36	31	29	30	37	46	—	10
1978	25	27	19	21	25	29	—	4
1972–1964	−3	−7	−16	−15	−8	—	—	
1978–1972	−11	−4	−10	−9	−12	−17	—	

Accommodations Intervention
(% Government should see to it)

1964	33	42	48	51	47	—	—	14
1974	49	58	54	65	72	81	—	32
1974–1964	16	16	6	14	25	—	—	

Open Housing
(% No discrimination)

1973	23	27	23	32	37	55	—	32
1983	35	27	29	35	48	55	61	26
1983–1973	12	0	6	3	11	0	—	

Sources: Table 1 in John G. Condran, "Changes in White Attitudes toward Blacks," *Public Opinion Quarterly* (1979):466; 1973, 1982, and 1983 General Social Surveys; 1964, 1972, 1974, and 1978 National Election Studies.

a. All the base Ns for the percentages in this table are more than 100 except for the oldest cohort in the most recent years. By 1983 the cohort born before 1906 contained only 51 respondents.

b. In order to make each cohort cover approximately ten years, we combined Condran's 1946–1950 and 1951–1955 groups by averaging the percentages for 1972 listed in his table 1.

gest that some shifts took place prior to 1963. Hyman and Sheatsley (1956), in the first of a series of articles on white racial attitudes that appeared in *Scientific American,* included data on the Same Schools question for respondents born from 1932 through 1935. In 1956, 53 percent of that cohort favored integrated schools, a percentage that can be roughly compared to the 70 percent in 1963 for the cohort born in 1926–1935 (table 3.5). The increase of 17 percentage points suggests that individuals may have become more liberal on this question at just as fast a pace during the 1950s as during the 1960s. Unfortunately the data do not allow us to determine whether this pattern holds for any of the other questions.

As in our other analyses, questions about implementation introduce more complex patterns that lead to somewhat different conclusions. In the first place, only two of the items, those dealing with public accommodations and open housing, exhibit increases in pro-integration attitudes within cohorts, and only in the case of public accommodations are these improvements as substantial for implementation questions as for principle and social distance questions. For the question on federal intervention to ensure school integration (table 3.2), which shows a decline for the population as a whole, the decline occurred within all cohorts. Second, it is impossible to compare the rates of change during the 1960s with those during the 1970s for most implementation questions, simply because the questions were not asked over a long enough period. If we use 1972 as a breaking point for the one question with a sufficient time span—Federal School Intervention—there is not a great difference in trend between the two decades for any of the cohorts.[16]

To examine changes from cohort to cohort, read across the rows rather than down the columns in table 3.5. For all of the years and questions listed, there is a nearly monotonic tendency for the percentages of pro-integration sentiment to increase as cohort age decreases. The differences between the oldest and youngest cohorts are substantial at every time point, except on the Federal School Intervention question. This result provides support for the proposition that younger generations have been more liberal than their elders, and it appears that pro-integration attitudes in the population as a whole have increased as a result of the replacement of older cohorts by younger ones.[17]

For an item such as Federal School Intervention, which shows within-cohort *decreases* in favorable sentiments toward racial integration, cohort replacement can operate to slow such changes for the overall population. Although the differences among the cohorts on this particular issue are modest compared to those for all other questions, they are solidly positive and act as a counterweight to the negative movement of individual attitudes. Thus the replacement of older cohorts by younger ones constrains the decline in approval of school intervention in the population as a whole, producing less regression than might be expected on the basis of intracohort trends alone. This proposition needs to be more systematically explored. At least one careful study of several nonracial General Social Survey items reached a similar conclusion—that demographic factors can work, though weakly, to foster liberal sentiments even when overall trends are conservative (Davis 1980).

In the case of the Federal School Intervention question, these inferences about within- and between-cohort attitude change are supported by panel data on high school seniors and their parents collected in 1965 and 1973 by Jennings and Niemi (1981). In panel data, exactly the same people are interviewed on more than one occasion, and thus the evidence for change in individuals is more direct than it can be for comparisons of two samples from the same cohort. As shown in table 3.6, between 1965 and 1973 both the youth and parent samples evidence substantial declines—of 20

Table 3.6 Panel results for Federal School Intervention item.

Response	Youth Panel		Parent Panel	
	1965	1973	1965	1973
Government see to it	70%	50%	59%	41%
Government stay out	24	42	35	47
No interest	6	8	6	12
Total	100	100	100	100
N	(1099)	(1035)	(896)	(888)

$X^2 = 87.04$, d.f. = 2, p < .001 $X^2 = 62.08$, d.f. = 2, p < .001
Three-way interaction: $X^2 = 5.58$, d.f. = 2, n.s.

Source: These results were obtained from a reanalysis of data originally gathered by Jennings and Niemi (1981). The table in their book (p. 413) is slightly different from this one because they exclude the "no interest" category but include a "depends" category.

percent and 18 percent respectively—in support for government intervention in schools. The declines within cohorts are confirmed quite clearly by these individual-level data. In addition, consistent with the results in figure 3.5, these declines are restricted entirely to Northern youth and parents (see Bobo 1984). Furthermore, at both time points the younger respondents are more supportive of federal intervention.

Although cohort replacement has acted to liberalize racial attitudes in the past, the results in table 3.5 suggest that it may not continue to do so in the future. For those questions with 1982 or 1983 time points, it appears that the youngest generation is not as sharply differentiated from its immediate predecessor as had been the case in 1972. In 1982, for the five questions with relevant data, the youngest cohort was more liberal than the next-youngest cohort by an average of only 2 percentage points. The comparable difference over the same five questions in 1972 was 12 percentage points. While this evidence of a slowdown in the process of cohort replacement is far from conclusive, it comes at a time when we might have expected widespread positive change as the first cohort raised during the civil rights movement reached adulthood.

Although our findings can only be suggestive, they highlight several conditions that should be monitored in the future. The slowing down of positive change within cohorts and the apparently greater homogeneity among the youngest cohorts in the population may be signs of negative developments in white attitudes toward racial matters, or they may be temporary phenomena that will be quickly reversed as additional cohorts born in the 1960s mature. One thing does seem clear: The positive changes that have occurred during the last decade have been largely the result of cohort replacement rather than of changes in the attitudes of individuals. In contrast, during the 1960s and early 1970s pro-integration trends resulted from the operation of both processes.

We have not been able to consider a related problem of interest—whether differences in educational levels across cohorts can account for their differences in liberalism about racial issues. Here again, a thorough investigation using many racial attitude items would be in order. However, there is research which shows that while education does explain some of the variation in levels of liberalism among cohorts, it seldom explains very much (Davis 1980; Taylor, Sheatsley, and Greeley 1978).

Conclusions about White Racial Attitudes

1. On questions concerning principles of equal treatment of blacks and whites in the major public spheres of life (jobs, residential choice, transportation, schools, public accommodations), there has been a strong and steady movement of white attitudes from denial to affirmation of equality, so much so that the figures often reach above 90 percent positive in the most recent years. The meaning of such affirmation is not self-evident, however, but must be drawn in part from other patterns of results.

2. Results for questions on government action to implement the principles just mentioned differ in two fundamental respects from results for questions on the principles themselves. First, there is considerably less support for the implementation of principles than for principles as such. Differences in question wording make it impossible to offer a precise estimate of these gaps in levels of support, but the gaps are quite consistent and fairly large across every sphere in which the data allow comparison of principle and implementation. A second and more surprising difference occurs in trends: unlike principle questions, implementation questions seldom show a clear positive trend over time. In fact, one implementation question (on schools) shows a negative slope and others (including several on economic assistance to blacks) reveal little or no movement at all over time.

3. One way of reconciling both the levels and the trends (slopes) for questions dealing with principles with those for questions dealing with implementation is to hypothesize a "lag effect": that is, to hypothesize that only after principles in a particular area (for example, nondiscrimination in housing) have been deeply internalized by much of the white population will there begin to be acceptance of concrete steps (for example, open housing laws) to implement those principles. Such a line of reasoning would fit well our findings for the areas of public accommodations and residential choice, and would not be inconsistent with the area of employment, for which the implementation question may have been

dropped from surveys too early to allow the lag effect to become apparent. Together with findings about a small gap in black attitudes toward principles and implementation, to be reported in the next chapter, the lag-effect hypothesis would explain a number of the discrepant trends reported in this chapter. However, there are other results for other areas, notably the implementation of school integration, which are clearly inconsistent with a lag effect, since in these areas the trends for implementation and principle are diametrically opposite in direction. Thus other hypotheses will have to be added to deal fully with all of the important results in this chapter. For example, it may be that when an issue becomes highly politicized at a national level, as has occurred with busing for school integration, the lag effect is interrupted. But the need for this and other special interpretations indicates the complexity of trends in white racial attitudes over the past four decades, and points to the need to resist glib generalization in a sphere where emotions and ideologies can too easily tempt one to bypass data.

4. Important as is the distinction between principle and implementation, it by no means captures all the meaningful variation in either level or trend in the set of questions examined. Perhaps the most noteworthy cross-cutting distinction has to do with the sphere of life covered by a question. At one extreme, when public accommodations in hotels and restaurants are at issue, even an implementation question calling for federal action shows a strong positive trend toward enforcement. At the other extreme, a question on laws against racial intermarriage that we interpret as primarily one dealing with principle shows a leveling off well below the near-100-percent ceiling reached by most other items. In all likelihood, the more impersonal and transient the interracial contact at issue, the more white support for integration; the more intimate and long-lasting the contact, the less the support. But relative numbers of whites and blacks are involved as well, as noted in point 5.

5. A third type of question that we examined concerns white willingness—insofar as this can be measured by asking about intentions and feelings—to participate personally in integrated situations. The clearest result for these items is that white response varies according to the proportion of blacks and whites in the hypo-

thetical situations described. Few whites object to school or residential integration involving a small number of blacks, but objections are much more frequent when substantial numbers of blacks are involved. This difference might be seen as related to the distinction between principle and implementation: the acceptance of one or a few blacks means that segregation and discrimination have been rejected as absolute principles, but nevertheless full-scale integration is also rejected.

6. On almost all questions throughout the entire time period, responses of Northern whites are more liberal than those of Southern whites. However, slopes for the two regions are usually similar, except where a ceiling is reached or where there was some traditional reason for the South initially to adhere much more strongly to segregation (as in the case of schools).

7. Greater education is associated with positive responses on principle questions, but this association tends to decrease or disappear when implementation is involved. For social distance questions, education is positively related to acceptance of integration when only a few blacks are involved, but the relation tends to disappear when the proportion of blacks increases.

8. Our limited consideration of the effects of age on racial attitudes suggests that the process of change has itself changed over time. In the 1960s the rise in pro-integration sentiments seems to have occurred as a result of both positive modifications in individual attitudes and the demographic replacement of older cohorts by younger, more liberal cohorts. However, the later increase in positive attitudes during the 1970s was apparently almost entirely the product of demographic replacement. Furthermore, there were signs by the early 1980s that even this process might cease to foster positive change in the future.

9. The results summarized in points 1–8 involve broad conclusions and omit some negative trends for particular questions. An item on the Ku Klux Klan shows somewhat increased tolerance for that organization in recent years; this support may be drawn from those whites most hostile to blacks, but quite possibly also in part from whites who are simply uninformed about the Klan. And despite the widespread and increasing endorsement of the principle of integration in most areas of life, one quite general question that

allows an intermediate response has shown a sharp turn away from integrationist sentiment in recent years (though this odd shift is probably due at least in part to question context effects). We do not think great emphasis should be placed on unusual trends for single items, especially given contextual and other effects discussed in Chapter 2. All racial items must be considered in relation to one another, so that the meaning of each is interpreted in terms of patterns provided by the others.[18]

4 Trends in Black Racial Attitudes

Trend data are much sparser for black racial attitudes than for white. During the 1940s and 1950s, survey investigators interested in racial issues saw the racial problem as almost entirely one of white acceptance of equal treatment across racial lines. After all, laws and administrative rules upheld racial segregation during much of that period, and large parts of the white population still supported segregation as a general principle. As Paul Sheatsley, one of the major initiators of research in this area, has commented: "It never occurred to us when we wrote questions in the Forties and Fifties to ask them of blacks because Myrdal's dilemma was a white dilemma and it was white attitudes that demanded study" (personal communication, 1984).[1] Added to this was the fact that some of the main issues inquired into, such as whether "whites should have the first chance at jobs," would have seemed demeaning if asked of blacks.

With the rise of new and diverse forms of political ideology, action, and organization among blacks in the 1960s, survey investigators (almost all of whom were white) realized that blacks were not merely passive players in the rapidly changing racial scene and that black attitudes should not be assumed to be either self-evident or fixed. A series of special survey studies of blacks were carried out during the 1960s: Brink and Harris (1964), Marx (1967), Murphy and Watson (1967), Campbell and Schuman (1968), Caplan and Paige (1968), Aberbach and Walker (1970), Sears and McConahay (1973). However, the very fact that issues important to blacks appeared to be changing so rapidly made for considerable discontinuity from one study to the next. Within a short period of time in the mid-1960s, for example, the term "militancy" changed from indicating nonviolent action against white-imposed segregation to suggesting support for violent rebellion and separatism. Furthermore, the samples used in these special surveys were seldom national and often quite different from one another. As a result of both these factors it is virtually impossible to draw on these studies, despite the theoretical importance of some of them, for the kind of trend analysis we have presented for white attitudes.

Also in the 1960s a few questions on racial issues began to be asked of blacks as well as whites on a regular basis by the major survey organizations. The problem with these data is one of small numbers of cases, for a typical national sample of 1500 to 2000 Americans yields only 150 to 200 black respondents.[2] These small samples mean that even overall distributions of answers lack the sampling reliability we were able to count on in the data for whites, and internal analysis by region and other variables is even less reliable. Additional problems result from possible race-of-interviewer effects (see Chapter 2) and from the fact that some questions originally designed for white respondents are less appropriate or less clear in meaning when asked of black respondents.

Despite these limitations, the available data from Gallup, ISR, and NORC on black attitudes are of considerable value. Comparisons between black and white answers to the same items are illuminating, and additional light is cast on certain of the findings for whites when we learn the extent to which blacks show similar or different trends. Therefore, keeping in mind that smaller sample sizes for the black data make it even more important here than in the discussion of white attitudes to avoid fixation on a single point in a time series, we will present results for the timelines that are of sufficient length to allow conclusions about trends in black racial attitudes. We will supplement the data with reference to other survey evidence on changes in black attitudes, though we will not attempt to cover the separate cross-sectional studies cited above, except insofar as they involved replication to measure change.[3]

Mirror Images

We begin with two questions that reveal the kind of divergence between black and white attitudes one might expect when the two racial groups evaluate civil rights progress over the past several decades. The first of these questions was not introduced earlier because it does not offer a clear positive-negative attitude dimension; yet in the present context it is useful to note the different trends that appear for blacks and whites. Figure 4.1 shows a nearly linear

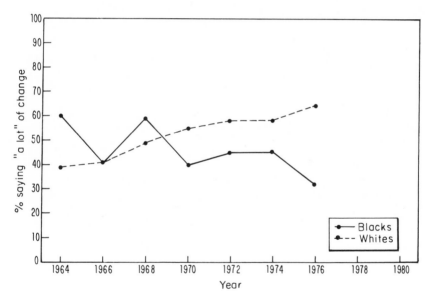

Figure 4.1. Attitudes toward civil rights progress, by race.
Civil Rights Progress (ISR): "In the past few years we have heard a lot about civil rights groups working to improve the position of black people in this country. How much real change do you think there has been in the position of black people in the past few years: a lot, some, or not much at all?"
1. A lot   2. Some   3. Not much at all

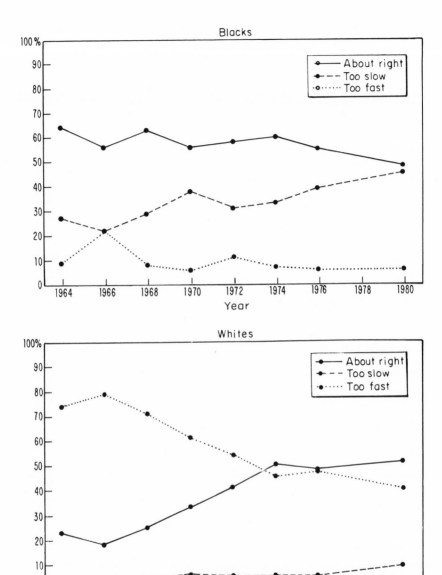

Figure 4.2. Attitudes toward "pushing" by civil rights leaders.

    Civil Rights Push (ISR): "Some say that the civil rights people have been trying to push too fast. Others feel they haven't pushed fast enough. How about you: Do you think that civil rights leaders are trying to push too fast, are going too slowly, or are moving at about the right speed?"

    1. Too fast   2. About right   3. Too slowly

upward trend for whites from 1964 to 1976 in the belief that "a lot" of progress had been made in the civil rights area, but a downward trend for blacks. (The less linear black trend is probably partly due to the smaller number of cases on which each black time point is based.) Likewise, figure 4.2 shows that as civil rights activism has declined over the past 15 years, whites have moved from believing that civil rights leaders are pushing "too fast" to saying their speed is "about right"; but blacks have moved from seeing the civil rights push as "about right" to believing it to be "too slow." These cross-race differences in trends should not be surprising, for most whites are likely to be satisfied with relatively little change in race relations in the United States, while most blacks are likely to wish for a great deal of change.[4]

Principle, Implementation, and Other Questions

In table 4.1 we present the record of black trends for five of the questions dealing with principles, eight of the questions on implementation, and two of the miscellaneous questions that were discussed for whites in Chapter 3. (No long-term trend data are available for blacks on social distance questions, though the principle question on intermarriage is obviously relevant to issues of social distance.) Unlike our trends for whites, however, which extend back to 1942 in some cases, the earliest date for black trends is 1958 and most questions were first asked in 1964 or later.

Principle Questions

Responses to three of the principle questions are very close to 100 percent at all time points: Virtually all black respondents say they would vote for a well-qualified black presidential candidate, think blacks should have a right to live anywhere they can afford, and believe black and white children should go to the same schools. Such unanimity is not surprising on the first two issues, but on the question of integrated schooling one might have expected a little more dissent based on some form of black separatism. On all three of these issues of principle there appears to have been a clear consensus among blacks for at least the number of years for which survey data are available. For two of these same three questions,

Table 4.1 Black responses to principle, implementation, and miscellaneous questions, 1958–1983.

Question	58	59	60	61	62	63	64	65	66	(
Principle questions										
Black Candidate (Gallup):										
% Yes	92	98	–	97	–	96	–	98	–	9
Black Candidate (NORC):										
% Yes	–	–	–	–	–	–	–	–	–	
Intermarriage (Gallup):										
% Approve	–	–	–	–	–	–	–	–	–	
Same Schools (NORC):										
% Same	–	–	–	–	–	–	–	–	–	
Residential Choice, 2 alts. (ISR):										
% Blacks have rights	–	–	–	–	–	–	98	–	–	
General Segregation (ISR):										
% Desegregation	–	–	–	–	–	–	78	–	–	
% In between	–	–	–	–	–	–	17	–	–	
Implementation questions										
Accommodations Intervention (ISR):										
% Gov't see to it	–	–	–	–	–	–	89	–	–	
% No interest	–	–	–	–	–	–	7	–	–	
Federal Job Intervention (ISR):										
% Gov't see to it	–	–	–	–	–	–	92	–	–	
% No interest	–	–	–	–	–	–	4	–	–	
Federal School Intervention (ISR):										
% Gov't see to it	–	–	–	–	–	–	82	–	79	
% No interest	–	–	–	–	–	–	10	–	12	
Aid to Minorities (ISR):										
% Gov't see to it	–	–	–	–	–	–	–	–	–	
% No interest	–	–	–	–	–	–	–	–	–	
Riots (ISR):										
% Solve problems	–	–	–	–	–	–	–	–	–	
% No interest	–	–	–	–	–	–	–	–	–	
Spending on Blacks (NORC):										
% Too little	–	–	–	–	–	–	–	–	–	
% About right	–	–	–	–	–	–	–	–	–	
Busing (ISR):										
% Busing	–	–	–	–	–	–	–	–	–	
% Haven't thought much about this	–	–	–	–	–	–	–	–	–	

	68	69	70	71	72	73	74	75	76	77	78	79	80	81	82	83	Last minus first
	–	100	–	95	–	–	–	–	–	–	94	–	–	–	–	96	+4
	–	–	–	–	–	–	97	–	–	–	96	–	–	–	97	–	0
	–	–	–	–	76	–	–	–	–	–	77	–	–	–	–	78	+2
	–	–	–	–	96	–	–	–	97	93	–	–	98	–	96	–	0
8	–	98	–	99	–	99	–	99	–	–	–	–	–	–	–		+1
9	–	79	–	69	–	62	–	74	–	56	–	–	–	–	–		−22
8	–	18	–	29	–	31	–	24	–	39	–	–	–	–	–		+22
3	–	92	–	92	–	91	–	–	–	–	–	–	–	–	–		+2
4	–	5	–	4	–	6	–	–	–	–	–	–	–	–	–		−1
5	–	–	–	85	–	82	–	–	–	–	–	–	–	–	–		−10
5	–	–	–	6	–	11	–	–	–	–	–	–	–	–	–		+7
0	–	85	–	81	–	76	–	68	–	60	–	–	–	–	–		−22
4	–	8	–	7	–	9	–	20	–	39	–	–	–	–	–		+29
	–	78	–	73	–	77	–	64	–	57	–	–	–	49	–		−29
	–	6	–	6	–	6	–	11	–	14	–	–	–	16	–		+10
	–	–	–	74	–	71	–	64	–	–	–	–	–	–	–		−10
	–	–	–	9	–	9	–	24	–	–	–	–	–	–	–		+15
	–	–	–	–	83	83	85	82	80	84	–	79	–	91	80		−3
	–	–	–	–	14	17	14	15	20	15	–	18	–	8	20		+6
	–	–	–	46	–	43	–	57	–	–	–	49	–	–	–		+3
	–	–	–	6	–	13	–	11	–	–	–	12	–	–	–		+6

Table 4.1 (continued)

Question	58	59	60	61	62	63	64	65	66	6
				Year of survey						
Implementation questions (continued)										
Busing (NORC):										
% Favor	–	–	–	–	–	–	–	–	–	
Miscellaneous questions										
Thermometer Rating of Blacks (ISR):										
Mean of 100-pt. scale	–	–	–	–	–	–	–	89	86	
Ku Klux Klan Rating (Gallup):										
% Unfavorable	–	–	–	–	–	–	–	7	–	
% Highly unfavorable	–	–	–	–	–	–	–	88	–	
Civil Rights Push (ISR):										
% About right	–	–	–	–	–	–	64	–	56	
% Too slow	–	–	–	–	–	–	27	–	22	
Civil Rights Progress (ISR):										
% Some	–	–	–	–	–	–	31	–	48	
% A lot	–	–	–	–	–	–	60	–	41	

whites have also reached a high level of support in recent years for integration in principle, though with not quite the same unanimity as for blacks; on one item (a black presidential candidate) the white level of support remains a good deal lower.

The other two principle items in table 4.1 show much more variation among blacks. On the Intermarriage item, black approval of intermarriage is much higher than white approval but still far from unanimous. More unexpected are attitudes toward segregation as a principle (the General Segregation item); black responses are not only divided but show a trend somewhat similar to that for whites discussed in Chapter 3. Figure 4.3 indicates that both blacks overall and higher-educated Northern whites have been less likely in recent years to choose the "desegregation" response, selecting instead the more ambiguous "in between" response. Rather than stopping to interpret the similarity in trend in this one case, we will pass on to some even more striking parallels with implementation items.

8	69	70	71	72	73	74	75	76	77	78	79	80	81	82	83	Last minus first
–	–	–	–	56	–	63	48	53	48	53	–	–	–	52	56	0
0	–	86	–	87	–	86	–	86	–	–	–	89	–	76	–	−13
–	–	4	–	–	12	–	–	–	–	16	–	–	–	–	–	+ 9
–	–	93	–	–	84	–	–	–	–	80	–	–	–	–	–	−8
3	–	56	–	58	–	60	–	56	–	–	–	46	–	–	–	−18
9	–	38	–	31	–	33	–	39	–	–	–	45	–	–	–	+18
3	–	47	–	48	–	46	–	51	–	–	–	–	–	–	–	+20
9	–	40	–	45	–	45	–	32	–	–	–	–	–	–	–	−28

Implementation Questions

Whites have always shown considerably less support for the implementation of principles than for the principles themselves. It is rather natural to interpret this difference, which we documented in detail in Chapter 3, as due to a failure of whites to live up in practice to what they claim to subscribe to in the abstract. In Chapter 5 we will discuss several theoretical approaches that attempt to deal critically with just this disjunction between principle and implementation, but it is important at this point to recognize that blacks also show something of the same disjunction (see table 4.1). True, black support for government intervention is much stronger than comparable white support; for example, an average of about 85 percent of blacks favor federal intervention to ensure fair treatment in jobs, as against figures for whites in the 36 percent to 39 percent range. Yet black responses on the implementation items are always below—and sometimes well below—the near–100 per-

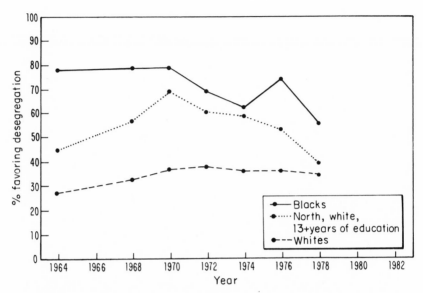

Figure 4.3. Attitudes toward desegregation as a principle, by race and social factors.

General Segregation (ISR): "Are you in favor of *desegregation*, strict *segregation*, or something in between?"

    1. Desegregation   2. Something in between   3. Strict segregation

---

cent levels blacks reach on several principle items. Furthermore, there is strong evidence that in recent years black support for government intervention has declined on some issues, while on no issue has it clearly risen.

A particularly striking example of a parallel between black and white trends is presented graphically in figure 4.4. From 1964 to 1978, *both* blacks and whites show declining support for federal intervention to integrate schools. The black decline is especially sharp—a drop from a peak of 90 percent in 1968 to only 60 percent in 1978. This 60 percent level in 1978 is some 35 percentage points higher than the white level, but it is more than 35 percentage points below the level of black support for the most closely related principle item, that dealing with attitudes toward black and white students attending the same schools.[5]

It might be assumed that the issue of federal intervention to pro-

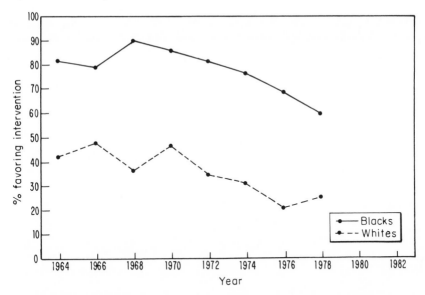

Figure 4.4. Attitudes toward federal intervention to ensure school integration, by race.

Federal School Intervention (ISR): "Some people say that the government in Washington should see to it that white and black children are allowed to go to the same schools. Others claim that this is not the government's business. Have you been concerned enough about this question to favor one side over the other?" (If Yes) "Do you think the government in Washington should see to it that white and black children go to the same schools, or stay out of this matter as it is not its business?"

    1. Government should see to it   2. Government should stay out
      3. No interest

mote desegregation of schools is quite unlike other racial issues, perhaps because of the intense controversy over busing, an issue on which, as we can also see from table 4.1, the black population is also split nearly down the middle. But figure 4.5 shows a similar drop, less sharp but still statistically significant, in black levels of support for federal intervention to equalize job opportunities, and figure 4.6 shows a very large decline in support of federal aid to minorities.[6] (In both of these cases white levels are low but stable, whereas black levels are relatively high but dropping.) Thus the declining trends for blacks are not limited to a single topic or area.

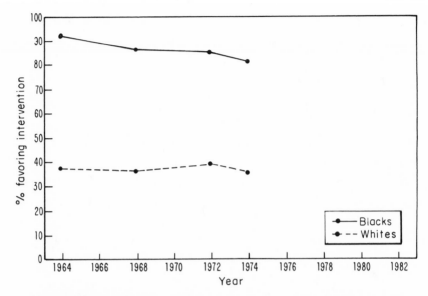

Figure 4.5. Attitudes toward federal intervention to ensure equal job opportunities, by race.

Federal Job Intervention (ISR): "Some people feel that if black people are not getting fair treatment in jobs the government in Washington ought to see to it that they do. Others feel that this is not the federal government's business. Have you had enough interest in this question to favor one side over the other?" (If Yes) "How do you feel? Should the government in Washington see to it that black people get fair treatment in jobs or leave these matters to the states and local communities?"

    1. Government should see to it   2. Government should stay out
       3. No interest

At the same time, a decline is not apparent on several other implementation questions in table 4.1: Accommodations Intervention, Spending on Blacks, and Busing. (Particularly puzzling is the fact that the NORC Spending on Blacks question shows little change between 1973 and 1978, whereas the rather similar ISR Aid to Minorities item shows a decline.) We have not been able to discover an explanation for this difference; it is possible that context effects could be a factor, since the NORC Spending on Blacks question is part of a long series of short items about various forms of national expenditure, whereas the ISR Aid to Minorities question is complex

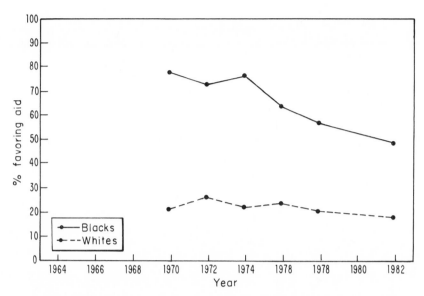

Figure 4.6. Attitudes toward federal aid to minorities, by race.

Aid to Minorities (*ISR*): "Some people feel that the government in Washington should make every possible effort to improve the social and economic position of blacks and other minority groups. Others feel that the government should not make any special effort to help minorities because they should help themselves. Where would you place yourself on this scale, or haven't you thought much about this?"

    1. Government help (1–3)   2. Minority groups help themselves (4–7)   3. Haven't thought much about this

and is asked as part of a diverse series of questions on race.)

There is one other item for which we find unexpected similarity between black and white trends. In Chapter 3 we reported that whites have become somewhat less rejecting of the Ku Klux Klan over the past decade or so. It is evident from table 4.1 that a similar trend occurs for blacks, though again absolute levels of rejection differ markedly for the two groups. As with whites, a small but significantly rising proportion of blacks have moved from an extreme unfavorable view to a somewhat less extreme unfavorable view of the Klan.[7] This may well be due to the lower visibility of the Klan in recent years and therefore simply to decreasing familiarity with it.

We should reiterate that even where there is no perceptible drop over time in black support for implementation, there is still a gap for blacks between principle and implementation questions on the same issue, although never as large a gap as occurs for whites. The ISR Residential Choice principle item in table 4.1 always registers 98 or 99 percent black support for "black people have a right to live wherever they can afford to." We do not present results for the question on open housing laws in table 4.1 because the data available for blacks are limited to too short a time span to establish any clear trend. However, during the period 1978–1983, in which NORC collected data on blacks, black support for a "no discrimination" law on the Open Housing item averaged 73 percent—that is, 25 percent less than the 98+ percent supporting the principle of black rights to free residential choice.[8] This 25 percent gap for blacks compares with a 53 percent gap for whites in 1976, the most recent year in which whites were asked both questions (one by ISR and one by NORC). Thus the gap for blacks is only half as large as the gap for whites, but both differences are substantial in absolute magnitude. Both blacks and whites find it easier to support the general principle of freedom of residential choice than the implementation of the principle by means of an open housing law.

Interpretations

We consider first the gap between principle and implementation questions, and then the decline in support for implementation that appears on certain questions. Before proceeding with these substantive interpretations, however, we need to consider possible problems in sampling or interviewing that might have created the effects just reported, especially the downward trends on several items.

Possible Artifacts in Sampling or Interviewing

One possible artifact could have been an increase in ideologically related refusals to be interviewed or other forms of nonresponse by blacks during the years when the apparent attitude changes were occurring (compare Farley, Hatchett, and Schuman 1979). There is evidence that survey refusals have been rising over the past two decades, and further evidence that this rise has been concentrated especially in large Northern cities (Steeh 1981). Thus it is possible that the samples of blacks interviewed in recent years contained an increasingly large *proportion* of rural or Southern individuals who might be more conservative on civil rights issues than blacks living in large Northern cities. If so, this would increase the apparent conservatism of the responses of the total black sample, and could lead to the downturn in trends that we have reported. However, examination of the demographic composition of both the ISR and NORC black samples for the past 20 years shows little change in either urban-rural or North-South composition. There is also little change in sex or age composition. The black samples do reveal a steady rise in educational level, but this reflects a real change in the composition of the population, not an artifact due to sample bias. Moreover, education is only slightly related to the questions shown in figures 4.4, 4.5, and 4.6. In sum, we have found no evidence that the trends portrayed in earlier figures are due to problems with sample completion or sample composition.

A second possible artifact is systematic changes in the racial composition of survey interviewing staffs. The considerable effect of race of interviewer on some responses to racial questions is well documented (Schuman and Hatchett 1974). Less well documented but fairly certain is that survey organizations increased their employment of black interviewers in the late 1960s, but that this staff compositional change leveled off and probably even reversed in the mid- and late 1970s. It is conceivable that as a result of these staff changes black responses became more conservative in recent years as blacks were increasingly being interviewed by whites. This is a difficult hypothesis to test because of the lack of systematic data on interview assignment by race of interviewer in most surveys. However, the 1974 ISR omnibus survey did record race of interviewer assignments, though they were not randomized, and there is no evidence that responses on the main items included in that survey (such as Federal School Intervention) varied by race of interviewer. This accords with other evidence (for example, Schuman and Converse 1971) that race-of-interviewer effects on black responses are largely limited to questions dealing directly with antiwhite attitudes, and do not extend to racial policy issues.

Having rejected two seemingly plausible artifactual explanations, we are left with the need for more substantive interpretations.

The Principle-Implementation Gap

As we have said, black support for principles of integration and equal treatment is generally very high, but support for the implementation of such principles is sometimes lower. Evidently the means used to put principles into practice raise problems for an appreciable number of blacks. For the most part we can only speculate as to what these problems are, but we have data from one relevant instance in which both blacks and whites were asked to explain in their own words their replies to an implementation question.

In 1976 the Detroit Area Study asked a sample of metropolitan Detroit residents a question on attitudes toward busing—not one of the same busing questions we have been using for trend analysis, but close enough to be of value for the present purpose. The closed busing question was followed in turn by a simple open question: "Can you tell me why you feel this way?" Responses of blacks and whites were coded into categories; these categories and the distributions of answers in them are presented in table 4.2.[9] We should note that exactly half the black sample (and 93 percent of the white sample) disapproved of busing, and our focus here is on these individuals.

The most frequently given reason for black opposition to busing is the belief that school quality is the paramount issue and that it can be achieved in better ways than through busing. Second in frequency is a concern for the inconvenience and related problems said to be created by busing. These two reasons together account for just over half of all explanations given by blacks who oppose busing, and for 35 percent of the explanations of white opponents. (Higher than either of these responses for whites is a "freedom of choice" explanation; for blacks, such an explanation is tied for third.)

Very few of the black explanations for opposing busing deal explicitly with racial reasons or with black-white conflict over busing, and it would be unwarranted to assume that such reasons underlie

Table 4.2 Respondents' explanations for opposition to busing (1976 De-troit Area Study).

Code	Black	White
1. *Be concerned with quality of schools instead.* Better quality of schools is solution, not busing. E.g., "They should take all that money for busing and upgrade the schools." "Move the teachers to schools that need them, not move the children." "It's more the quality of the school that counts."	31.5%	17.6%
2. *Inconvenience—not specifically related to safety.* Busing is inconvenient for either children or parents. E.g., "The kids have to leave home early, when they get back its dark again." "It creates a problem for the parents." "The children give up sports, close friends and everyday school activities." Include here references that education is affected as a result of the inconvenience, e.g., "Cuts down on education because kids are tired from riding the bus."	20.8	17.2
3. *Freedom of choice.* People should have the right to choose where to send children, where to live, etc. E.g., "I wouldn't mind if it was voluntary." "You can't force the issue on people." "Parents have a right to decide about their kids." "I feel everyone moves to an area that they want their children to go to school in."	9.0	19.4
4. *Safety of children.* Specific expression of fear for safety, or health, or general well-being of children, if they are forced to ride buses or go to distant schools. E.g., "I am opposed to busing not because of racial problems, but because busing is dangerous for the child's safety—the fights on the buses." "There's too much fighting in the schools they'll be bused to."	9.0	8.0

Table 4.2 (continued)

Code	Black	White
5. *Vague reference to neighborhood concept.* Prefers neighborhood schools, but no explanation given. *Low* priority relative to 2, 3, 12, e.g., "Let every area take care of its own children."	9.0	9.6
6. *High black proportion nullifies busing.* "You can't integrate schools in Detroit because it's mostly black, so you're just shuffling kids around."	5.6	2.3
7. *Racial reasons.* Better not to integrate the schools, or blacks and whites want to go to their own separate schools. E.g., "I don't think it's fair for coloreds to have to mix with whites." "They like to be with their own kind."	5.6	2.6
8. *Integrated neighborhoods is the solution.* Positive expression of belief in residential integration as resolution of problems that motivated busing. "Because I believe that the way to integrate is to integrate the neighborhoods. I think they're going backward."	4.5	2.5
9. *There is no problem for busing to solve.* Denies there is a problem. "Equal opportunity already exists." "The schools already have blacks."	1.7	1.3
10. *Waste of money, no specific reference to schools.* Do *not* code here if money is to be spent on improving schools; code 1 instead. "Puts a lot of extra burden on taxpayers."	1.1	7.7
11. *Other specific reasons for opposing busing.* Not a residual category. Reason must be clear and specific.	1.1	1.8
12. *Emphasis on community concept.* Emphasis on "community" nature of school. "School and community should be tied together, so the school represents the community." Include here also statements that R pays taxes for the schools in		

Table 4.2 (continued)

Code	Black	White
a particular area. "I pay taxes here so why should my children be bused."	0.6	8.2
13. *Problems with blacks.* Black schools are inferior, black children are inferior, or black children destroy the schools. E.g., "I don't want to bus my kids to a district where people aren't interested in education." "Now there's vandalism, sarcasm, and meanness in the children coming into the neighborhood."	0.6	1.8
	100	100
	(160)	(585)

Note: Respondents were first asked: "Turning now to a different issue, the courts ordered busing for some Detroit school children this past winter. What do you think of busing as a way to integrate the schools of the city of Detroit? Do you strongly approve, approve, disapprove, or strongly disapprove of busing for integration in Detroit?" Respondents were then asked: "Can you tell me why you feel that way?"

The table is based on all categories used to code responses that explain opposition (disapprove or strongly disapprove) to busing. The categories have been ordered here in terms of black percentages.

all of the nonracial explanations. If busing had had the enthusiastic backing of white authority figures and much of the white population, there probably would have been greater support for it among blacks as well; yet even then it seems likely that some black opposition would have remained, for the types of reasons given in table 4.2.

We do not have similar follow-up explanatory responses for blacks on other implementation items, but it is not too difficult to imagine what they might be. The Federal School Intervention question could yield answers related to busing and therefore to the categories in table 4.2. The Open Housing question would have to produce a rather different set of explanations, but the same blacks who give a "freedom of choice" reason for opposing busing might offer a similar explanation for opposing (or for supporting) open housing laws. We can only speculate about what other responses would be given, but there is no reason to assume that reasonable-sounding explanations would be lacking to account for dissenting black voices on various implementation steps.

A useful way to view implementation questions is in terms of the psychological forces supporting or opposing a particular response. Since there are some legitimate reasons for questioning almost any nonvoluntary change—whether it is a step to promote racial integration, or a step to increase safety through a mandatory seat belt law, or some other required action—one must ask what forces support implementation in each case. One force in the case of laws promoting equal treatment is a strong commitment to the principle being implemented, and another force is a personal stake in the success of the implementation. Blacks tend to have both of these to a high degree on issues such as implementing free residential choice by means of open housing laws. Therefore it makes sense that *most* blacks should support such steps toward implementation. Whites, never having been denied freedom of residential choice on the basis of race, do not see any personal gain at stake, and the principle itself is probably so much taken for granted in their own case that commitment to it as a necessary bulwark is not deeply felt. Thus the reasons for black and white opposition to busing can in good part be the same, yet the balance of forces can be different enough to lead to quite different proportions of blacks and whites that finally support or oppose this particular form of implementation.

This is not the whole story, for many whites also appear to react as a group to what they perceive as an intrusive threat from another group, a point we raised earlier when discussing white objections to situations where they lose majority status. Such white concern may be especially manifested in the "freedom of choice" category in table 4.2, the response for which white proportions are most out of line with black proportions. We will return to the importance of a group-conflict perspective in later chapters.

The Decline in Black Support for Implementation

Black support for the implementation of certain types of racial change has declined over the past few years. Analysis of several of the trends by age, education, and region indicates that the decline is fairly general, rather than being limited to any one demographic or social category. Two of the analyses are shown in table 4.3, using region, education, and a dichotomized measure of time as predictor variables. (Because of the small samples, it was necessary to collapse time points into a simple dichotomy of early versus late; moreover, the division could not be identical for all items, but had to make use of time points available in each instance.)

For the two questions presented in table 4.3, black support for government intervention—in the one case to promote school desegregation and in the other to provide economic aid to blacks and other minorities—has declined in every regional and educational category. And to the extent that the other predictor variable, early versus late time period, shows effects, they are opposite for the two items. For the Federal School Intervention question, the decline tends to be greater in the North, though not significantly so. For the Aid to Minorities question, the decline is significantly greater in the South. (Education does not show a clear effect alone or in either region separately, and in a parallel analysis using age there is also no clear effect.) Thus the two downturns in support for implementation seem to occur differently in the two regions—but the more important point is that both downturns occur in both regions of the country. (Results for the General Segregation question, not shown in table 4.3, are very similar to those for the Federal School Intervention question.)

There are two plausible and possibly overlapping explanations for these unexpected negative trends, with some evidence in favor of each explanation. One is that after the tremendous emphasis by blacks on various forms of civil rights protests during the 1960s, there was some natural falling away during the 1970s as the salience of these issues decreased. Evidence for this proposition can be found in the fact that the drop in support for federal intervention to ensure school integration is not accompanied by an increase in opposition to federal intervention, but rather by a rise in the "no interest" response (see table 4.1). (The same movement from support to a "no interest" or similar position also occurs, to a lesser degree, for the other items in figures 4.4, 4.5, and 4.6.) This line of reasoning is also consistent with trend data reported for the black population of Detroit concerning "alienation from white society"

Table 4.3 Responses to the Federal School Intervention and Aid to Minorities questions, by region, education, and early vs. recent survey years.

Question	Region	Education	% Positive and base N	
			1964–1970	1972–1978
Federal School Intervention[a] % Government see to it	South	0–11	77.8 (378)	67.5 (246)
		12	87.5 (112)	71.3 (108)
		13+	91.4 (35)	79.7 (74)
	North	0–11	85.9 (255)	73.4 (124)
		12	91.0 (122)	74.7 (103)
		13+	92.0 (74)	70.3 (91)
			1970–1974	1976–1982
Aid to Minorities[b] % Government see to it	South	0–11	75.3 (215)	52.5 (158)
		12	85.7 (77)	49.4 (83)
		13+	76.5 (34)	58.2 (55)
	North	0–11	73.1 (104)	65.5 (84)
		12	73.0 (74)	57.3 (75)
		13+	67.3 (49)	65.8 (82)

a. See figure 4.4 for wording.
b. See figure 4.6 for wording.

(Schuman and Hatchett 1974; Farley, Hatchett, and Schuman 1979). Survey indicators of alienation rose sharply from 1968 to 1971, then declined with equal sharpness between 1971 and 1976. Such trends fit those reported here for our quite different questions, and both patterns can be explained by the increase in civil rights militancy in the 1960s followed by some decrease in the 1970s.[10]

A second possible explanation is that some blacks may have re-treated from the use of federal force for desegregation because of their perception that such methods were so intensely opposed by whites as to be impractical. Efforts at school desegregation, espe-cially in the North, provide a clear case; the fierce white opposition to busing might have dissuaded some blacks from supporting any such approach to desegregation. Thus the *decline* in black support for federal intervention to desegregate schools could be largely a reaction to white intractability on this issue. Evidence in support of this interpretation can be drawn from the association between the decline in black support for federal intervention in this area and black objections to busing specifically. The association becomes larger over time ($r = .21$ in 1972 and $.36$ in 1976), indicating that blacks are increasingly linking the general issue of federal school intervention and the specific issue of busing.[11] Such a linkage does not demonstrate the reactive hypothesis, but it is consistent with such a hypothesis.

Neither of the two explanations we have offered seems entirely satisfactory, and certainly at present the evidence in favor of either is slim. Thus in this chapter, by documenting a downturn in black support for certain important steps toward implementing equal op-portunity, we have identified more problems than we have solved. The same is true for the more general gap between support for principles and support for implementation. What we can assert with confidence is that it is important to bear black racial attitudes in mind when attempting to interpret white trends. The assump-tion that the latter are entirely a white phenomenon is considerably shaken by the finding of similarities in kind, even though not in de-gree, for black trends. In their attitudes, as in their lives more gen-erally, blacks and whites in the United States are inescapably connected in many ways, and these connections are easily missed when only one group is considered at a time.

At the same time, blacks' perceptions of the amount of progress and the need for further change do differ systematically from those of whites. Blacks appear to have been more optimistic than whites during the early and late 1960s, when major protests were taking place, significant legislation was enacted, and national attention was focused on black grievances. Whites were considerably less likely at that time to view such actions positively, even though they recognized racial issues as a pressing national priority. The same sort of difference in sensed need for change probably played a crucial role in the widespread black support for the Reverend Jesse Jackson's bid for the Democratic presidential nomination in 1984. Yet the substantial black consensus concerning the need for change evidently does not mean there is complete agreement among blacks as to means, or probably even equal intensity of commitment to goals. Blacks may overwhelmingly perceive a need for further change and even be in near agreement on the desirability of a specific goal like school integration, yet not speak with one voice on how best to effect the change.

5   Theoretical Interpretations of White Trends

There have been a number of attempts to interpret the nature and direction of trends in white racial attitudes. The interpretations are often linked by a concern—sometimes direct, sometimes indirect—with the gap between attitudes toward matters of principle and attitudes toward the implementation of principle, or indeed between attitudes of any kind and "real behavior" outside the survey interview. Depending upon how such a gap is treated, the interpretations tend to support one or the other of the three broad perspectives on racial change discussed in Chapter 1: Progressive Trend, Underlying Racism, or Progress and Resistance.

In considering these past efforts at interpretation, it is useful to bear in mind exactly what trend data were available to interpreters at particular points in time. Table 5.1 indicates in what year a second set of data became available that was at least four years past the initial inclusion of the question in a national survey—that is, the first point at which a *trend* could be established for the item. The choice of a four-year minimum is necessarily arbitrary, but we judge it to be the least time needed between two points for durable trends to be noted. It can be seen that NORC trend data on questions dealing with principles of racial equality became available

Table 5.1 Years at which trend data became available on white racial attitudes.

1956	Same Schools (NORC) (3.1)
	Segregated Transportation (NORC) (3.1)
	Same Block (NORC) (3.3)
	Intelligence (NORC) (3.4)
1963	Equal Jobs (NORC) (3.1)
	Black Candidate (Gallup) (3.1)
	Few (Gallup) (3.3)
	Half (Gallup) (3.3)
	Most (Gallup) (3.3)
	Next Door (Gallup) (3.3)
	Great Numbers (Gallup) (3.3)
1968	Residential Choice (ISR) (3.1)
	Residential Choice (NORC) (3.1)
	Laws against Intermarriage (NORC) (3.1)
	General Segregation (ISR) (3.1)
	Federal Job Intervention (ISR) (3.2)
	Federal School Intervention (ISR) (3.2)
	Accommodations Intervention (ISR) (3.2)
	Thermometer Rating of Blacks (ISR) (3.4)
	Civil Rights Push (ISR) (3.4)
	Black Push (NORC) (3.4)
1970	Same Accommodations (NORC) (3.1)
	Black Dinner Guest (NORC) (3.3)
	Ku Klux Klan (Gallup) (3.4)
1972	Intermarriage (Gallup) (3.1)
1974	Aid to Minorities (ISR) (3.2)
1976	Black Candidate (NORC) (3.1)
	Busing (ISR) (3.2)
	Busing (NORC) (3.2)
	Riots (ISR) (3.2)
	Neighborhood Preference (ISR) (3.3)
1977	Spending on Blacks (NORC) (3.2)
	Few (NORC) (3.3)
	Half (NORC) (3.3)
	Most (NORC) (3.3)
1978	Open Housing (NORC) (3.2)

Note: Date given is the first year by which a question had been replicated at least four years beyond its initial administration. Numbers in parentheses indicate tables in Chapter 3 that provide full dates, question wording, and national trends.

first (1956); Gallup trend data on social distance later (1963); and ISR trend data on the implementation of principles last (1968).

This general congruence between types of questions and dates was in part a reflection of the underlying changes that such surveys were attempting to measure: principles of integration and equal treatment were still very much at issue in the 1940s and 1950s, whereas in later years the implementation of these principles became the more salient problem. The congruence is also one cause of certain of the differences in interpretation that have emerged. Some of the writings we will discuss provide a relatively optimistic perspective on trends over the past forty years, and some a more pessimistic view; the differences seem to be partly a function of the particular items that were available for analysis at a given time. We begin with a more optimistic line of interpretation.

The *Scientific American* Reports

Probably the best-known reports of trends in white racial attitudes have appeared in *Scientific American,* in four articles by social scientists associated with NORC (Hyman and Sheatsley 1956; Hyman and Sheatsley 1964; Greeley and Sheatsley 1971; and Taylor, Sheatsley, and Greeley 1978). These four reports rely largely on NORC data, which were the only trend data available when the initial report was published.[1]

The 1956 *Scientific American* report focuses on three questions concerning the integration of schools, transportation, and neighborhoods, as shown at the top of table 5.1. Consistent with the national trends for these questions (tables 3.1 and 3.3), Hyman and Sheatsley report large positive shifts on all three items between 1942 and 1956. They also draw on the Intelligence item (table 3.4), pointing out the substantial rise between 1942 and 1956 in white belief in black-white equality in intelligence, and suggest that this rise provided an important basis for the general shift toward acceptance of integration. They find positive associations between integrationist sentiments on the three main questions and both younger age and higher education, implying that a new and better-educated generation would give increased support to integration. Their conclusions about change are perhaps best summarized as follows:

the long-term trend is steadily in the direction of integration. It has moved far in 15 years, and it may be accelerating. Certainly there is no evidence that it will soon, if ever, reverse itself, for it is supported by revolutionary changes in ancient beliefs about Negroes and by the continued influx of better educated and more tolerant young people into the effective adult public. (Hyman and Sheatsley 1956:39)

The second *Scientific American* report in 1964, by the same authors, focuses on the same four items. By this time equalitarian responses on the Intelligence question had leveled off, but responses to the other three questions continued to move strongly in an integrationist direction, and the associations with education (positive) and age (negative) continued to hold. The article also provides evidence that personal acceptance of integration often followed government actions that created integrated situations, as when Southern attitudes changed soon after schools in a Southern community were desegregated. In general, despite the leveling off for the Intelligence item and some evidence that the youngest (21–24) age group among Southerners might no longer be a leading force for integration in that region, the authors' conclusions remain optimistic:

the unbroken trend of the past 20 years, and particularly its acceleration in the past decade of intensified controversy, suggests that integration will not be easily halted. In the minds and hearts of the majority of Americans the principle of integration seems already to have won. The issues that remain are how soon and in what ways the principle is to be implemented. (Hyman and Sheatsley 1964:23)

Note that the authors clearly recognize a distinction between principle and implementation. But because their results related largely to the former, the distinction may well have been lost on many readers.

In the 1971 *Scientific American* report, Greeley and Sheatsley open by summarizing the trend since 1942 as "distinctly and strongly toward increasing approval of integration." This conclusion is based on the Same Schools and Segregated Transportation items employed in the previous reports plus five newer questions for which NORC trend data had become available: Same Accommodations, Black Dinner Guest, Residential Choice, Laws against

Intermarriage, and Black Push (see table 5.1 for references to tables in Chapter 3 that give wordings and trends for these questions). (Nothing is said in this or the fourth report concerning the Intelligence and Same Block questions, neither of which had been asked in 1970.) Most of the new items continue to focus on principles; none deals directly with the implementation of these principles. The only two time points available for all seven items were 1963 and 1970. All but the question about attitudes toward blacks "pushing themselves where they're not wanted" (Black Push) show increased support for integration during this period. Moreover, younger age and higher education continue to be associated with more integrationist answers; the possible reversal for young white Southerners noted in 1964 is not evident in the 1970 data.

In stating conclusions, the authors appear to be somewhat ambivalent about the meaning of the continued strong positive shift indicated by their data. On the one hand, for example, they write of the results as suggesting that the trend for attitudes toward integrated education (Same Schools) was proceeding so rapidly that in just a few years (1977 is the date they project) "desegregating schools [will have] ceased to be a significant issue." On the other hand, they also emphasize that "a change of attitude does not necessarily predict a change in behavior," and write of the shifts "as creating an environment for effective social reform," rather than as being reform itself. In a follow-up three years later, Greeley and Sheatsley (1974) also include data on the overwhelming white resistance to busing, and they note the distinction between principle and practice, though without altering substantially their emphasis on progress toward acceptance of integration.

The 1978 *Scientific American* report, by Taylor, Sheatsley, and Greeley, continues to record change in an integrationist direction, with the special additional point that the two-year period 1970–1972 saw an unexpected "leap forward in racial tolerance." This conclusion is based on trend data through 1976 for five of the seven items employed in the 1971 report. The remaining two, Segregated Transportation and Same Accommodations, were dropped because of having earlier reached ceilings. In fact, of the items originally used in 1956, only the Same Schools question remains in the 1978 analysis. Younger age and higher education continue to be related to pro-integration responses, and region is identified as having taken on special importance: the "liberal leap" of 1970–1972 appears to have occurred mainly in the South.[2]

In sum, the picture presented by these four reports is one of almost unvarying movement in an equalitarian and integrationist direction. Although qualifications concerning both implementation and actual behavior are introduced in each article, the thrust of the quantitative results is clearly toward progress in white support for integration in all major areas under inquiry.

The four *Scientific American* reports have served as a major source of data on and interpretation of trends in white racial attitudes during a period of great national change in terms of court decisions, executive and legislative actions, organized social movements, and outbursts of collective behavior, as well as during a more recent period in which racial issues have receded somewhat from public attention. The main message of the reports is that despite much talk about "white backlash" against both government actions on civil rights and black protests, there was virtually constant movement toward acceptance of basic principles of racial integration. Moreover, the reports produce evidence that direct government efforts to enforce integration seemed to shift white attitudes in that same direction, so that the pace of change was likely to be determined more by acts of leadership than by the acquiescence of leaders to the state of public opinion at any given time. And since the younger and better-educated generation was particularly sympathetic to integrationist goals, underlying demographic and social currents also favored integrationist trends.[3]

As might be expected given our heavy use of the same NORC data, we agree with many of the major findings and conclusions of the *Scientific American* reports. There has indeed been a great deal of change, and the varying of amount of change by area of life (with the most change in the least personal areas, such as public transportation) fits fairly well the ordering of integrationist sentiment in the NORC data. Yet a reader of our previous chapters will not have come away from them with the same sense of nearly unambiguous positive movement in racial attitudes. Nor do we think that most observers of the American scene over the past four decades will have perceived as much actual racial change as is suggested by the

NORC survey data (for example, the disappearance of school integration as a significant issue).

How can we reconcile these two pictures? The obvious answer is that the *Scientific American* reports draw almost entirely on questions that do in fact show steady positive change, primarily principle and minimal social distance questions, but do not include any government implementation or other more complex questions. Only the Intelligence question, which was dropped after the second report (and dropped from NORC surveys after 1968), and the Black Push question, which both the *Scientific American* authors and we consider too ambiguous to deserve much emphasis, challenged the strong positive trends shown by the other items. Thus these authors were not faced with compelling survey evidence that might have prompted them to qualify more strongly their claims of progress toward integration. Survey investigators have long known that responses to items at a single time point can be misleading if not recognized as the product of a particular question. The same can be true for trends over time: they also are a function of the exact questions asked.

With the benefit of hindsight, it appears that the items used in the *Scientific American* reports were too restricted in form and content to give an adequately rounded picture of racial attitudes, especially in recent years. Yet it would be a mistake to attribute the restriction to misjudgment on the part of these or other investigators. The baseline questions used by NORC in the 1940s dealt with fundamental issues and were hardly platitudinous for their time. It was both natural and desirable to replicate them in later years in order to study trends. And once such a set of items was established for replication, it no doubt tended to occupy the questionnaire space available for studying racial issues and therefore to limit the number of new items that could be entertained. Only in the 1970s did NORC introduce new trend questions that presented a somewhat different picture of racial change, and these questions (Black Candidate, Open Housing, Busing, Spending on Blacks, and the Few, Half, Most series) were not referred to in the 1978 *Scientific American* report, perhaps because they were not part of the basic set that had been tracked in the previous articles.

What happened in these reports is probably best thought of in terms of the sociology of knowledge (Merton 1957) applied to the construction of survey questionnaires, rather than as a matter of individual judgment. The main available set of distinctively different survey items, those concerning implementation of principles (as implicitly called for by Hyman and Sheatsley in their 1964 article) grew out of ISR election surveys, which were designed specifically to study the political process and were therefore rather naturally concerned with what "the government" should or should not do. Moreover, these items are not better than, but merely different from, those in the NORC replication set. Questions asked in surveys are inevitably products of the social context in which their creators work.

In sum, the *Scientific American* reports are accurate and important in what they say, but they also leave out much that can now be seen to be significant in the evolution of racial attitudes and behavior in America. Largely omitted are the struggles over how to implement principles and over the proportions of blacks "acceptable" to whites (and, of course, of whites acceptable to blacks) in particular life settings. In addition, average differences in social class between blacks and whites are not considered—and in the case of the Same Block item they were explicitly eliminated by the wording of the question (see table 3.3).[4]

The problems caused by these omissions can be demonstrated by a consideration of the basic item employed in the *Scientific American* reports to tap attitudes toward the integration of schools: "Do you think white students and black students should go to the same schools, or to separate schools?" This is a good question as far as it goes, straightforward in phrasing and not obviously loaded in any direction. And it has clearly captured fundamental trends in white American attitudes over the forty years it has been asked, moving from 32 percent to 90 percent choice of the first alternative. Yet it cannot capture the degree to which the *proportions* of black and white children matter in school integration, not to mention perceived problems due to differences in social class or other factors ignored by the question. But it is evident from other questions that proportions do make an important difference to many people. Such people, faced with the question's dichotomous choice, are likely to select the first, integrationist alternative, since they probably have no preference for segregated schooling in any absolute sense—but this choice does not indicate a commitment to all kinds and degrees of integration. The point is that the question does not encourage or even allow people to indicate the complexities underlying real-life attitudes and behavior, but instead assumes an absolute commitment to one of two abstractions called "integration" and "segregation." The choice is too simple for most respondents in the 1980s, and thus in the end it may be the question and not the answer that is misleading. A single dichotomous question simply cannot capture the complexities of attitudes toward school integration.[5]

Despite the problems we have discussed, the *Scientific American* reports and the NORC data on which they are based are of great importance for recording fundamental changes in the values of white Americans. The data indicate that there is no longer an attempt by any significant number of Americans to justify segregation in principle, and that this evolution occurred steadily during the period 1940–1980 regardless of more salient short-term stresses and opposition. The change extends even to questions on racial intermarriage, although this and closely related symbols of complete integration have not moved as far, or as inexorably, as have attitudes in more clearly public spheres of life. Without the NORC trend data on principles we would have a much more impoverished and inaccurate picture of trends in white racial attitudes and behavior. Behavior as well as attitudes must be emphasized, for the appointment and election of black Americans to high government positions, as well as many other signs of the crumbling of symbols of absolute segregation, could have come about only as part of a major change in modal white values. These behavioral changes may be regarded as small, but they are nevertheless important, and they would be difficult to understand without the existence of the NORC trend data.

Superficial Tolerance

A second, more indirect interpretation of trends in white racial attitudes can be drawn from Mary Jackman's (1978) discussion of "general" versus "applied" measures of tolerance. Jackman's concern is primarily with the relation of education to white racial attitudes at any one time, but her main thesis and findings have implications for trends over time also.

Jackman primarily uses the four ISR items we have termed General Segregation (our table 3.1), Residential Choice (table 3.1), Federal Job Intervention (3.2), and Federal School Intervention (3.2). The first two she considers measures of general or abstract support for integration; the latter two measures of applied or policy-relevant support for integration. The distinction is essentially the same as the one we drew in Chapter 3 between questions concerning principles and questions about the implementation of principles. What is most relevant for us about Jackman's argument is her initial assumption that implementation items provide a touchstone of genuine commitment to integration, whereas principle items do not. Given this basic assumption, when she finds that education is positively associated with endorsement of integrationist alternatives on the two principle items, and is unrelated or more weakly related to similar endorsement on the two implementation items, she argues that "increasing years of education leads to a greater familiarity with the appropriate democratic position on racial integration," but not to greater commitment to that position (p. 322). She does not claim that more-educated respondents deliberately lie to interviewers, but rather that they have a superficial adherence to principles and no greater tendency than the less educated to call on these principles when real-life issues are at stake. (See Stember 1961 for a somewhat similar analysis that challenges the assumption that education reduces prejudice.)

The implication of Jackman's argument for our analysis is that if responses to principle questions are wholly superficial then the massive shifts recorded on principle items between 1942 and 1982 have little meaning, since most implementation items do not show a similar degree of change. Moreover, the shift over time on principle items was always in the direction of the position held initially by the more educated respondents; it might be seen as merely a process whereby democratic slogans were learned first by the more educated and then passed on to the less educated. In sum, just as the association of principle items with education would be much less important than it at first appears, so their association with "time" would also lose much of its apparent meaning about real change in white racial attitudes and behavior.

We therefore need to examine Jackman's assumptions and evidence carefully. The main criticism that has been offered thus far is that Jackman's analysis ignores the fact that the applied or implementation items confound attitudes toward integration with attitudes toward federal intervention more generally (Margolis and Haque 1981; Kuklinski and Parent 1981). Thus, for example, more-educated respondents might have a genuine commitment to integration but be so opposed to intrusion by the federal government that they would not endorse concrete steps toward integration on the two items Jackman employs. Jackman has answered this criticism by showing fairly convincingly that a negative attitude toward federal power or coercion as such is not strongly related either to education or to the implementation items (Jackman 1981a, 1981b). (See also our discussion of objections to government intrusion later in this chapter.)

Nevertheless, Jackman's conclusions do seem to need modification in several important respects. First, on one government implementation item—the one concerning federal intervention to desegregate public accommodations—there are strong positive trends over time, as well as a moderately strong association with education (see pp. 98–101). Evidently, under some circumstances there is increasing white support for government intervention.

Even in areas more central to American race relations, Jackman's results may be somewhat less general than they at first appear. All of the associations with education that she analyzed in her 1978 article involved just two principle questions and two policy-related questions, and may have been unduly affected by idiosyncratic features of the form, wording, or context of those specific questions. Some hint in this direction is provided by data from a 1968 survey of racial attitudes in fifteen American cities (Campbell and Schuman 1968). This survey included a slight variant of the ISR Residential Choice principle question used by Jackman and by us in Chapter 3 (see table 3.1), followed by an original implementation question concerning support for laws against residential discrimination. *Both* these questions show large and essentially similar associations to education, with the gap between the lowest and highest educational categories being about 25 percent for the principle question and about 23 percent for the implementation question (see table 5.2). The two items do differ in overall levels of

Table 5.2 Responses to principle and implementation items from the 1968 fifteen-cities study, by education.

Principle Question: "Which of these statements would you agree with—first, white people have a right to keep Negroes out of their neighborhoods if they want to, or second, Negroes have a right to live anywhere they can afford to, just like white people?"	Education		
	0–11	12	13+
1. Whites have right to keep Negroes out	41.3%	27.9%	15.9%
2. Depend, DK, Other	7.8	10.2	8.4
3. Negroes have right	51.0	61.9	75.7
(Base N)	(889)	(743)	(580)
Implementation Question: "How about laws to prevent discrimination against Negroes in buying or renting houses and apartments? Do you favor or oppose such laws?"			
1. Favor	37.3%	53.2%	59.7%
2. Undecided	7.1	10.0	9.4
3. Oppose[a]	55.6	36.8	31.0
(Base N)	(885)	(737)	(570)

Source: Based on a reanalysis of data for whites from Campbell and Schuman 1968.
a. Includes those who answered "Whites have right to keep Negroes out" to preceding question

support, as we have found regularly for principle and implementation questions for both whites and blacks, but their associations to education do not vary greatly. We do not wish to argue that the implementation question shown in table 5.2 is a better item than those used by Jackman; we simply note that under certain circumstances more-educated respondents appear to provide more support than less-educated respondents for implementing a principle.[6]

Jackman's assumption that white respondents who endorse school or residential integration in the abstract but oppose government implementation lack a real commitment to integration is also inconsistent with other results we reported in Chapter 3. We see no reason not to give considerable credence to social distance questions indicating rising support for integration in the sense of small numbers of black families moving into previously white neighborhoods, or very high levels of support for "a few" black children in previously all-white schools. Jackman seems to consider these types of questions unimportant because hypothetical, but in one sense they are closer to real-life contact with integration than are general questions about government implementation. In any case, they provide a different picture from *either* principle or implementation questions. Our results with such items in Chapter 3 only partially question Jackman's thesis about education, since the associations of education with social distance items vary from large to essentially zero, but our findings are directly relevant to trends over time. In particular, in the area of residential integration there has been steadily rising support for white acceptance of "integration" in the sense of a black family moving next door or onto the same block. Unless one treats these responses as completely misleading—a claim we will consider later, but one not made by Jackman—they indicate real change in an area of life that is of considerable importance in terms of both social status and social contact.

Unfortunately there is not a similar trend question regarding employment, but it seems likely that such questions would show lack of change only if a ceiling were reached, as happened with the question about a few black children in a school. In the 1968 white cross-sectional sample from fifteen cities, respondents were asked: "Suppose you had a job where your supervisor was a qualified Negro. Would you mind that a lot, a little, or not at all?" At that time, 86 percent of the whites interviewed answered "Not at all" (Campbell and Schuman 1968). Presumably the figure would be near 100 percent by now.

Of course, it can be argued that questions about a qualified black supervisor or a black family moving next door or a few black children in a school do not grapple with serious issues such as integration at closer to fifty-fifty proportions, or affirmative action steps, or other concrete policies that have raised substantial controversy and considerable white opposition. These issues quite likely have much less support—and less growth in support—among whites, as is suggested by the nearly unanimous white opposition to busing and the decline in support for federal intervention to integrate schools. But to insist that questions about principles and social distance are essentially superficial because they do not involve support for busing or for affirmative action is again to make the assumption, noted earlier in connection with the *Scientific American* reports, that real attitudes toward integration are as dichotomous as the survey questions that are generally posed: that people must be 100 percent for integration or 100 percent opposed to it. A little thought will show how unrealistic such an assumption is: it would be easy to suggest steps toward integration or black progress that virtually nobody would accept. Many positions on racial issues are captured by responses in support of "integration," and many of these positions are probably at the level of acceptance of a black family, or a few black children, or a qualified black supervisor. Support for this sort of change may be insufficient to solve racial problems in American society, but that is another matter than attempting to understand the nature and meaning of trends in white racial attitudes.[7]

Symbolic Racism

David Sears and his colleagues, in developing their theory of "symbolic racism," have indirectly addressed the issue of the different patterns of white support for principles of equality and for the implementation of those principles. They have reported their results in a large number of articles and chapters; here we rely heavily on Sears, Hensler, and Speer 1979, and to a lesser extent on Kinder and Sears 1981. (See also Sears and Allen 1984, which includes references to other work by Sears and his colleagues.) The primary focus of these articles is on the sources of attitudes toward types of implementation such as busing or actually voting for a black candidate. (Only passing comments are made regarding upward trends in attitudes toward principles, though they are said by Kinder and Sears to represent "a momentous . . . change.") Reduced to what we see as its essentials, the main argument can be summarized as follows:

1. Many whites acquire antiblack (prejudiced, racist) attitudes during their preadult years, and these persist in adulthood.
2. Underlying antiblack attitudes are not expressed today by overt support for segregation and discrimination (presumably because such support is no longer culturally appropriate).
3. But antiblack attitudes can be expressed today in the form of opposition to busing, or to a black candidate, or to preferential

treatment for blacks. Moreover, such issues take on a "symbolic" connection to deeper fears; for example, deep-seated rejection of blacks can be expressed as fear of what will happen to white children bused into black neighborhoods.

4. This further suggests that white resistance to changes in the racial status quo may be due less (or perhaps not at all) to a defense of personal interests (for example, school quality for one's own child or job security for oneself), and more to animosities having little relation to specific vested interests.

The total argument is more elaborate than this outline suggests. In particular, symbolic racism is said to be "a blend of antiblack affect and the kind of traditional American moral values embodied in the Protestant Ethic" (Kinder and Sears 1981:416), such as individualism and self-reliance, with blacks felt to be violating these values.[8][9]

Two types of evidence are used to support this argument. On the one hand, Sears, Hensler, and Speer show, for example, that white opposition to busing is moderately correlated with a variety of more obvious measures of prejudice (such as support for segregation in general). On the other hand, they present evidence that such opposition to busing has little, if any, relation to personal self-interest in the sense of having children who might be bused. Thus busing is a "symbolic" issue, a focus for expressing general antiblack attitudes in terms that seem culturally appropriate (for example, in terms of the importance of neighborhood schools), rather than an instrumental response to a situation involving immediate practical needs (such as disruption of one's own child's schooling).[9]

Since Sears and his colleagues do not focus on many of the survey questions discussed in our report, or on trends over time (but see Kinder and Rhodebeck 1982 for a related short-term trend analysis), inferences from their work to the main issues confronting us are indirect. But it seems likely that they would assign less importance to the pro-integration trends over time on principle items than do the *Scientific American* authors, and that they would interpret the lack of positive change on most implementation items as more indicative of the true state of white racial attitudes over the past four decades. "From overt racism to symbolic racism" might well be their way of describing trends since 1942.

We find the evidence presented by Sears and his colleagues against the importance of personal self-interest to be persuasive. It does appear from their data that attitudinal opposition to busing is not mainly the result of white parents' personal concern about the educational experience or physical security of their children, since having a child who might be involved in busing shows little or no association with opposition to busing. Furthermore, other indicators of immediate personal risk from various forms of government implementation do not correlate well with opposition to such implementation. Indeed, these findings on racial issues seem to reflect a larger discovery that personal self-interest is not generally transformed in any simple way into political belief and action (see, for example, Kinder and Mebane 1983).

However, the evidence that most of the opposition to busing, or to black candidates, or to various forms of affirmative action, can be seen as symbolic racism is less persuasive. We find several serious problems with the evidence:

1. The absolute levels of white opposition to busing shown in our table 3.2 approach 90 percent. If this opposition reflects a new form of racism, symbolic racism, then virtually the entire white population (and a substantial part of the black population) must be characterized as racist. This position certainly can be (and has been) claimed, but it must be done in the face of much survey data that show white support for some forms of racial integration (for example, near unanimity in not objecting to "a few" black children in a previously white school).[10] Moreover, if the latter kind of unanimity is seen as merely platitudinous, perhaps opposition to busing has also become something of a platitude. Indeed, because the distribution on the busing item is so skewed, Sears, Hensler, and Speer are identifying not "symbolic racists" but rather "symbolic antiracists"—that is, the small part (10 to 15 percent) of the white population that defends busing in the face of opposition from the great majority.

2. The argument that old-fashioned racism is largely transformed today into more indirect or symbolic forms is undermined by the fact that Sears, Hensler, and Speer's main evidence involves the correlation between overt "racial intolerance" (for example, support for segregation in general) and antibusing answers. Although this evidence can be used to show that opposition to busing is asso-

ciated with prejudice, it hardly suggests that prejudice *needs* the busing issue as a vehicle for expression. On the contrary, there must be a fair amount of overt "racial intolerance."[11]

3. The fact that such correlations exist is hardly surprising. Correlations simply show that the orderings on two variables are much the same. It seems almost inevitable that those who support "segregation in general" will oppose busing to end segregation, and this is bound to produce a correlation of some magnitude. In other words, the discovery of correlations between antiblack attitudes and antibusing attitudes tells us very little. The real questions concern the size of the correlations and the absolute level of opposition to busing.

4. The sizes of the correlations reported by Sears and his colleagues are not trivial by social science standards, but they are far from suggesting that antibusing sentiments can be identified with racial intolerance. Sears, Hensler, and Speer's most straightforward summary correlation is .36, between their "racial intolerance scale" and a seven-point antibusing item (1979:374). Unless most of the remaining variation on the pertinent items is due to chance, this leaves a substantial amount of variation in antibusing sentiments unexplained by "racial intolerance" as it was directly measured, and presumably caused by other factors.

5. Finally, as Bobo (1983b) has argued, Sears and his colleagues' conception of "self-interest" is probably too narrow and lacking in political definition. A clash of personal interests, such as direct interpersonal competition for some resource between people of different racial backgrounds, is certainly one form that racial conflict can assume. Conflict can also, however, stem from the linkage that often exists between personal and collective interests. For example, a very high proportion of the black population seems to be opposed to the Reagan Administration, yet many of these blacks have been no more personally threatened by President Reagan's actions than childless whites are affected by busing. Perhaps such blacks oppose Reagan merely as a symbol, but if so he is seen as a symbol of a larger threat to blacks as a group. It becomes difficult for onlookers to distinguish symbolic threats from real threats in this case, just as it may be for whites who oppose busing. Once issues are defined in terms of political conflict between racial groups, political threat does become "personal."

Discounting Positive Responses Entirely

Neither Jackman (1978) nor Sears and his colleagues claim that pro-integration responses to questions about principles are meaningless, but they do not give much credence to white protestations of support for integration in principle unless backed up by support for strong implementation. Thus, it is only a small step to entirely discounting positive answers to survey questions such as those dealing with principles of school integration or nondiscrimination in employment, treating such responses as merely lip service to equalitarian values. From this perspective, the massive shifts shown in table 3.1 (and more dramatically in figure 6.1) become merely slopes of hypocrisy, glaring examples of the gap between verbal responses to surveys and both true thoughts and actual deeds.

No single author or paper is especially associated with this position, but there are several types of evidence that provide some support for it. Race-of-interviewer studies show that white respondents give more pro-integration responses to black than to white interviewers, with the differences sometimes very large (Hatchett and Schuman 1975–76). This suggests that such responses either are highly situational in nature or represent deliberate falsifications for the benefit of the black interviewers. In either case, this finding makes the validity of responses to white interviewers uncertain as well, for interviewers also may be perceived to represent values different from the actual values of the respondent. In Chapter 2 we provided evidence involving regional differences in interviewing staffs that invites just such an interpretation.

More direct evidence of the need to use care in interpreting responses to survey questionnaires comes from an occasional investigation of discrepancies between attitudes and behavior. Silverman (1974) sent some incoming white college students a supposedly genuine inquiry from their college about having a black roommate, and sent a comparable group a purportedly "scientific" survey on the same subject. Students were significantly more likely to appear favorable toward having a black roommate on the "scientific" questionnaire than on the supposedly real inquiry, but the number of students is not given and the nature of the scale used makes it possible that only a small proportion of students were involved in the discrepancies. Somewhat less easy to interpret are a series of "bogus pipeline experiments" that show whites giving more anti-black answers when under the impression that they are hooked up to a "lie detector" than under more ordinary conditions (for example, Allen 1975). The results are ambiguous because it is possible to interpret them as due to the experimental situation, especially if one assumes that white Americans are often ambivalent and insecure in their racial views, as some social psychologists argue (Poskocil 1977; Katz 1981).

Still another source of evidence on what might be called "covert racism" comes from the literature on unobtrusive research, where race has been introduced as a variable in studies of helping, nonverbal behavior, and the like. A recent review by Crosby, Bromley, and Saxe concludes that "discriminatory behavior is more prevalent in the body of unobtrusive studies than we might expect on the basis of survey data" (1980:557). However, the authors do not test this conclusion directly, since few of the investigations they review gathered any survey data at all. In addition, as we have seen in previous chapters, the degree to which negative sentiments toward blacks are revealed in surveys depends heavily on the specific questions asked; it is a serious mistake to summarize all "survey data" as implying that discriminatory attitudes are rare (compare Schuman 1972).[12]

It seems to us likely that at least some white responses to survey questions today are affected by social pressure to give racially liberal answers. But this in turn means that norms in the United States have changed radically over the past forty years, so that antiblack speech and action that were once acceptable and common are now almost completely taboo in the public arena and perhaps even in that special semipublic setting known as the survey interview. It is striking to recall that the first and classic demonstration of attitude-behavior discrepancy (LaPiere 1934) showed verbal responses to a questionnaire to be discriminatory and actual behavior to be equalitarian! That our concern today is with exactly the opposite problem indicates how great has been the change from the 1930s to the 1980s. The same radical shift is equally evident in many other ways, such as in the difference between the blatantly racist job advertisements of the 1930s and those which today proclaim a commitment to "equal opportunity." We are dealing with a fundamental transformation of social norms and with the issue of what this transformation means at the individual level. It would be as simplistic to regard such a sweeping change as merely "lip service" as to take at face value all pro-integration responses given in surveys. Because this is such a large and difficult issue, we defer further discussion of it to our concluding chapter.

Equalitarianism versus Individualism

A quite different perspective on racial attitudes is provided by Lipset and Schneider, who review a wide range of survey questions (though not mainly trend data) and conclude that "on the central issues involving racial discrimination . . . the American consensus is powerfully *against discrimination* . . . The consensus breaks down, however, when *compulsory integration* is involved . . . Many whites deeply resent efforts to force racial integration on them, not because they oppose racial equality, but because they feel it violates their individual freedom" (1978:44). Lipset and Schneider see the basic conflict as one "between two values that are at the core of the American creed—individualism and egalitarianism" (1978:43). They also note that there is a fair amount of white support for "compensatory treatment" for blacks, such as special educational programs, but that white public opinion is strongly opposed to preferential treatment in the form of quotas or similar procedures in school or work situations.

The data cited by Lipset and Schneider do clearly show decreasing white support as one moves from antidiscrimination principles, at the one extreme, to preferential treatment for blacks, at the other. And Lipset and Schneider's view that this is a logically defensible sequence in terms of national values, rather than merely a matter of overt versus covert racism, provides a useful foil to several of the theoretical approaches considered previously in this chapter. At the same time, their own data and arguments, as well as other available evidence, raise serious questions about their more general conclusions. For one thing, as they indicate at the beginning of their article, whites do not necessarily endorse full integration even when stated as a principle, with neither coercion nor affirmative action measures involved. Clearly something more is going on than resistance to external pressures or a defense of individualistic values. Moreover, Lipset and Schneider provide evidence elsewhere in their article that most white support of civil rights legislation and judicial decisions was provided by *Northern* whites as the agents, or at least acquiescers, and *Southern* whites as the targets—which sounds as much like the operation of some form of self-interest as like the operation of individualism. A convincing case for the high importance of individualism with regard to racial issues requires framing questions that oppose the value of individualism to self-interest—not align it with self-interest.

This is not to deny the usefulness of the distinctions Lipset and Schneider make. It seems clear that whites are more likely to endorse nondiscrimination in education or employment than compensatory training programs for blacks, and more likely to endorse compensatory training than preferential quotas or other advantages for blacks involving actual employment or promotion. These differences in response deserve to be given serious interpretation, rather than simply dismissed as superficial variants of basically prejudiced attitudes.

Objections to Government Intrusion

The difference between trends for questions dealing with principles and trends for questions dealing with implementation is sometimes attributed to a confounding of racial attitudes with attitudes toward government intervention in general. For example, federal intervention to enforce school integration might be opposed not because of any reluctance to see schools integrated but because of a belief that the federal government should not intrude into such a sphere, or perhaps simply an objection to the further growth of "big government." This point has been made most often in critiques of Jackman's thesis about the connection between education and racial attitudes, which we discussed earlier, but it also provides a possible explanation for the differences in level and slope of trends in attitudes that we reported in Chapter 3.

Our consideration of the available evidence indicates that opposition to government intervention per se cannot explain differences in the *slopes* (that is, the direction and rate of change) of principle and implementation trends, but that it may explain part of the difference in trend *levels*. With regard to slopes, table 3.2 shows that between 1964 and 1974 support for federal intervention to enforce school integration dropped by 9 percentage points (and by an additional 10 points two years later), but that support for federal intervention to enforce integration in public accommodations rose by 22 percentage points over the same period (unfortunately the question was not asked after 1974). It is most plausible to see these diametrically opposing trends as due not to changes in concern over federal intervention as such, but to the more threatening nature of integration in the one sphere than in the other. A quite different piece of evidence is the lack of systematic decline in support for government intervention in some areas that are remote from racial attitudes. For example, attitudes toward federal support for universal health care, tracked by an ISR election survey question, showed little net change between 1970 and 1978, the dates closest to those for the racial items. Nor is there evidence that a general rejection of government spending in various domains occurred between 1972 and 1978 (Davis 1980). In sum, the available evidence does not provide much support for an explanation of our trend results in terms of some general increase in rejection of government intervention, whatever loss of faith may have occurred in government efficacy, honesty, and the like (House and Mason 1975).

However, our data reveal not only variations in the slopes of trends, but also a wide difference in levels of support for principle as against implementation of principle, and the latter difference might conceivably be accounted for by general objections to government intrusion. Even in the area of public accommodations, where principle and implementation slopes have shown a similar positive upward movement, approximately 30 percent more of the population sampled supported the principle than supported implementation. The size of this persistent gap cannot be specified with great precision, since pairs of principle and implementation questions are not precisely comparable and there are other complicating factors such as sampling error, but the substantial and consistent magnitude of the gap is unmistakable in comparisons of tables 3.1 and 3.2.

Several pieces of evidence bear indirectly on whether a general

concern about government intrusiveness is involved in this difference in levels, though the evidence is neither as consistent nor as
unambiguous as in the case of slopes. First, objection to *federal* intervention as such can hardly be the source of the principle-implementation gap, for the gap is as striking for residential integration
as for other types of integration (see figure 3.6), yet the implementation item in this area speaks of a "community-wide vote" on an
open housing law, with no mention of the federal government. Second, in one clear case where we can correlate several racial implementation items with a nonracial implementation item (the
question on federal support for health care), the correlations tend
to be small but statistically significant; for example, when the federal school intervention and federal health care items are correlated, the median correlation is .15 (p < .001). The interpretation
of such correlations is not without ambiguity, but one might argue
that *general* objection to government intervention (as tapped by
the health item) can account for a small amount of the variation in
the racial implementation items, but also that it almost certainly
leaves a good deal of the variation unaccounted for.

There is one broader consideration that should also lead to some
skepticism about hypotheses concerning a general rejection of government intervention, whether that be seen as constant or as increasing. If we consider all forms of government intervention, there
has always been a certain kind of inconsistency on the issue of federal intervention per se. Those of liberal persuasion tend to support
government intervention for equalitarian ends, but are more wary
of government intervention when it comes to censorship, federal
police activities, or other civil libertarian concerns. Those of conservative persuasion tend to feel the opposite. This difference suggests that *general* opposition to government intervention may be a
very rare phenomenon, and that it is probably a mistake to look toward such an explanation for the principle-implementation difference in the racial data.

We followed one other tack in attempting to clarify the reluctance of many whites to endorse the implementation of principles
they support. The main ISR implementation questions can be
criticized for being somewhat vague; respondents do not know precisely what they are being asked to endorse. For example, the question on federal intervention to support school desegregation asks

Table 5.3 Experiments on support for enforcement of nondiscrimination in housing.

Government Version		Laws Version	
On another subject, suppose a black family plans to move into a house in an all-white neighborhood, and some white people in the neighborhood want to stop them from moving in. Do you think the government should enforce the black family's right to live wherever they can afford to, *or* that it should be left entirely up to the white neighborhood residents to decide? (If "other" volunteered, accept and record.)		On another subject, suppose a black family plans to move into a house in an all-white neighborhood, and some white people in the neighborhood want to stop them from moving in. Do you think there should be laws to enforce the black family's right to live wherever they can afford to, *or* that it should be left entirely up to the white neighborhood residents to decide? (If "other" volunteered, accept and record.)	
1. Government enforce	52.2%	1. Laws to enforce	56.1%
2. Leave it up to white neighbors	15.9	2. Leave it up to white neighbors	4.9
3. Other types of response		3. Other types of response	
a. Says laws already exist	0.7	a. Says laws already exist	4.1
b. Favors nondiscrimination but does not support enforcement	21.7	b. Favors nondiscrimination but does not support enforcement	23.6
c. Opposes enforcement, no other comments	2.9	c. Opposes enforcement, no other comments	1.6
d. Other vague responses: "depends," "don't know"	6.5	d. Other vague responses: "depends," "don't know"	9.8
(Base N)	(138)	(Base N)	(123)

Note: "Laws already exist" (3.a) is treated as support of enforcement. All other volunteered responses are treated as lack of support for enforcement and in this sense can be combined with "Leave it up to white residents." If this consolidation is used to create a complete two-by-two table (governments/laws, enforcement/nonenforcement), $X^2 = 1.39$, d.f. = 1, n.s. If only the two closed alternatives are used, ignoring all volunteered response, $X^2 = 7.16$, d.f. = 1, p < .01.

whether "the government in Washington should see to it that white and black children go to the same schools," but "the government" is not really defined (Congress? the President? the FBI? or what?), nor are the means or limits of enforcement specified (busing, magnet schools, funding incentives, and so on). In order to provide a more sharply defined focus on implementation, we carried out the experiment shown in table 5.3.

An ISR national telephone survey in November 1983 included two forms of a question we prepared on enforcing nondiscrimination in housing, with each form administered to a random half of the sample. Our experimental manipulation of wording distinguishes between enforcement by the "government" and enforcement by "laws," the latter presumably suggesting a more orderly and judicious procedure than the former. In addition, both forms of the question speak of "a black family" (that is, a single family) in order to reduce the possible fear by white respondents of a mass influx of blacks, and thus to concentrate on the issue of legal enforcement as such. Finally, in order to avoid pressuring respondents to fit their answers into a simplistic dichotomy, we instructed interviewers to accept and record volunteered "other" responses, which in fact more than a third of the respondents did offer. (In the end we classified most of the "other" responses as implying rejection of legal or government enforcement, despite the frequent affirmation of support for the *principle* of nondiscrimination.)

The experimental results in table 5.3 suggest that specification of "laws" rather than "government" may make it somewhat easier for respondents to support implementation, but the difference does not reach statistical significance for the most crucial test and, in any case, is not very large. Furthermore, although the proportion supporting "laws to enforce" nondiscrimination in housing is higher than most figures for implementation items in table 3.2, it is considerably below the 88 percent that in 1976 supported nondiscrimination in housing in principle (see table 3.1), and even below the 66 percent that in 1974 supported government intervention to prevent discrimination in hotels and restaurants (table 3.2).[13] It seems evident that an important segment of the population upholds the right of black people to live wherever they wish *but* is unwilling to see legal means used to enforce that right. Unfortunately, our experiment did not probe further to discover explanations for this apparent inconsistency.

The results and reasoning offered in this section point to a problem in great need of additional research—research carefully designed to illuminate difficult issues, rather than to bolster any particular ideological position on the nature of racial attitudes in America. A substantial number of white people—and, it is important to recall from Chapter 4, a noticeable number of black people as well—oppose the use of government coercion to enforce nondiscrimination, despite their claim to support nondiscrimination and even integration in principle. This opposition varies by area of life, however, and does not seem adequately explained by reference to a general objection to government intervention in private life.

Our own tentative interpretation is that it is constraint of any kind that is disliked, and that the extent to which respondents accept constraint is heavily influenced by the *degree* to which they support a particular policy goal. Those with a very strong commitment to a policy goal will usually also express support for the use of government authority to reach that goal. This does not mean that those who support a principle but not its legal implementation are without any real commitment to the principle. Such an attempt to separate people into the truly committed and the uncommitted is an oversimplification, far removed from the realities of life. Thus, many of those who support residential integration in principle and oppose government implementation of such integration show their modest commitment to the principle by positive answers to social distance items (see figures 3.9, 3.10, and 3.11).[14] Both commitment to a principle and commitment to its implementation must be seen as continuous dimensions, and the exact balance between them is always problematic for each member of the population at any given time.

Conclusions

Each of the theoretical approaches considered in this chapter offers insight into the trends in white racial attitudes we reviewed earlier, but the trends are more complex than any of the theories would allow. We will need to draw from all of the theories, as well as from other ideas, to arrive at an adequate understanding of the changes that have occurred over the past four decades.

The *Scientific American* reports provide the fullest record of major shifts in white attitudes between the early 1940s and the present. During that period, most white Americans ceased to defend segregation in public spheres of life and came to accept, at least in principle, the idea that race should make no difference when it comes to buying a house, gaining employment, or enrolling in a school. But because the survey items used did not address difficult issues of implementation, the *Scientific American* articles did not represent adequately all important trends in racial attitudes.

Partly in reaction to the picture of a nearly continuous progressive trend presented in the *Scientific American* reports, a number of social scientists expressed skepticism about the large changes in attitudes concerning principles of equal treatment. Some went so far as to challenge the truthfulness of answers given in survey interviews, suggesting that instead of revealing their genuine feelings respondents merely say what they think interviewers want to hear. Doubtless some such deception does occur, but it is implausible to assume that whites are unwilling to express reservations about various steps toward integration, especially since responses are quite sensitive to the type of issue presented and degree of integration posed. In addition, to recognize that there has been an important change in social norms that affects individual behavior in the interview situation, yet to deny that the change is at all internalized, is to assume a separation between individual attitudes and cultural norms that is hard to make sense of. If there were not important changes in racial attitudes generally, why should respondents assume interviewers to be so different in their expectations in the 1980s than in the 1940s? Norms do not exist in thin air, and in the absence of legal or other coercion they must receive some support from personal attitudes. Furthermore, if one believes that attitudes vary greatly from situation to situation, then one must recognize that whatever social pressures exist in the interview exist in many other situations as well: for this reason behavior outside the interview will often resemble behavior in the interview.

More sophisticated critiques of the emphasis on progressive trends are offered by two other approaches we examined. Both Jackman and Sears acknowledge as real the changes reported in the *Scientific American* articles but regard the changes as too superficial to have real impact on the significant racial issues of today. White Americans may have come to believe in equal treatment or in integration or in economic progress for blacks, but the beliefs are said to be fine-sounding abstractions that do not influence other attitudes or behavior. According to Jackman, unless an individual subscribes to the implementation of principles through government action, the principles themselves lack real meaning. Sears and his coauthors also seem to take commitment to concrete implementation to be the touchstone of important change at present.

In this basic sense, the Jackman and Sears critiques are much the same. They differ in assumptions and in the evidence they present. Jackman regards the importance of implementation as essentially self-evident; her main interest is in showing that an individual's educational attainment, though related to the endorsement of principles, is not related to the endorsement of implementation, and thus that more educated people have no greater commitment to tolerance than the less educated. To the extent that this is the case, she regards her data as consistent with (though not a direct demonstration of) her assumption about the difference between implementation and principle. Sears and his colleagues attempt to provide more direct evidence for their stress on implementation, primarily by showing that when whites oppose implementation it is not because of personal self-interest but because of underlying racist beliefs.

Where Sears and Jackman differ most sharply is in their larger theoretical frameworks. Jackman writes from a Marxian perspective and views whites as a dominant group that creates a set of racial attitudes (an ideology) primarily to help maintain its dominance, altering the attitudes as necessary to fend off challenges from the subordinate group (blacks). Moreover, she does not view racial attitudes as fundamentally different from attitudes on social class or gender: each area involves power and its intellectual rationalization for the benefit of members of the dominant group. Sears and his colleagues, in contrast, see "symbolic racism" as the residue from childhood of a set of internalized attitudes, presumably peculiar to our and perhaps some other cultures, and certainly more characteristic of some white people ("racists") than of other white people. Their larger concern is not with the way self-interest arises and is pursued out of the structural relations between groups; on the contrary, they attempt to show that with respect to race (and other social issues as well) people act primarily on the basis of deep-seated psychological sentiments rather than on the basis of the rational pursuit of self-interest.

We believe that both Jackman and Sears have identified important reasons not to rely exclusively on the kinds of questions that form the basis of the four *Scientific American* articles. At the same time, we think their interpretations are too completely guided by the assumption that anyone who claims to be unprejudiced at the level of principle must confirm this by subscribing fully to all forms of implementation. This dichotomous view of social life is unrealistic. It does not fit the wide variation that we find across questions about government enforcement of principles of equal treatment, and it fits even less well variations across a set of social distance questions about personal willingness to be involved in integrated situations. It is also inconsistent with the variation our data show in black attitudes toward implementation.

Lipset and Schneider's approach bears interesting relations to two of the theories already summarized. Lipset and Schneider are close to the *Scientific American* reports in emphasizing the degree to which Americans have come to believe in equal treatment of blacks and whites. However, they are mainly concerned to distinguish nondiscrimination and voluntary integration from strong affirmative action steps and enforced integration. They see this distinction as involving basic conflicts in values, primarily between "individualism" and "equalitarianism." There is a useful contrast here between Lipset and Schneider on the one hand and Sears and his coauthors on the other. Both regard individualism as an important American value, but Lipset and Schneider see it as a legitimate basis for opposing some forms of government implementation, without implying antiblack sentiments. Sears, in contrast, sees individualism as a "conservative value" that is merged with antiblack attitudes to create "symbolic racism." It is really in their own attitudes toward "individualism" that these authors differ from one another.

The final theoretical approach we discussed attempts to explain differences in trends for principle and implementation items by hypothesizing a general rejection by whites of government intervention, quite apart from racial issues. Our own and other data do not support such an explanation for differences in the slopes of trends. There is more support for the explanation when considering the difference in *levels* of support for principles and implementation, but we believe it is more useful to emphasize the reluctance to accept constraints of any kind on behavior in cases where commitment to the goals of integration is relatively weak. This is a problem that is particularly in need of further research, since the data available are not adequate for a conclusive analysis and interpretation.

The six theoretical approaches that we have discussed range from those close to a Progressive Trend view of recent race relations to those close to the Underlying Racism view. Our own interpretation, based on as wide a perspective as we could obtain from our data, is presented in the next chapter.

6   Conclusions

Seek simplicity and distrust it.
                                        —A. N. Whitehead

Since the early 1940s, white support for racial integration and related issues has risen, fallen, or remained virtually unchanged, depending upon the question analyzed. Thus it is essential to consider the specific content and sometimes even the form of the questions that provide the basis for analysis of trends.

It appears that segregation of and discrimination against black Americans were supported as *principles* by a majority of white Americans in the early 1940s, and no doubt in the preceding decades as well. By the early 1970s, however, support for overt discrimination in employment had nearly vanished, so that questions about it were no longer included in surveys after 1972, and in most other public spheres of life—public accommodations, public transportation, and even public schools—the proportion of the white population insisting on segregation in principle was both small and shrinking. In figure 6.1 we present a summary of national trend data for all but one of the survey items that we classify as dealing with general principles (see table 3.1 for question wordings).[1] Separation of the trends by region does not substantially alter the picture given in figure 6.1, except that absolute percentage levels are higher at most points in the North, lower in the South; some other specific regional differences will be noted later.

This overall picture of change points to a broad cultural shift in

193

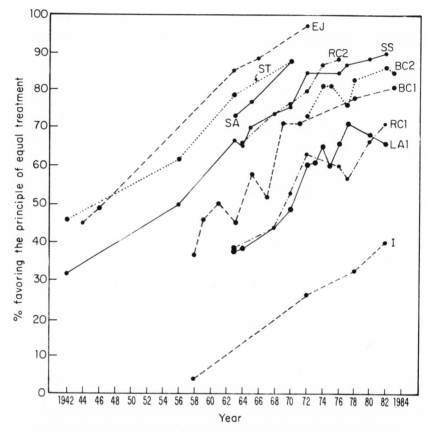

Figure 6.1. Attitudes toward principles of equal treatment: national trend lines. (For question wordings and exact percentages, see table 3.1.)

EJ = Equal Jobs	BC2 = Black Candidate (NORC)
ST = Segregated Transportation	BC1 = Black Candidate (Gallup)
SA = Same Accommodations	RC1 = Residential Choice, 1 alter-
RC2 = Residential Choice, 2 alter-	native (NORC)
natives (ISR)	LAI = Laws against Intermarriage
SS = Same Schools	I = Intermarriage

the norms that influence white attitudes toward the treatment of blacks in America. Despite irregularities in particular instances, ten questions asked about different issues and by different organizations show the same basic upward trend. Yet this shift was by no means a simple turnabout, whether that be taken to mean a sudden profound transformation in values or a sudden new superficial expression of socially desirable responses. The overall normative change affected different issues to different degrees; some persons ready to favor integration or nondiscrimination in one sphere of life were unready to show the same support in another sphere. For example, in 1972, when virtually the entire white population claimed to believe that blacks and whites should be judged equally in terms of employment, there was at least one job—that of President of the United States—for which a quarter of the white population made an exception. The Intermarriage question makes the point even more clearly: by 1983 approval of integrated marriage had reached only the same level that approval of integrated transportation had reached in the early 1940s. Thus, despite the striking increase in support across all of these issues, some still remain very much a matter of controversy in the 1980s, even at the level of abstract principle.

The importance of resistance on particular issues is further indicated by questions that seem to have leveled off, at least for a period of years, well below a theoretical ceiling. Responses to the Laws against Intermarriage question, for example, show little change over the past decade. In this case, the spread of the norm of nondiscrimination to the specific issue appears to have been halted, or at least slowed down, for a lengthy period.[2] Thus again there is evidence against the simple view that white attitudes on principles of racial equality have merely shifted from "no" to "yes" without regard for the particular issue under consideration. In fact, on a broad question about the desirability of segregation in general, there was even a partial reversal of trend in the early 1970s (see note 1). Although this reversal is probably the indirect result of the busing issue and its contextual effect on other questions, it does show that many white Americans were quite capable of expressing internally discrepant views about racial issues even at the level of general principle.

White responses to questions of principle are therefore somewhat more complex than is often portrayed, but they nevertheless do show in almost every instance a positive movement over time. A different and much more variable pattern is apparent in figure 6.2, which summarizes national trends for all questions that deal with the implementation of principles (see table 3.2 for question word-

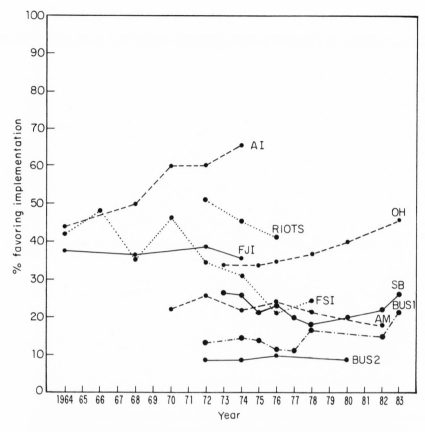

Figure 6.2. Attitudes toward the implementation of principles: national trend lines. (For question wordings and exact percentages, see table 3.2.)

AI = Accommodations Inter-
   vention
RIOTS = Riots
   FJI = Federal Job Intervention
   OH = Open Housing
   FSI = Federal School Interven-
   tion

SB = Spending on Blacks
AM = Aid to Minorities
BUS1 = Busing (NORC)
BUS2 = Busing (ISR)

ings). A question on public accommodations reveals a substantial rise in support for government intervention; a question on school integration reveals a substantial drop; and questions on job discrimination and on economic assistance to blacks show little or no change. Thus the trends in the support for implementation seem to be even more issue-dependent than support for principles as such.[3] The implementation questions do resemble one another in one way: they always reveal a much lower level of support for government intervention to promote principles than for the principles themselves. Furthermore, the level of support for intervention is almost always low in absolute terms; in only one case— government intervention to support equal treatment in hotels and restaurants—does it clearly rise above 50 percent of the white population.

The third type of question available in sufficient numbers and time points to allow broad trend analysis, the social distance questions, are summarized in figure 6.3 (see table 3.3 for question wordings).[4] These items ask white respondents whether they are personally willing to be involved in one way or another in situations with varying degrees of integration. The questions are especially useful because they sometimes hold constant the type of situation and specify varying proportions of blacks and whites. The basic finding is that very few whites indicate any resistance to the presence of one or a few blacks in a neighborhood or a school, but that resistance increases as the proportion of blacks mentioned in the question increases. However, even when the proportion specified is large (say, half), a surprisingly high percentage of whites claim to have no objection. It is important with all these questions to keep in mind the differences in verbs used to represent personal acceptance of integration: sometimes white respondents are asked if they would "have any objection to" integration; sometimes if they would move from a neighborhood in order to avoid integration; sometimes if they would actually prefer an integrated situation. The effects of these variations in wording are hard to disentangle from other differences in the questions, but some of the absolute differences in percentages are likely to be explicable in terms of degree of enthusiasm for integration, as against simple acceptance or rejection of it.

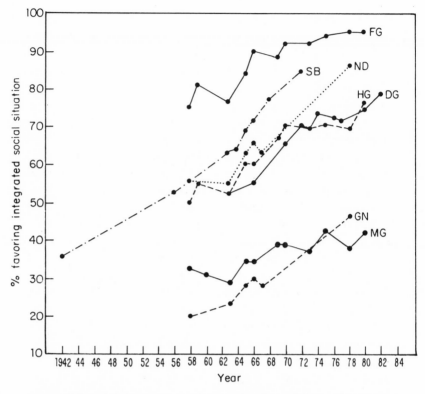

Figure 6.3. Social distance questions: national trend lines. (For question wordings and exact percentages, see table 3.3.)

FG = Few (Gallup)	HG = Half (Gallup)
SB = Same Block (NORC)	GN = Great Numbers (Gallup)
ND = Next Door (Gallup)	MG = Most (Gallup)
DG = Black Dinner Guest (NORC)	

The three types of questions summarized in figures 6.1, 6.2, and 6.3 are not the only ones on which it would be useful to have trend data. It would be valuable if questions concerning white beliefs about blacks had been regularly repeated, if questions on various definitions of affirmative action were available, and if certain other issues (such as integration of voluntary associations) had been explored over time. Unfortunately the first of these topics is limited to a single item on possible black-white differences in intelligence, which was asked only between 1942 and 1968 and then dropped despite having shown first a sharp rise much like those in figure 6.1 and then an equally clear leveling off after the mid-1950s. Affirmative action is too new an issue to have generated useful trends, and other issues have simply been omitted from major surveys, perhaps by oversight or for lack of space. Thus the trend data we have available, though fairly extensive for a single social problem, are nevertheless far from complete in topic or in time points.

Our analysis is not limited to overall national trends. We also look systematically at trends by region and by education, and less systematically we include age, relations among attitude questions themselves, and certain methodologically important variables. The results for region are the simplest to summarize: Southern whites are always less supportive of integration and nondiscrimination than non-Southern whites, but trends for the two regions usually tend to be similar, and on a number of questions the South begins to "catch up" to the North wherever the North approaches the ceiling of 100 percent support for integration.

The relation of education to racial attitudes is more complex than that of region. Educational categories generally do not differ appreciably in direction or slope of change over time. However, on most broad principle questions and on certain other questions dealing with the integration of small numbers of blacks into white settings, more-educated respondents show higher levels of support at all time points. The differences by education are smaller on most items calling for government implementation, and tend to disappear entirely on social distance items that place whites in settings in which they are no longer in the majority. Furthermore, on questions where negative trends occur (for example, the decline in support for the implementation of school desegregation), respondents with more education account for much of the drop. In such cases, the educational categories converge in their levels of response as the college educated drop toward the levels of the less educated.

More limited consideration of the effects of age on racial attitudes suggests that the process of change has itself changed over time. In the 1960s the rise in support for integration seems to have occurred as a result of both positive modifications in individual attitudes and the demographic replacement of older cohorts by younger, more liberal cohorts. The later upward movement of positive attitudes during the 1970s, however, was largely a result of demographic replacement. Furthermore, there were signs by the early 1980s that even this process might cease to foster additional positive change in the future. It appears that the civil rights movement and the events leading up to it greatly influenced the attitudes of white people in the United States, creating effects that are still being felt, but that the effects from that earlier period are diminishing and further impetus will be necessary if the momentum of change is to be sustained.

All of the above summary statements refer only to white Americans. Our data on trends for black Americans, while more limited, are nonetheless illuminating. On most available questions dealing with principles, blacks are nearly 100 percent in favor of integration, but black support for the implementation of principles is always somewhat lower than black support for the principles as such. The gap between responses for principle and implementation is only about half as wide for blacks as for whites, but that it exists for blacks at all is an important finding, since it is exactly this type of gap that has given rise to skepticism about the meaning of upward trends in white attitudes. Moreover, on several questions blacks have shown a turn away from integration that either parallels white trends or converges toward lower white levels to a surprising degree. These comparisons between blacks and whites suggest that the distinction between principles and implementation is more complex than is often assumed; it is too simple to treat support for principles as merely lip service and support for implementation as genuine commitment. We do not mean to suggest that blacks and whites view racial issues in the same way—but neither are their two vantage points as diametrically opposed as one might easily assume.

Both the similarities and the differences in white and black responses are brought out well by questions dealing with busing to bring about school integration. Both groups show less support for school busing than for any other issue mentioned, but the support is still much greater among blacks (about 50 percent) than among whites. Moreover, when black and white opponents of busing are asked to explain their answers, there is a good deal of similarity—

both groups say busing does not solve problems of educational quality and is inconvenient—but whites are much more likely than blacks to mention objecting to being coerced. If the black answers are taken at face value, then many whites resemble blacks closely in their reasons, while a fair number do not. Without trying to put exact numbers on these proportions, it appears that any theory that assumes white objections to be totally different from black objections is likely to go astray.

In addition to the substantive results of our study, we have also dealt with both methodological issues and theoretical interpretations relevant to these trend data. We note here especially the importance of context effects on responses to survey questions, and the need to be certain that unusual trends are not the result of such artifacts, as seemed to be the case for the General Segregation question (see Chapter 3).

Interpreting the Trends

No simple and sovereign theory will explain the diverse trends we have described. They represent too many different and conflicting forces to be reduced to a single concept, no matter how broad or attractive it may be.

Relations between blacks and whites in this country have been based since the beginning on a conception of two socially distinct groups, defined largely in terms of physical characteristics, though with social categorization enforced even where the physical characterization would be ambiguous—as in the occasional case of someone who seems "white" in appearance but either elects or is forced to be viewed as "black." There is no evidence that this virtually absolute differentiation of the American population has been reduced by any of the changes of the last four decades. Indeed, it may even have increased as a result of the growth in black consciousness and in the use of racial enumeration procedures as a way of monitoring progress in civil rights. America is not much more color-blind today than it ever was, and despite some small increase in the rate of racial intermarriage (Wilson 1984), a melting-pot solution to racial differences in America has not occurred, nor is it likely to in the foreseeable future.

What has changed is the normative definition of appropriate relations between blacks and whites. Whereas discrimination against,
and enforced segregation of, blacks was taken for granted by most
white Americans as recently as the 1940s, today the dominant belief is that blacks deserve the same treatment and respect as whites,
and that some degree of racial integration is a desirable thing.
Questions like the ones summarized in figure 6.1 reflect this change,
with aggregate responses in some cases having moved along almost
the entire percentage scale within a generation. Further important
issues are how far back in time these upward trends go and what
led to the initial movement of whites toward principles of equal
treatment. The available survey data, with a first measurable trend
appearing in 1946, unfortunately do not allow us to trace the movement to its sources; this must remain a challenge to be pursued in
other ways and at a later point.

Meaningful Responses

Do the changes in measured attitudes mean anything? It is difficult
to believe that they do not, for the evidence is all around us of important and pervasive changes in the public relations between
blacks and whites in the United States—though how much responses to attitude questions reflect the cause and how much the effect of such changes is much more difficult to determine. Beyond
the total elimination of a vast structure of legal segregation
throughout the South and Southwest and within the U.S. armed
forces, there is an abundance of nonsurvey evidence of genuine
change in white actions toward blacks. Black Americans today hold
a wide range of high elected and appointed political positions, and
not by any means only in areas with black majorities. Blacks also
hold positions of prominence in television and film, in major uni-
versities and colleges, and to a greater or lesser degree in many
other public spheres of life. In most of these spheres blacks are still
greatly underrepresented in proportion to their numbers in the
total population, but this does not alter the fact that the change
from the early 1940s has been substantial. Only because so much of
the population of the United States is now too young to remember
race relations circa 1940 can there be any doubt about the magnitude of the change.[5]

Do these changes in either survey responses or forms of public behavior represent true inner change by white Americans, or are the changes some kind of veneer that conceals continued profound racism on the part of most or all white Americans? This is a complicated question; in the language of sociologists, it asks whether the new norms have been internalized. One response is to insist that change in public norms is important in itself, especially as it is reflected in white actions. If a white president appoints a black lawyer to the Supreme Court, or if a substantial part of the white electorate in California votes for a black gubernatorial candidate, it is not of critical importance whether they do so because in their hearts they are genuinely nondiscriminatory, because they have temporarily put aside their racism to make that particular decision, or because they actually prefer to appoint or vote for blacks. All of us conform to norms that we may or may not have internalized deeply, but which guide our actions in ways that are of considerable consequence for our relations with others.

Another way to address the question is to admit that persons who respond to a survey question on the principle of school integration by saying "blacks and whites should go to the same schools" probably run the full gamut from those deeply committed to that idea to those who feel quite otherwise but are embarrassed to admit it to the interviewer. We have no way of knowing exactly what the distribution along this continuum is, but quite likely most people fall somewhere in the middle: they feel some genuine belief in the norm but also have other beliefs that leave them in conflict on the issue. Outright lying is probably rare in these data; there is compelling evidence that most people assume that others—in this case white interviewers—agree with their own views, and therefore feel little need for deception (Schuman and Kalton, in press). On the other hand, it is clear from other trend questions and from trends in actual behavior that many white respondents do feel conflict about school integration and similar issues, and that their responses in support of integration in principle are unlikely to be translated directly into action. It is essential to try to understand the sources of these conflicts.

Underlying Forces and Motives

Questions such as Same Schools simply ask in dichotomous fashion about "segregation" versus "integration," without allowing consideration of either the amount or the form of integration. Yet the questions we reviewed on white willingness to be personally involved in integration, as well as other survey data (Levine 1971; Farley et al. 1978; Rothbart 1976; Smith 1981), make it quite clear that whites are much more positive toward a situation with a white majority and a black minority than toward one approaching fifty-fifty or with a black majority. Given the history of white dominance in this country and the persistence of color as a significant dividing line, this is not a surprising finding; nor is it out of keeping with the way majority ethnic and racial groups behave in other countries (including black African countries). These tendencies are at least as much a matter of power and control—and of fear of being controlled by others—as they are of "prejudice" as a separate and self-contained psychological state.

One sign of this fact of life about intergroup relations in America is the ability of a black candidate to obtain far more white votes when blacks are in a clear minority (as in the Los Angeles mayoral elections of 1969 and 1973) than when blacks obtain or approach a majority (as in recent Detroit or Chicago elections). In the latter situation, whites are apt to perceive blacks as "taking over the city," whereas in the former case the black candidate is more likely to be treated as an individual. White voting in instances where blacks approach a majority tends to be determined not so much by attitudes toward the race of the candidate as by the perceived balance of power between blacks and whites as groups.

Resistance to government intervention in support of black employment, school integration, or open housing is probably at least partly due to the same perceived conflict between blacks and whites as competing groups. Government intervention to overcome discrimination or segregation against *one* or *two* black individuals would probably receive greater white support. Most questions about government intervention, including those dealing with busing, are phrased more in terms of large-scale group change, and they probably suggest a degree of integration that most whites do not wish to accept (Bobo 1983b, 1984).

Other factors are also involved in the distinction between principle and implementation. In Chapter 4 we saw that black as well as white Americans are less likely to endorse the implementation of principles than the principles themselves, although the gap is not nearly as wide for blacks as for whites. Evidently once methods of implementation are brought to the fore, objections are raised in the minds of some people, blacks as well as whites.[6] There is evidence that black objections to some forms of implementation have been increasing over the past decade or so, though the precise reasons for this are not clear from the available data. In fact, it is exactly in providing clues as to reasons that survey data are most deficient, partly because of the failure to ask open follow-up questions about reasons for choices on standard closed questions. Such explanations need not be accepted at face value, but they are clearly of use in interpreting data from forced-choice questions (Schuman 1966, 1969).

Finally, the fact that whites are much less likely to support concrete implementation of principles than principles themselves testifies to conflicts over the extent and types of possible integration. The principles have some force, but they often lose out when they conflict with other principles (such as "individualism"), with personal goals (such as the maintenance of a seniority system beneficial to one's own group), or with personal preferences (such as for living in a largely white neighborhood). This does not mean that the integrationist principles are without any efficacy, but rather that in race relations as in other areas of life, a single principle is not the only or even the major determinant of behavior.[7] For example, a respondent might believe that blacks should be able to live in whatever neighborhood they wish, but that whites should have the same right, including the right to leave a changing neighborhood in favor of a largely white neighborhood. Unfortunately, most survey questions fail to simulate real-life conflicts between one principle and another, or between principles and personal preferences, and therefore survey results are probably more limited to the abstract plane than need be (Schuman 1972).

Difficulties of Generalization

It is not easy to generalize about implementation from the available trend data, for the various implementation items behave differently. Support for open housing laws appears to be growing, though slowly and from a low level. Support for government intervention in the area of public accommodations is strong and grew rapidly. Support for moves to enforce school integration is low and dropping, and one of the more effective methods of school desegregation, busing, has virtually no support within the white population. Support for government implementation of nondiscrimination in employment seems to be static, but this issue may recently have become confounded in the public mind with various forms of affirmative action. In sum, no simple generalization is likely to explain the complexity of attitudes about the implementation of principles. The only convincing general statement is that implementation is always a good deal more problematic than are principles taken one at a time.

It is important that future surveys of racial attitudes include ways of achieving better understanding of the intra-individual conflicts, ambivalences, and compartmentalized inconsistency that are present in most whites and perhaps most blacks as well (compare Katz 1981). Simple questions that assume that people are either for *or* against integration can be very misleading, given the psychological and sociological complexities of race relations in the United States. Any attempt to use survey data to sketch broad trends must necessarily simplify the real situation somewhat, but present puzzles in the trend data would almost certainly become more understandable with additions and improvements in the available set of questions. It is also important to continue to ask many of the questions for which trend data already exist, in order to follow future change. Responses to attitude questions are not merely data for possible grand generalization; they are an important source for historical understanding of the past and its development into the ever-emerging present.

Some Practical Implications

The strong and still growing commitment to equalitarian principles among whites, combined with the serious inconsistencies on issues of application, indicates the importance of strategic choices and actions by leaders who favor implementation of such principles. During the 1950s some of those who resisted the implementation of specific forms of integration by the federal government claimed that it was necessary to change people's hearts before trying to change their behavior. A number of social scientists argued, however, that attitudes often change more quickly as a *consequence* of behavioral change, and in fact the attitudinal shifts in the South that we and others have reported seem to bear this out. But it is too extreme to go on to claim that attitudes can be treated as epiphenomena and that determined leadership (as in the desegregation of the military) is all that is needed to bring about behavioral change, with attitudes likely to follow thereafter. This point of view tacitly assumes situations in which leaders have their authority protected from serious challenge. Where an electorate can exercise ultimate control over its leaders, attitudes do count. For example, in 1979 the Los Angeles school board president was recalled, and ultimately a statewide antibusing amendment was passed in a referendum, both primarily as a result of an attempt by the Los Angeles school board to use busing to achieve court-ordered desegregation. More generally, it seems likely that antibusing attitudes are so strong that substantial two-way busing to achieve desegregation cannot proceed at this time without serious challenge in most communities. Public attitudes are certainly malleable, and unless crystallized in a politically relevant way they are often ineffective; yet once aroused and pervasive, they must be viewed seriously. This is not to say that they are merely to be accepted, but it does mean that leaders who seek positive racial change will need to combine clear emphasis on principled ends with carefully chosen means that can win majority support when challenged. When means that are not likely to win substantial support become necessary, efforts at implementation must be accompanied by equal efforts at persuasion.

Epilogue: History and Social Psychology

At various points we have mentioned an "attitudinal record," the recorded answers over time of national samples of Americans to more than thirty questions. For the survey analyst, this attitudinal record takes the place of the historian's trail of documents as a source for understanding some period of history or some major event. The data and interpretations we have discussed are efforts to understand from one vantage point the complex and changing meaning of race in America.

When President Truman's Committee on Civil Rights reported

in 1947, Jim Crow laws were still alive and constituted in many places an unchallenged set of social rules. Black Americans were second-class citizens, often impoverished, poorly educated, and widely disdained by the white majority. The prosperity and social dislocation brought about by World War II, the importance of black manpower to the war effort, the growing influence of black urban voters within the Democratic coalition, and the heightened impatience of black leaders (driven in part by their increasingly urban, educated, and politicized constituencies) were some of the factors that placed a challenge to Jim Crow high on the national agenda.

Many of those who tried to understand America's glaring racial discrimination in the postwar era emphasized prejudice as the core of the problem. Prejudice, in turn, was regarded primarily as the product of ignorance. From this viewpoint, prejudice could be attacked by teaching tolerance and by facilitating contact between the races not structured by Jim Crow. The emotional roots of white contempt for blacks depended upon the regular symbolic humbling of blacks—through petty exclusions, separate and starkly unequal facilities, a demand for "traditional" deference, and an occasional lynching. If the government could intervene in these practices, both the symbolic and the concrete social relations required by Jim Crow would be weakened. Contact on new terms would gradually reduce the level of prejudice and set us on the path toward becoming a color-blind society.

In many ways, this analysis of the American racial dilemma bore fruit in the 1940s and 1950s. The slow, steady decline of prejudice is consistent with, for example, the strong educational differentials in response to racial principle items, the liberalizing impact (at least up until the 1980s) of the cohort-replacement process, the positive changes in the attitudes of individuals, and the striking though incomplete upward movement in whites' assessment of the intelligence of blacks.

These shifts in public opinion seemed to support Myrdal's belief that, at core, Americans maintained a value for equality (surely equality before the law), a value that had already brought Jim Crow into question before World War II. This value would break through more plainly as soon as the intellectual and emotional underpinnings of prejudice began to dissipate. In general, this seemed a period of progress. Government played its role through court decisions (like the *Brown* ruling) and executive actions (like Truman's order to desegregate the armed forces). Prejudice seemed an enemy that could be overcome. Categorical inequalities overtly premised upon notions of innate inferiority fell as the government intervened, backed by public opinion that not only increasingly rejected such views but was moving toward endorsement of the principle of racial equalitarianism. This process was fueled by insistent and often integrated civil rights demonstrations, which not only focused national attention upon black grievances but served an educational purpose and pressed the government to act more urgently in racial matters.

There was a growing consensus to all of this, and in the Johnson years the government began to move beyond the paradigm of reducing prejudice through integration—though this goal had by no means been achieved—to the often implicit paradigm of increasing the economic and political standing of blacks; that is, to treating the race problem as more a matter of social inequality than of prejudice. The landmark legislation of these years, to be sure, came in answer to a demand that would not be silenced. The demand was delivered most prominently with the consensus-seeking moral force of Martin Luther King, Jr.

But during these same years, the civil rights movement was becoming not only more visible but more variegated. In many of its important branches, it was no longer integrated. The thrust of the demand for change was decreasingly toward integration and increasingly toward redistribution. The sudden rise and then decline of the riots and the Black Power Movement; the assassination of Martin Luther King, which silenced the most widely listened to voice for nonviolent racial change; and Richard Nixon's victory over Hubert Humphrey, the national political figure then most closely associated with civil rights legislation, were both symbols and partial causes of a halt, or at least a pause, in government action in favor of racial equality.

The struggle against formal racial exclusion and the attitudes supporting it had been nearly completed. But the shift to a concern with larger, more complex, and more deeply entrenched forms of racial inequality and the attitudes supporting them did not meet with immediate success. The drive for racial equality began to involve spheres of life and types of change that were less likely to be accepted by the white majority.

The issues changed from removing an absolute color bar to eliminating the pervasive inequalities that the bar had created. There were no longer struggles over allowing *one* or *two* black students to enroll at a public university; instead, there were struggles over city-wide desegregation plans. Our data indicate that survey researchers were attentive, though not always consciously, to these changing issues and social contexts. More questions on the implementation of racial principles were asked around 1964, and more were added again in the early 1970s. The results show that enthusiasm for large-scale policy change was lacking. Whether the issue was open housing laws, school busing, or federal efforts to end job discrimination, support for the abstract ideals of fairness or integration moved well ahead of relevant forms of implementation.

The changes of the past four decades are many, complex, and seldom of completely transparent meaning for students of racial attitudes. Nonetheless, our examination of the attitudinal record—this venture in historical social psychology—points to some important considerations for those grappling with the gap between principles and implementation; with the paradoxical decline of "prejudice" and tendency to resist potentially more profound racial change. One is that the social foundations of change in attitudes are sometimes established in unintended ways. It was by no means obvious at the time that the mechanization of Southern agriculture and the lure of Northern war-industry jobs would create a black voting bloc. Nor was it clear that these black ballots would, over the years, serve to make civil rights a salient issue. The current period of relative stasis in racial matters has perhaps equally obscure implications. The low levels of support for many of our implementation items suggest that change in these attitudes may come quite slowly, especially given the homogenization of cohorts. On the other hand, though we have no direct data, the period from 1900 through the 1930s probably saw little movement in American racial attitudes—yet that period of stasis was followed, as we have shown, by one of dramatic positive change.

Perhaps a more important point is that racial change has always involved some element of conflict and resistance. This is clearly evident in political behavior and is surely suggested by our finding of a gap between attitudes toward principles and those toward implementation. Actual historical experience does not provide a record of linear progress and achievement, nor does our examination of the attitudinal record. Both these sources point to a process of defining and redefining issues as activists and established leaders clash and shape public opinion and public institutions. The changes may in fact be of an abrupt and surprising nature. Those years involving the most open dispute and conflict seem also to have resulted, at least for questions of principle, in the most positive change in attitudes.

A third point is that the problem of race has always been complex. For that reason we set out to study a broad pool of questions that would address various issues in different ways. The task we undertook once this pool of questions had been established was twofold: (1) to present the results in a manner that, so far as possible, allowed respondents to "speak their own minds"; and (2) to draw theoretical meaning from these responses insofar as the data allowed. We suggest that the gap between principles and implementation is a real substantive issue, both for individuals and for social researchers. Among the factors contributing to this gap are the sometimes conflicting interests of blacks and whites, which result from their enduring social identities and the enduring social inequalities between them; the difficult task of implementing any large-scale social change; and the ambivalent nature of both American values and American racial attitudes.

Considering all of the information we have reviewed, we cannot simply conclude that racial attitudes are characterized by a sweeping progressive movement. Nor can we draw the equally simple conclusion that racism is here to stay and remains fundamentally unchanged. The progress on principles of racial integration and equality have too many contemporary social manifestations to be disregarded or downplayed. Simultaneously, the weaker or nonexistent progress on issues of implementation is also important. Perhaps the main moral of this investigation is that simple generalities based in conceptions of either complete positive transformation or

complete stagnation are too extreme. What has occurred is a mix-
ture of progress and resistance, certainty and ambivalence, striking
movement and mere surface change. The balance among these lies
in the future, with political leadership one of the important elements that will determine the shape of that future.

Appendixes

Notes

Index

APPENDIX A

Locating and Selecting
Trend Questions

When we began our study of racial attitudes, we were faced with the task of identifying both relevant questions and the precise number of times each had been asked. Fortunately, a number of excellent compendiums of survey questions had already been published. Among the more general of these were Hadley Cantril's *Public Opinion, 1935–1946* (1951); Hastings and Southwick's *Survey Data for Trend Analysis* (1975), written as a guide to the Roper Center archives; and Hazel Erskine's various articles in the *Public Opinion Quarterly* during the 1960s. Collections specific to a single survey organization proved very helpful as well. We consulted the *Cumulative Codebooks* for the NORC General Social Surveys; *A Continuity Guide to the American National Election Surveys* (1980), compiled at ISR by the Center for Political Studies and the Interuniversity Consortium for Political and Social Research; George Gallup's *The Gallup Poll* (1972) and the monthly *Gallup Opinion Index*; Miller, Miller, and Schneider's *American Election Studies Data Sourcebook* (1980); Converse, Dotson, Hoag, and McGee's *American Social Attitudes Data Sourcebook* (1980); and Martin, McDuffee, and Presser's *Sourcebook of Harris National Surveys* (1981).

We did not rely solely on these references. A considerable amount of time was spent reviewing actual questionnaires from ISR and NORC surveys, the two organizations whose interview schedules were accessible to us, and searching the scholarly literature for items or replications that might have otherwise escaped our notice. In addition, the Roper Center documented which racial-attitude questions had been archived by Gallup since the publication of its 1975 guide, and the Harris Archive Retrieval System of the University of North Carolina used keywords to generate for us a list of race-related questions.

After compiling information from these sources, we possessed a list of approximately 120 items, questions that had been asked of cross-sectional samples of white American adults more than once and variants of those questions. We began the process of selecting items for analysis by considering the most obvious variants as simple replications. This substantially consolidated the original list. For example, the Gallup Black Candidate item was initially represented by four slightly different questions, each asked in a different year. The wording varied only in the introductory sentences (see note to table 3.1). Since it did not appear likely that these changes systematically influenced answers to the main question, we combined all the items into a single time series. (All important variants of our chosen questions are noted in tables 3.1 through 3.4.) The NORC question about voting for a qualified black presidential candidate can be regarded to some extent as another version of the Gallup question, but we present data for each version separately in table 3.1.

The decision to restrict our use of data from the Harris organization, for reasons noted in our text, further reduced the list of questions. From those remaining, we selected all items that had been asked at least twice over a period of ten or more years and that gauged individual racial attitudes along a positive-negative dimension. These criteria eliminated questions asked over too brief a time span and questions that dealt with more objective factors, such as the actual racial composition of schools, neighborhoods, and friends. The latter decision was made reluctantly, but it was necessary to keep the magnitude of our analysis within practical limits.

Several questions of possible interest were eliminated because they had not been replicated over a long enough period. Since these items were repeated in quick succession, their content seems particularly confounded witn time period. In addition, some of them address concerns that no longer have much current meaning: for example, a Gallup item assessing public approval of the U.S. Supreme Court's ruling against segregated schools, asked for the last time in 1961. However, we have included four questions with slightly shorter time spans than our limit (Riots, the two Neighborhood Preference items, the ISR Busing item, and Same Accommodations), because each provides a useful perspective on important aspects of current white racial attitudes.

APPENDIX B

Statistical Testing Procedures

In this appendix we describe our main procedures of data analysis and provide examples of detailed test results for logit-linear models for several questions discussed in the text. After conducting a comparison of ordinary least squares regression (OLS), log-linear models, the Davis-Taylor survey metric approach (Davis 1975; Taylor 1980), and logit-linear models (or logistic regression), we decided to employ the last mentioned as our main data-analytic tool. In practice, we found the four techniques to yield largely similar results in terms of the significance of trends and the presence (or absence) of ceiling effects or other curvilinear trends (for a more complete summary of these comparisons, see Bobo 1983a).

We begin by discussing logits and logistic regression using an example with some of our own data. Then we report results of trend analysis for three of our main questions for whites and three for blacks. These examples represent selected cases of no change, linear change, and more complex nonlinear patterns of change.

Logit-Linear Models

Logit-linear models are useful for studying cross-classifications of proportions where there is an interest in explaining variation in a dichotomous dependent variable with one or more predictor variables included in the cross-classifications. Specifically, a logit is a log transformation (usually natural log) of the ratio of positive to negative (or negative to positive) cell frequencies of the dependent variable within conditions or levels of the explanatory variable(s). For example, the Same Schools question (table 3.1) is a dichotomous dependent variable where we treat survey year as one key "predictor" or explanatory variable. Table B.1 shows the responses to the Same Schools item by year for a subset of the available time

217

Table B.1 Same Schools by year.

Response	$j = 1$ 1942	$j = 2$ 1956	$j = 3$ 1963	$j = 4$ 1972	$j = 5$ 1982
Same, $i = 1$	.3158 (1091)	.4991 (1644)	.6522 (1579)	.8409 (2029)	.9015 (1117)
Separate, $i = 2$	.6842 (2364)	.5009 (1650)	.3478 (842)	.1591 (384)	.0985 (122)
Logits	−.773	−.004	.629	1.665	2.214
Variance	.0013	.0012	.0018	.0031	.0090

Same Schools: "Do you think white students and black students should go to the same schools or to separate schools?"   1. Same   2. Separate

Note: Table shows a subset of the time points available. N's appear in parentheses.

points. A logit for each year can be obtained by calculating the ratio of "same" to "separate" responses and then taking the natural log of that quantity. The logits for these data are shown in the third row of the table.

Figures can be derived using either proportions or cell frequencies. Thus, for 1942 we can arrive at the logit (−.773) with proportions,

$$L_1 = \ln(.3158/.6842) = \ln(.4616) = -.773$$

or with the cell frequencies,

$$L_1 = \ln(1091/2364) = \ln(.4615) = -.773;$$

or, more generally, in the case of proportions,

$$L_j = \ln(p_{1j}/1 - p_{2j})$$

and cell frequencies,

$$L_j = \ln(f_{1j}/f_{2j}),$$

where L designates the logit and j indexes categories of the explanatory variable.

Although the logarithmic metric is not as widely familiar as proportions or percentages, logits can paint an accessible portrait of the data. For instance, if the proportions of respondents saying "same" schools and "separate" schools were each .5, the log of the odds of saying "same" as opposed to "separate" schools would be zero. As the proportion saying "same" increased, the log of the odds, the logit, would become a larger positive number. Conversely, as the proportion giving the "same" response dropped below .5, the logit would become an increasingly large negative number. That is, as a proportion approaches 1.0 the logit goes to $+\infty$, and as the proportion approaches 0.0 the logit goes to $-\infty$. As is evident in table B.1, the proportion giving the "same" schools response was fairly low in 1942, approximately .32, but increased steadily to .90 in 1982. Correspondingly, the log odds of saying "same," the logits, increase from $-.773$ to 2.214.[1] Since we always treat the frequency saying "same" as the numerator in calculating the logits in table B.1, we speak of modeling the log odds of saying "same," or more formally, modeling the log of the odds of saying "same" as opposed to "separate."

Logits have several desirable properties when the aim is to model a rate or proportion. First, with logits as the dependent quantity it is possible to avoid the problems of heteroskedasticity that arise in OLS regression when modeling a binary dependent variable (Hanushek and Jackson 1977). Second, because the logits are bounded by $+\infty$ and $-\infty$, predicted values under different models cannot lie outside the range of possible values. One undesirable property of using actual proportions as a dependent quantity is that predicted values below 0.0 and above 1.0 may result. Third, because the logit can be used as the dependent variable in a regression framework, we may exploit more fully the year variable in our cross-classifications. Although years are treated as discrete ordered categories when presented in tabled form, with logits as the dependent quantity in a logistic regression, year can also be treated as a continuous predictor variable.

We use the Generalized Linear Iterative Modeling (GLIM) program (see Baker and Nelder 1978). GLIM performs a maximum-likelihood iterative weighted least squares analysis in order to estimate coefficients of the logit-linear model. The data are weighted because cell proportions based on different numbers of cases do not have equal variances, since proportions based on larger numbers of cases are more efficient estimators of population values (that is, have smaller variances). This is especially relevant in our analysis where survey sample sizes vary from year to year.

When examining national trends, we performed a forward selection procedure comparing three increasingly complex models. The first of these, and the simplest, is a "null" model, which fits only a grand mean or average logit term to the data:

$$L_i = B_0. \tag{B.1}$$

This model can be compared to a simple linear model where a continuous year variable is added:

$$L_i = B_0 + B_1 X_1, \tag{B.2}$$

where X_1 is year (actual year of survey minus 1900). Finally, in order to test for the presence of ceiling effects or other curvilinear trends, we estimate a third model, which adds a year-squared variable:

$$L_i = B_0 + B_1 X_1 + B_2 X_1^2. \tag{B.3}$$

The three models described in (B.1), (B.2), and (B.3), for ease of presentation, are labeled the *no change, linear trend,* and *curvilinear trend* models, respectively. All models are estimated in nested steps. A variable or term added at step 2 is included, therefore, at any subsequent steps. Thus, the linear trend model always includes an intercept (constant) term, and the curvilinear trend model always includes the intercept and linear component terms.

Table B.2 contains the analysis of the data shown in table B.1. In

Table B.2 Logit analysis of Same Schools modeling log-odds of saying "same."

National trend (subset of time points) for whites (1942–1982)

Model	chi-square	d.f.	prob-value
1. No change model	2514.00	4	p < .001
2. Linear trend model (year)	65.40	3	p < .001
3. Curvilinear trend model (year^2)	30.04	2	p < .001
Linear improvement over no change (1–2)	2448.60	1	p < .001
Curvilinear improvement over linear (2–3)	35.36	1	p < .001

Final model: significant curvilinear trend
Coefficients: $-1.441 + -.020(\text{year} - 1900) + .001(\text{year} - 1900)^2$
Standard errors: (.4667)   (.0166)   (.0001)

Summary: There is a substantial linear trend and a curvilinear component. The final model describes a trend of linear improvement with a period of more rapid change in later years.

order to assess the adequacy of different models, chi-square indicators of goodness of fit are compared. Chi-square tests are reported
for each model and also for differences (labeled "improvement")
between less and more complex models. For example, the second
chi-square reported is that for the linear trend model ($\chi^2 = 65.40$,
d.f. = 3, p < .001). The difference between the fit of the no change
and linear trend models ($\chi^2 = 2448.60$, d.f. = 1, p < .001) is reported in the fourth row. In the same way the improvement of the
linear trend over the no change model can be ascertained, so the
contribution of specifying a curvilinear trend over the linear trend
model can be assessed. The curvilinear trend is a significant improvement over the linear trend model, ($\chi^2 = 35.36$, d.f. = 1,
p < .001), although it is evident that most of the difference between the no change and curvilinear trend models is accounted for
by the linear trend.

Using the coefficients shown in table B.2, we can calculate the
predicted logits from the following equation:

$$\hat{L}_j = -1.441 + -.020(\text{year}-1900) + .001(\text{year}-1900)^2.$$

The figures are as follows:

$$\hat{L}_1 = -1.441 + -.020\ (42) + .001\ (1764) = -.517$$
$$\hat{L}_2 = -1.441 + -.020\ (56) + .001\ (3136) = .575$$
$$\hat{L}_3 = -1.441 + -.020\ (63) + .001\ (3969) = 1.268$$
$$\hat{L}_4 = -1.441 + -.020\ (72) + .001\ (5184) = 2.303$$
$$\hat{L}_5 = -1.441 + -.020\ (82) + .001\ (6724) = 3.643$$

Thus, the model fits a clear linear trend, but with a more rapid pace
of change in later years (hence, the curvilinear component).

The results of the analysis of the data from table B.1 are displayed graphically in figure B.1. This figure presents the trend line
as predicted under the logit model selected (the dashed line), as
well as the actual percentages (the solid line), and the actual logits
(the dotted line). The predicted logits are not an exact fit to the
data, as the chi-square for the curvilinear model indicates
($\chi^2 = 30.04$, d.f. = 2, p < .001). But, this model is a statistically significant improvement over less complex models, and as the graph
suggests, the model is a reasonable approximation of the actual
trend.

Two further points should be noted. First, in tests reported in

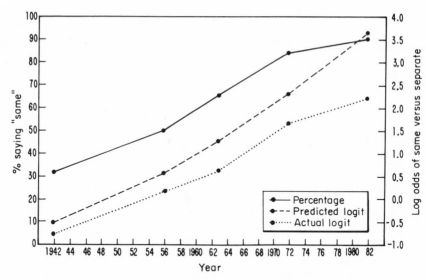

Figure B.1. Comparison of percentages and actual and predicted logits.

notes to the chapters of our text, we sometimes employ dummy variables. These dummy variables are no different from those used in standard OLS regression, save for the fact that the dependent quantity is the logit. Dummy variables in this instance allow for differences in average logits between whites and blacks, between principle and implementation questions, and so on. Second, where we are interested in differences in slopes over time, we add interaction terms. For example, a race dummy variable is multiplied by year in order to test for differences in trends between blacks and whites on a particular question. Such tests for interaction are also performed when comparing trends for principle and implementation items.

For those wishing to read more about logistic regression, two accessible discussions are available (see Little 1978; and Swafford 1980). More technical discussions are provided by Haberman 1978, Hanushek and Jackson 1977, and Fienberg 1978.

Trend Test Examples for Whites

Three further applications of our test procedure, using data for white respondents, are provided here. These examples, which are based on the full time-series data, illustrate different types of trend results and highlight several important considerations. The first, shown in table B.3, is an example of a significant linear trend using data for the Same Accommodations item (see table 3.1 for wording). The results indicate that the linear trend model (as in equation B.2) is a clear improvement over the no change model (improvement $X^2 = 84.61$, d.f. = 1, p < .001). Also, no curvilinear component is necessary to provide a good fit to the Same Accommodations trend. This example is especially instructive because it involves one of the shortest time spans (only seven years), uses data from only three surveys, and involves a modest amount of change (+10 percent). As these results suggest, given the large sample size, a change of 10 percent or more (actually between 6 and 10 percent at the national level for whites) will usually yield highly significant test results (p < .001).

An example of no significant change, using the Federal Job Intervention item, is provided in table B.4 (see table 3.2 for wording). Despite the large number of cases involved (n = 5668) and a full

Table B.3 Logit analysis of Same Accommodations modeling log-odds of saying "yes."

National trend for whites (1963–1970)			
Model	chi-square	d.f.	prob-value
1. No change	85.15	2	p < .001
2. Linear trend model (year)	.54	1	.50 < p < .70
3. Curvilinear trend model (year^2)	0	0	1.0
Linear improvement over no change (1–2)	84.61	1	p < .001
Curvilinear improvement over linear (2–3)	.54	1	.50 < p < .70

Final model: significant linear trend
Coefficients: −7.73 + .14(year − 1900)
Standard errors: (1.02)   (.02)
n = 3576
Summary: There is a highly significant and positive increase in white support for the principle of equal accommodations.

Table B.4 Logit analysis of Federal Job Intervention modeling log-odds of saying "government should see to it."

National trend for whites (1964–1974)			
Model	chi-square	d.f.	prob-value
1. No change	4.36	3	.20 < p < .30
2. Linear trend (year)	4.30	2	.10 < p < .20
3. Curvilinear trend (year^2)	3.96	1	
Linear improvement over no change (1–2)	.06	1	.80 < p < .90
Curvilinear improvement over linear (2–3)	.40	1	.50 < p < .70

Final model: no change
Coefficient: −.50
Standard error: (.03)
n = 5668
Summary: White support for federal efforts against job discrimination is below 50 percent and does not change over time.

ten-year time span, there is no significant change in the level of white support for federal intervention to prevent job discrimination, hence the model in equation B.1 fits the data best. The linear trend model is not an improvement over the no change model (improvement X^2 = .06, d.f. = 1, n.s.). Nor is the curvilinear model an improvement over the linear model (improvement X^2 = .40,

Table B.5 Logit analysis of Laws against Intermarriage modeling log-odds of saying "no."

National trend for whites (1963–1982)			
Model	chi-square	d.f.	prob-value
1. No change	775.90	11	p < .001
2. Linear trend (year)	93.26	10	p < .001
3. Curvilinear trend (year^2)	58.37	9	p < .001
Linear improvement over no change (1–2)	682.64	1	p < .001
Curvilinear improvement over linear (2–3)	34.89	1	p < .001

Final model: significant curvilinear component
Coefficients: −20.80 + .510 (year − 1900) + −.003 (year − 1900)^2
Standard errors: (2.625) (.073)   (.000)
Summary: Although there is considerable positive increase in opposition to laws forbidding racial intermarriage, this rise in opposition levels off in recent years.

d.f. = 1, n.s.). A large case base does not invariably produce statistically significant results.

An example of a more complex, curvilinear trend is presented in table B.5, which uses the Laws against Intermarriage item (see table 3.1 for wording). The model of curvilinear change (as in equation B.3) is a significant improvement over the simple linear trend (improvement $\chi^2 = 34.89$, d.f. = 1, p < .001). The negative sign of the slope coefficient for the year-squared variable indicates that, as depicted earlier in figure 3.2, the trend on this item flattens out in more recent years.

Trend Test Examples for Blacks

We provide separate examples for blacks because the case base for blacks is always considerably lower than that for whites. In order to establish a significant trend, well over a 10 percent change is required. Table B.6, using the Civil Rights Push item (see table 3.4 for wording), presents an example of significant linear change using our data for blacks. The linear model is a significant improvement over the no change model (improvement $\chi^2 = 22.39$, d.f. = 1, p < .001). The Civil Rights Push item is an example of the lower

Table B.6 Logit analysis of Civil Rights Push modeling log-odds of saying "too slow."

Model	chi-square	d.f.	prob-value
National trend for blacks (1964–1980)			
1. No change	30.42	7	p < .001
2. Linear trend (year)	8.03	6	.20 < p < .30
3. Curvilinear trend (year^2)	7.92	5	.10 < p < .20
Linear improvement over no change (1–2)	22.39	1	p < .001
Curvilinear improvement over linear (2–3)	.11	1	.70 < p < .80

Final model: significant linear trend
Coefficients: −4.145 + .048 (year − 1900)
Standard errors: (.728) (.010)
n = 1857

Summary: There is a significant and positive increase in tendency of blacks to believe civil rights leaders are moving "too slowly."

Table B.7 Logit analysis of Residential Choice (ISR) modeling log-odds of saying "afford."

National trend for blacks (1964–1976)			
Model	chi-square	d.f.	prob-value
1. No change	2.74	5	.70 < p < .80
2. Linear trend (year)	2.07	4	.70 < p < .80
3. Curvilinear trend (year^2)	2.06	3	.50 < p < .70
Linear improvement over no change (1–2)	.67	1	.30 < p < .50
Curvilinear improvement over linear (2–3)	.01	1	.95 < p < .90

Final model: no change
Coefficients: 4.333
Standard errors: (.231)
n = 1467
Summary: Black support for the principle of free residential choice has always been high and does not change over a 12-year period.

limit of statistically discernible change among blacks; a change of between roughly 15 and 18 percent is necessary to yield highly significant results (p < .001).

Table B.7, using the ISR Residential Choice item, presents an example of no change among blacks. Despite covering a 12-year

Table B.8 Logit analysis of Federal School Intervention modeling log-odds of saying "government see to it."

National trend for blacks (1964–1978)			
Model	chi-square	d.f.	prob-value
1. No change	78.99	7	p < .001
2. *Linear trend (year)*	33.82	6	p < .001
3. Curvilinear trend (year^2)	7.63	5	.10 < p < .20
Linear improvement over no change (1–2)	45.17	1	p < .001
Curvilinear improvement over linear (2–3)	26.19	1	p < .001

Final model: significant curvilinear component
Coefficients: $-69.350 + 2.084 \text{ (year} - 1900) + -.015 \text{ (year} - 1900)^2$
Standard errors: (14.980)   (.424)   (.003)
n = 1756
Summary: After an initial small increase, black support for federal school integration efforts drops sharply.

period and involving 6 surveys and more than 1400 cases, this item shows no statistically significant change in the high level of black support for the principle of free residential choice.

An example of a significant curvilinear trend among blacks is provided in table B.8, using the Federal School Intervention item. In this case, the curvilinear trend model is a significant improvement over the linear trend model (improvement $X^2 = 26.19$, d.f. $= 1$, p $< .001$). After a slight increase in support, black endorsement of federal school integration efforts dropped sharply.

Notes

1. Perspectives and Historical Background

1. Despite their bleak and deeply pessimistic predictions, Jefferson and Tocqueville were convinced that slavery was a moral wrong fundamentally at odds with democratic principles. Both of these beliefs—that a peaceful society where blacks and whites were equals was unattainable and that black slavery was a doomed antidemocratic institution—make Jefferson and Tocqueville exemplars of moderate elite opinion in their times.

2. There were those at the time who objected to the *Plessy* ruling, including Justice John M. Harlan, who said in a strong dissenting opinion: "The arbitrary separation of citizens, on the basis of race, while they are on a public highway, is a badge of servitude wholly inconsistent with the civil freedom and the equality before the law established by the Constitution. It cannot be justified upon any legal grounds. If evils will result from the commingling of the two races upon public highways established for the benefit of all, they will be infinitely less than those that will surely come from state legislation regulating the enjoyment of civil rights upon the basis of race. We boast of the freedom enjoyed by our people above all other peoples. But it is difficult to reconcile that boast with a state of law which, practically, puts the brand of servitude and degradation upon a large class of our fellow-citizens, our equals before the law. The thin disguise of 'equal' accommodations for passengers in railroad coaches will not mislead anyone, nor atone for the wrong this day done" (p. 561).

3. Some authors contend that the use, or potential use, of blacks as strikebreakers and the general apprehension of whites regarding black competition for jobs were the main sources of racial animosity between black and white workers. See, for example, Bonacich (1972, 1976) and William J. Wilson (1980).

4. Meier and Rudwick say at a later point: "black workers who joined the CIO unions did indeed benefit substantially. Not only were their wages and working conditions improved along with those of all union members, but racial differentials in wages paid for identical work, prevalent in the South, were wiped out, and black union officers, previously a rarity, became fairly common" (1976:329).

228

5. This figure is an average of segregation index scores for 107 cities reported in Taeuber and Taeuber (1965:35–36).

6. The case was *Guinn v. United States;* the suit was actually brought by the Department of Justice. The NAACP submitted an amicus curiae brief. See Lawson (1976:17–18).

7. The letter appeared in many prominent publications at the time and eventually became a major chapter in King's book *Why We Can't Wait* (1963).

8. The actual extent of intimidation and violence used against blacks generally, and civil rights activists more specifically, is not easily documented. Most of the incidents we note here drew considerable national attention, in no small part because the violence was directed at whites as well as blacks. But, as others have noted, these notorious cases involving whites "cannot convey the magnitude and the impact of repression during this era when many blacks were beaten, bombed, fired from jobs, or shot" (Morris 1984:30).

9. The nature of acceptable affirmative action programs is still being decided by the courts. The case of *United Steelworkers of America v. Weber* (99 S. CT. 2721 [1979]) established that preferential hiring programs were acceptable under Title VII of the Civil Rights Act of 1964. Claims that the act forbids any consideration of race in hiring practices were repudiated. Such an interpretation, the Court held, was tantamount to construing the act to prohibit voluntary efforts to make up for past and lingering discrimination. In *Fullilove v. Klutznick* the Court held that Congress had the authority to make "race-conscious" decisions. The case concerned a provision of the Public Works Employment Act of 1977 stipulating that 10 percent of all public works contracts must go to minority businesses. The Court upheld this provision. More recently, the Court ruled that affirmative action goals could *not* take precedence over seniority in making layoff decisions. The court held that "bona-fide" seniority programs had a protected status under the 1964 act. In the most celebrated affirmative action case, *Regents of the University of California v. Bakke* (438 U.S. 265 [1978]), the Court ruled that the racial quota at the Medical School of the University of California at Davis, which set aside 16 of 100 slots for minority or disadvantaged students, was unconstitutional. The Court did not, however, reject all preferential treatment for minorities; it rejected only state-imposed rigid quotas that had the effect of discrimination against whites. Although the precise legal mandate of affirmative action is still being defined, such efforts are credited with improving blacks' educational opportunities, occupations, and incomes (Burstein 1979a). Some point out, however, that much of the economic progress may have been confined to the South (McCrone and Hardy 1978).

2. Studying Changes in Racial Attitudes

1. If the relation between individual attitudes and individual actions is always problematic, so much more so is the relation between the individual level and what sociologists call "collective behavior." It is not often, for example, that mass uprisings—the urban riots in American cities in the 1960s, or the Solidarity movement in Poland in 1980—are predicted in advance on the basis of individual-level data. But in these instances there may be as much or more discrepancy between the preceding ordinary individual *behavior* and the collective outbursts as between the latter and individual attitudes.

2. As part of the preparatory work for Gunnar Myrdal's *American Dilemma*, several questions were included in a survey conducted for *Fortune* magazine by Roper in September 1939. These questions are quite similar in content, though not in precise wording, to some of our items. The questions and the distributions of responses across regions are reported in Horowitz (1944).

3. This includes not only the 273 points represented by table 2.1 but also various replications at the same time points, plus several other racial items not conceptualized along a positive/negative dimension.

4. Gallup and NORC code race as white, black, or other except during the mid to late 1960s when NORC used the categories white, black, Oriental, and other. From internal analysis it appears that almost all Hispanics included in the interview samples were classified as white. The ISR election studies, in contrast, shifted in 1966 from the simple trichotomy to a more complex coding scheme that specified Mexican (later Mexican-American and Chicano), Puerto Rican, American Indian, and Oriental, as well as white and black; at the end of the 1970s another category, other Hispanic, was added. In an attempt to be consistent across all surveys at all time points for all organizations, we chose to include as whites or blacks only those respondents explicitly designated as such. In sum, we systematically excluded from our analysis Orientals and American Indians who were so identified. A tiny number of Hispanics (no more than 3 or 4 persons classified as "other" for a given year) were probably excluded from the analysis for Gallup and NORC; somewhat larger numbers were excluded for ISR, ranging from a low of 10 in 1966 to a high of 73 in 1978. In retrospect, it appears that exclusion of Hispanics was probably undesirable. In order to make certain that the exclusion had not affected our basic results, we reran several analyses with ISR 1978 and 1982 data, including as white all persons labeled Mexican-American, Chicano, Puerto Rican, or Hispanic. No trend point changed by as much as one percent.

It should be noted that the shifting classifications employed by the survey organizations reflect the fact that the recognition of Hispanic groups as having a distinct ethnicity has been evolving over the past several decades, and it would be very difficult at this point to determine exactly what was done by interviewers twenty years ago. It should also be noted that all three of the survey organizations regularly exclude from their final interview samples those people who do not speak English well enough to respond to the questionnaire.

5. "Sampling error" refers to the variation in survey results that occurs when different samples are drawn by the same random method from a particular population. The variation of one sample's result from another's—or from the result that would be obtained if the entire population were enumerated—is due to chance and is termed sampling error. When random selection procedures are used, the amount of sampling error can be estimated from the survey data themselves. (Other forms of error related to the survey process can also occur, such as the inability to locate a respondent who has been drawn into a sample; these will be discussed later.) When sample statistics from two or more time points are being compared, each is subject to sampling error, and an apparent difference between them may be due to chance factors. If on the basis of statistical testing one can reject chance as an explanation for such a difference, the difference is termed statistically significant.

6. With full probability methods, every step in the selection of persons to be interviewed is strictly controlled and nothing is left to the discretion of the interviewer. ISR has always used full probability designs, and during 1975 and 1976 the NORC General Social Survey shifted to full probability sampling. With modified probability designs, blocks are selected by probability methods, but quotas are introduced at the block level to determine respondents. The interviewer does not list the composition of the household and does not apply a selection table, but administers the questionnaire to the first person who is at home and who fits a quota description, such as an employed woman or man under 35 years of age. All surveys conducted by NORC from the early 1950s to 1975, by Gallup since the early 1950s, and by the Harris Poll, have relied upon modified probability designs or probability sampling with quotas, as it has sometimes been called. (The Harris Poll also tries to ensure a nearly accurate sex distribution by requiring its interviewers to select half men and half women as respondents.) Available comparisons suggest that these differences in sampling design should ordinarily not have important effects on results (Stephenson 1979), though of course such discrepancies are especially undesirable from the standpoint of making comparisons across surveys.

7. Modified probability samples are also open to some bias of this type, and one organization, Gallup, has devised a weighting procedure that attempts to correct for this deficiency (Glenn 1975).

8. It is not always possible to maintain perfectly identical wording on items. For one thing, as in this example, references to "Negroes" changed to "blacks" in survey questions around 1972, and there is nothing we can do to correct for this. In other cases, introductions to items vary somewhat from one survey to another. In our work with these data

we paid careful attention to variations in wording, and wherever such variations might possibly have an effect on results we try to note this for readers.

9. The leveling off is clearer and smoother if the NORC 4-point scale is dichotomized between "strongly agree" and the other three points. The percentages over time then become: 60, 69, 71, 78, 78, 78, 84, and 86. (See the further discussion of this division of the scale in Chapter 3.) With logistic regression we explicitly tested for differences in trends between the two Residential Choice items. A series of models were estimated, ranging from a simple model hypothesizing no change over time for either question to one allowing for differences in curvilinear trends. The latter, fairly complex model provided the best fit. There was a significant difference (p < .01) in curvilinear trends. The NORC version leveled out, while the ISR version showed a somewhat steeper trend in later years ($\chi^2_8 = 85.22$, d.f.= 82, p < .001). Appendix B provides a more complete discussion of this type of test.

10. The 1976 experimental study included three other racial items that are not part of our trend data. All three show the same tendency for responses to be more positive (liberal) on the telephone, and for this tendency to be stronger for Southerners than for Northerners. In two of the four cases (including the Neighborhood Preference question), the three-way interaction of response by mode of administration by region is significant at the .05 level.

11. We did carry out one further context experiment on the Federal Job Intervention item, but in this case the experiment was methodologically motivated. In this experiment, two of our main racial items—Accommodations Intervention and Federal Job Intervention (see table 3.2)—were included contiguously in Survey Research Center monthly surveys in a "split-ballot" design, with Accommodations Intervention asked first in a random portion of the interviews and Federal Job Intervention asked first in the remaining portion. The results indicate no context effect at all on the Accommodations Intervention item (55 percent endorsement on both forms), but for the Job Intervention question there is greater support (41 percent as against 29 percent; p < .01) when it appears after rather than before the Accommodations Intervention item. We suspect that respondents who have agreed to federal intervention on the less controversial accommodations issue feel some pressure to agree to similar government action in the more sensitive area of jobs. In practical terms, the results show that the relatively low levels of support for federal intervention (discussed in Chapter 3) are not entirely fixed, though the increase is not great here.

3. Trends in White Racial Attitudes

1. "Missing data" are omitted from percentaging in table 3.1, as explained in Chapter 2. Data from a single question asked more than once

within a single year by the same organization have been averaged and are presented as a single time point. For a description of the sample sizes on which the percentages in tables 3.1, 3.2, 3.3, and 3.4 are based, see Chapter 2.

2. For 1983 for these Gallup data, we did not have specifically designed cross-tabulations but relied on a recent issue of the monthly *Gallup Reports* (no. 213, June 1983). This required us to estimate educational and regional effects separately for whites, since race is not controlled in this publication.

3. Implicitly in the sense that the percentages of nonpositive responses that are not shown in figure 3.4 are composed of *both* negative and "no interest" answers.

4. A strong case can be made for not omitting "no interest" responses, but rather for assuming that they tend to be merely a more polite form of the negative response that they seem to replace over time. See, for example, figure 3.12, which is supported by other cross-tabulations. In addition, we conducted an experimental split-ballot comparison in December 1982, with the Federal Job Intervention question in its original form and in a form modified to omit the "no interest" option. The "no interest" percentage dropped by 26 percent, and nearly two-thirds of the difference shifted to the "government stay out" alternative.

5. The General Segregation item varied in position from immediately after the School Intervention item to following it but with several intervening items. However, contiguity is not required for a context effect to operate (Schuman, Kalton, and Ludwig 1983).

6. We tested for a difference in trends at the national level between the ISR Residential Choice question and the Open Housing question (using data for 1964–1980). We estimated a series of logistic-regression models, from a simple model specifying no change over time for either question, to one allowing different time trends for each question. The results indicate a clear difference in trends, with the Residential Choice question having a steeper positive slope than the Open Housing question. A model specifying an interaction between question and year $(X^2 = 12.20$, d.f. $= 7$, $p > .05)$ fits the data best. This model provides a significant improvement in fit over a model that specifies only a linear trend for year, a difference in absolute levels of support, but no difference in trends (improvement $X^2 = 43.31$, d.f. $= 1$, $p < .001$).

7. For the Residential Choice principle question from 1964 to 1983, the difference between the low and high educational categories in percentage choosing the nondiscrimination alternative averaged 23 percent; after 1972 ceiling effects reduced this difference artifactually. For the Open Housing implementation question, from 1973 to 1983 the difference between the same two educational categories averaged 16 percent. In both cases the range around the mean for different years was small (several percentage points).

8. The curvilinear component is a significant improvement over a model specifying only a linear trend (improvement $X^2 = 21.06$, d.f. $= 1$, $p < .001$).

9. This analysis is based on dichotomizing the item into favorable and unfavorable categories. However, the 7-point scale can be used more fully in order to calculate means. When this is done, the only change is that the differences among educational categories, which are fairly clear at the beginning of the time period (1970) in the North, disappear or are even slightly reversed in 1978. (In this case, "don't know" and "no interest" responses can be placed in the middle category, number 4, or can be omitted altogether. We have carried out the analysis both ways, and the way chosen makes little difference.)

10. In the experiment a random half of a national telephone sample in January 1983 was given the Half question preceded by the Few question, while the remainder of the sample was given the Half question without any preceding racial item. Contrary to prediction, the Few/Half sequence produced a significantly ($p < .05$) *smaller* proportion of responses accepting integration. The experiment was replicated in March and showed the same trend, though nonsignificantly. We are uncertain whether any context effect occurs, but if so, it lowers rather than raises the acceptance of integration in the sequence regularly used by Gallup and NORC.

11. The 1978 and 1982 General Social Survey (NORC) asked similar questions of blacks about sending their children to school with whites and found the same hierarchy of responses, but considerably less objection to a school that was "more than half" white.

12. The discussion in Chapter 2 uses experimental results not shown in table 3.3: in 1976 version B was asked also face-to-face in order to allow precise comparison of modes of administration with question wording held constant.

13. There are small but clear differences by region and education (South and less educated more negative) in whites' ratings of blacks between 1964 and 1974, but by 1976 and in 1980 both types of differences disappear. This is not due to sharp change in one region as against the other, though what change occurs is somewhat greater in the South than in the North. Similarly, for education, the change is greater for low than for high education, but there is some change in each group.

14. Interpretation of the trend for the Intelligence question is complicated by related but discrepant trend data from a fourth survey organization. Between 1963 and 1978, the Harris organization asked whites nine questions about black characteristics, including intelligence. (The others included ambition, concern for family, morals, criminal tendencies, wanting handouts, and general inferiority.) Only national trends for certain of the items have been published (in *Newsweek*, February 26, 1979, p. 48), but we obtained data for 1966, 1967, and 1976 from the

Harris Data Center and examined the trends separately by region as well. The results are puzzling in two respects. First, there is little or no regional difference for the two earlier time points. Second, a large regional difference does appear at the third time point because a substantial positive change is registered for the North but none at all for the South. Both of these results are out of keeping with the trends for the NORC Intelligence item, though the survey dates are different enough to allow for some apparent inconsistency. In addition, the Harris data are out of line with virtually all of the other results we present in this chapter. We regularly find North-South differences at almost all points in time, especially early points, and the one other set of items on which there is sharp regional variation in trends (the Few, Half, Most items in figure 2.4) is quite different in pattern and much more readily interpretable. Therefore, because we cannot make much sense of these Harris data and have no other relevant Harris data or information about Harris sampling to give us confidence in their reliability, we feel it necessary to largely discount the results. If the unusual North-South findings are ignored and the data are collapsed, they do show a positive trend on all items over the 10-year period, and in this sense they are similar to the trends for the principle questions. They do not, however, correspond with the leveling off shown for the NORC Intelligence item. (The Harris Poll also collected data on these same questions in 1963, 1971, and 1978, but according to archivists at the Louis Harris Data Center at the University of North Carolina, the 1963 and 1971 data are presumed lost, and the 1978 data have an oversample of Jews that is not identifiable on the tape to allow adjustment to a standard white cross-sectional sample.)

15. A third type of change sometimes identified is that caused by the aging process itself; for example, individuals might become more conservative as they age. This seems less relevant to racial attitudes than to some other kinds of personality characteristics, but in any case it would be basically similar to the first type of change we describe, since both have to do with attitude change at the individual level. Other assumptions are also necessary and reasonable for our discussion of age effects: for example, that mortality is essentially random in relation to racial attitudes. For a general discussion of issues that arise in the kind of analysis presented in this section, see Glenn 1977.

16. Other analyses that utilize all the data for this question suggest that 1970 might be a better breaking point; if this date is used, more substantial differences in trend do appear: the overall direction of change for most cohorts becomes modestly positive in the 1960s and overwhelmingly negative in the 1970s. These results fit better with those for the principle and social distance questions, with the 1960s appearing to be a period of definite positive change within cohorts and the 1970s a period of much slower growth and in some cases a reversal in direction.

17. We also examined 20 items at the time of their most recent repli-

cation using the three age categories 18–29, 30–49, and 50+. For 16 of these items the cross-sectional relationship was highly significant, usually beyond the .001 level, and the direction of the relationship was as predicted, with younger people expressing more liberal racial attitudes than older people. These analyses provide corroboration for the conclusions drawn from table 3.5.

18. Overall results from the 1984 NORC General Social Survey became available as we were completing this book. They show a small but uniform increase in pro-integration attitudes on seven racial trend items asked of the white population. Of particular note are increased support for open housing laws (50 percent would be the 1984 figure to enter in table 3.2) and the first rise in several years in opposition to laws against intermarriage (72 percent in 1984). The latter, though only one point above a figure that had been reached earlier in 1977, may signify the end of the plateau noted in the text. Higher support is also registered for the principle of black residential choice and for increased government spending on blacks. Whether these and other smaller positive changes (on the Same Schools, Black Dinner Guest, and Black Push questions) point to continued growth in pro-integration and pro-black attitudes among whites can be determined only by monitoring future General Social Surveys.

4. Trends in Black Racial Attitudes

1. Myrdal (1944: lxxii) stated: "Although the Negro problem is a moral issue both to Negroes and to whites in America, we shall in this book give *primary* attention to what goes on in the minds of white Americans . . . All our attempts to reach scientific explanations of why the Negroes are what they are and why they live as they do have regularly led to determinants on the white side of the race line. In the practical and political struggles of effecting changes, the views and attitudes of the white Americans are likewise strategic. The Negro's entire life, and, consequently, also his opinions on the Negro problem, are, in the main, to be considered as secondary reactions to more primary pressures from the side of the dominant majority."

2. Total black sample sizes for Gallup are not available, but all N's are known to be approximately 180. Total sample sizes for ISR and NORC for the questions shown in table 4.1 are as follows (all these figures include missing data, so the actual base N's for the percentages in table 4.1 are slightly smaller):

Year	ISR	NORC
1964	422	
1966	136	
1968	265	
1970	243	

1972	244	242
1973		176
1974	149 (129)	166
1975		155
1976	210	122
1977		164
1978	217	145
1980	149	129
1982	148	146
1983		160

We draw on two ISR surveys for 1974: an omnibus survey, N = 149, for most items and an election survey, N = 129, for the Riots, Busing, and Aid to Minorities items.

3. Although Harris carried out (see Brink and Harris, 1964) the first large-scale survey of black attitudes in 1963, a second survey in 1966, and several later surveys, we have not been able to use Harris data on blacks in this book. The most substantial Harris report (1978) covering an adequate span of years for trend study gives only a small number of cross-tabulations by time, and these do not add appreciably to the data we have from Gallup, ISR, and NORC. Harris also frequently makes changes in the wording of questions, and some of the early Harris data (for example, from 1963) appear to have been lost. Despite these obstacles, it would be useful for someone to attempt a thorough analysis of whatever data on black attitudes are available from Harris, since so few other black data sets exist at a national level.

4. For analysis of two related questions on civil rights protests, see Bobo 1984. We have not focused on items dealing with evaluations of protest and progress because such items are often unclear in meaning unless anchored to a particular time point or form of protest. Hyman (1969), however, has suggested that it is important to study black and white attitudes toward the "state" of race relations, arguing that such beliefs tap the "root of conflict." More recently, Sears and Allen (1984) and Bobo (1983b) have emphasized the utility of the Civil Rights Push question in predicting racial policy attitudes like opposition to school busing, that is, in carrying out a kind of correlational analysis among attitudes that we have not been able to pursue in this book.

5. As we noted in Chapter 3, there appears to be a contextual link between the Federal School Intervention question and the General Segregation question, a link that could hold for blacks in exactly the same way as for whites.

6. For the Federal Job Intervention question, the negative linear component is a significant improvement over the no change model: improvement $\chi^2 = 13.61$, d.f. = 1, p < .001. For the question on Aid to Minorities also, the negative linear trend is a significant improvement over the no change model: improvement $\chi^2 = 47.95$, d.f. = 1, p < .001.

7. The negative linear component of the trend is a significant improvement over the no change model: improvement $X^2 = 6.72$, d.f. $= 1$, $p < .01$.

8. The percentages of blacks choosing the "no discrimination" response to the Open Housing implementation item were as follows for 1978, 1980, and 1983, respectively: 71.4 percent (N = 140), 71.0 percent (N = 124), and 75.2 percent (N = 149).

9. The 1976 Detroit Area Study gathered a total of 1134 interviews, using a cross-sectional sample of the Detroit SMSA, supplemented by a further cross-section of blacks from most census tracts in the city of Detroit. The survey was directed by Reynolds Farley and Howard Schuman. A 1976 sampling report is available from the Detroit Area Study, University of Michigan.

10. It should be noted that not all types of responses in support of black consciousness decreased in the Detroit data. Responses to a more cultural question (interest in the study of an African language) showed a marked increase between 1971 and 1976.

11. The difference between the two correlations does not reach significance ($p < .20$), but the sample sizes are small. Since a similar increase occurs for whites, we believe the difference is a real one.

5. Theoretical Interpretations of White Trends

1. Three other reports were based on these same data: Sheatsley 1966; Schwartz 1967; Greeley and Sheatsley 1974. Schwartz also discusses a number of questions asked by other organizations, but most of these are from single time points, not part of a trend series.

2. We were uncertain as to whether this "liberal leap" in the South would show up beyond the NORC surveys relied upon by Taylor, Sheatsley, and Greeley. Examination of Gallup and ISR data for approximately 1970–1972 does indicate that change was almost always appreciably greater in the South than in the North during that period. Why that happened remains a mystery.

3. Further support for the roles of age and education comes from a multivariate analysis of the NORC data by Condran (1979); education is generally the stronger of the two independent variables.

4. We used experimentation to test whether equating for social class affects answers. A slightly amended version of the NORC residential integration social distance question was used, with one form describing a black family as having "the same income and education as you" and the other form omitting the phrase. The experiment was administered as a randomized split-ballot to 321 respondents in a national telephone survey in January 1984 (159 respondents on one form, 162 on the other). The results show a tendency for blacks of "the same education and income" as the respondent to be accepted more readily into the neighborhood (85 percent of the white respondents saying they would "mind not

at all," as against 78 percent for the form with no mention of income or education), but the difference is small and does not approach significance ($\chi^2 = .99$, d.f. = 1, n.s.). We later learned that in 1966 NORC had carried out a within-subject experiment on the same issue, using its residential integration item, and had obtained similar results, though the possibility of order effects makes interpretation of these data more difficult. We are indebted to Patrick Bova and Paul Sheatsley for identifying and obtaining results from the NORC experiment for us; see also Hyman 1969. Further experimentation on the same basic issue of social class, but with other items and larger samples allowing internal analysis, would be useful.

5. Beginning in 1972, NORC included in its General Social Survey the Few, Half, Most series on acceptance of varying proportions of black children in schools; the responses clearly show that integration is not perceived as an all-or-nothing choice. But these items do not figure in any of the *Scientific American* reports. (It is also possible that some respondents might misinterpret the Same Schools question, taking "same" to mean "same quality" of schools. A probe would be useful to clarify this point.)

6. The questions presented in table 5.2 appear contiguously in the questionnaire, and there was probably contextual pressure on respondents favoring integration in principle to be consistent when asked about enforcement. However, this is not different from what happens in ordinary life when implementation measures are under consideration. (The ISR implementation questions used by Jackman also have limitations: for example, the unspecified nature of what is being proposed.) The Fifteen Cities survey included a number of other complex questions on implementation (for example, on whether whites would be willing to see their taxes go up if that was "necessary to prevent riots"), and these too generally show a positive relation to education.

7. Our discussion has drawn largely on Jackman's (1978) emphasis on the distinction between principle and policy-related (implementation) attitudes. In a recent paper dealing with attitudes on issues of race, gender, and class (Jackman and Muha 1984), Jackman has revised somewhat her view of the ways whites and other dominant groups, especially the more-educated members of such groups, defend their position in contemporary society. They do this, she argues, by stressing one principle in particular, the principle of individual achievement as the basis for advancement, thus opposing any claims based on group interests as such.

8. In a personal communication to us in 1984, Sears emphasizes that "symbolic racism" is not just a socially acceptable way of expressing prejudice, though he notes that one of his past coauthors, McConahay, does interpret it this way (see McConahay, Hardee, and Batts 1981). However, if Sears's use of the term "symbolic racism" does not refer to an underlying racism that is inhibited in expression by current norms of ra-

cial tolerance, then it is difficult to see how it differs from old-fashioned racism except in the fact that issues have changed. Sears also contends that negative attitudes toward blacks are no longer based on a belief in the inherent superiority of whites, but if this is the case it is unclear why the term "racism" is used, since the essence of that term has usually been the assumption of inherent racial differences. Finally, he states that he regards increases in support for principles of racial equality as important, but insufficient for achieving full equality.

9. Sears and Allen (1984) refine these conclusions somewhat, but do not change their basic tenor.

10. The symbolic racism researchers have also treated voting against a black mayoral candidate as a form of racism. Yet in terms of actual voting, 86 percent of white voters in Los Angeles in 1973 opposed busing to achieve desegregation, but only 51 percent favored Mayor Sam Yorty, the white incumbent, over his black challenger, Tom Bradley (Kinder and Sears 1981). Thus some 35 percent more of the white population seem to have expressed their "racism" by opposing busing than by favoring Yorty, a rather odd finding.

11. In Kinder and Sears 1981, opposition to busing is in turn related to attitudes toward the Bradley-Yorty mayoral contests in Los Angeles in 1969 and 1973. Overt "racial intolerance" is thus represented indirectly in that study by opposition to busing.

12. Another problem with many of the experiments reviewed by Crosby, Bromley, and Saxe (1980) is the ambiguity of the behavior reported. For example, the fact that whites sit farther away from blacks than from other whites has a number of possible interpretations other than "covert discrimination."

13. Differences in dates, modes of administration, and other survey features make these comparisons only approximate, but the basic conclusion here is unlikely to be altered by more exact data.

14. Although we generally do not have correlations between pairs of items (for example, principle and social distance items dealing with nondiscrimination in housing), we can plausibly infer the existence of such a correlation from the aggregate response distributions for each item at a particular time.

6. Conclusions

1. The one principle question omitted here is the General Segregation item. As figure 3.3 shows, the trend on this item is curvilinear, but we argue in Chapter 3 that the curvilinearity is best interpreted as an artifact due to a set of alternatives too general to escape contextual pressures from other more specific implementation items.

2. This leveling on the Laws against Intermarriage question is largely confined to the South, where it appears also on the Gallup Intermarriage question.

3. North-South differences in response to implementation questions are largely restricted to percentage levels and generally do not affect slopes. For one exception to this generalization, see figure 3.5 and the text discussion of it.

4. In order to reduce the complexity of figure 6.3, we have omitted five social distance items. Three of these are the NORC Few, Half, Most school integration questions, which closely duplicate the Gallup trends for the same items (see figure 2.3). The other two omitted items, concerning Neighborhood Preference (for integration) covered a relatively short time span. Percentages over time for all five omitted items can be found in table 3.3.

5. Additional evidence of substantial, though not total, change can be found in two special studies carried out in connection with the research reported in this book: Humphrey and Schuman (1984) used content analysis to assess changes in the presentation of blacks in magazine advertisements; Schuman, Singer, Donovan, and Selltiz (1982) measured changes in discriminating behavior in restaurants by means of observation.

6. The strength of this objection for whites was assessed by the experiment reported in Chapter 5 concerning enforcement of residential nondiscrimination when only a single black family was involved. Evidently the fear of large numbers of blacks will not explain all white resistance to such enforcement.

7. A famous example of a laboratory demonstration of a clash of principles is Milgram's (1974) study of what happens when "obedience" to authority is opposed to the norm against harming another person. Milgram does not argue that the latter norm is meaningless—in fact, he demonstrates quite the opposite—but only that in certain situations it has weaker effects on behavior than does the acceptance of direction from authority.

Appendix B. Statistical Testing Procedures

1. Any logit can be quickly converted to a proportion with

$$p = 1/[1 + e^{-L}].$$

Thus, the logit of −.773 for 1942 can be translated back into a proportion as follows:

$$p = 1/[1 + e^{.773}] = 1/[1 + 2.166] = 1/3.166 = .3158.$$

References

Aberbach, Joel D., and Jack L. Walker. 1970. "The Meanings of Black Power: A Comparison of White and Black Interpretations of a Political Slogan." *American Political Science Review* 64:367–388.

Ajzen, Icek, and Martin Fishbein. 1977. "Attitude-Behavior Relations: A Theoretical Analysis and Review of Empirical Research." *Psychological Bulletin* 84:888–918.

Allen, Bem P. 1975. "Social Distance and Admiration Reactions of 'Unprejudiced' Whites." *Journal of Personality* 43:709–726.

Allport, Gordon W. 1954. *The Nature of Prejudice.* Garden City: Doubleday Anchor Books.

Ashmore, Harry S. 1982. *Hearts and Minds: The Anatomy of Racism from Roosevelt to Reagan.* New York: McGraw-Hill.

Baker, R. J., and J. A. Nelder. 1978. *The GLIM System, Release 3.* Oxford: Royal Statistical Society.

Begley, Thomas M., and Henry Alker. 1982. "Anti-busing Protest: Attitudes and Actions." *Social Psychology Quarterly* 45:187–197.

Bobo, Lawrence. 1983a. "A Comparison of Four Methods for Studying Trends in Public Opinion Data." Project Memorandum, Survey Research Center, University of Michigan.

———1983b. "Whites' Opposition to Busing: Symbolic Racism or Realistic Group Conflict?" *Journal of Personality and Social Psychology* 45:1196–1210.

———1984. "Racial Hegemony: Group Conflict, Prejudice, and the Paradox of American Racial Attitudes." Ph.D. dissertation, University of Michigan.

Bogardus, Emory S. 1928. *Immigration and Race Attitudes.* Boston: D. C. Heath.

Bogart, Leo, ed. 1969. *Social Research and the Desegregation of the U.S. Army.* Chicago: Markham.

Bonacich, Edna. 1972. "A Theory of Ethnic Antagonism: The Split Labor Market." *American Sociological Review* 37:547–559.

———1976. "Advanced Capitalism and Black/White Race Relations in the United States: A Split Labor Market Interpretation." *American Sociological Review* 41:34–51.

Brannon, Robert, Gary Cyphers, Sharlene Hesse, Susan Hesselbart, Roberta Keane, Howard Schuman, Thomas Viccaro, and Diana Wright.

1973. "Attitude and Action: A Field Experiment Joined to a General Population Survey." *American Sociological Review* 38:625–636.

Brauer, Carl M. 1977. *John F. Kennedy and the Second Reconstruction.* New York: Columbia University Press.

Brink, William, and Louis Harris. 1964. *The Negro Revolution in America.* New York: Simon and Schuster.

———1967. *Black and White.* New York: Simon and Schuster.

Burstein, Paul. 1979a. "Equal Employment Opportunity Legislation and the Income of Women and Nonwhites." *American Sociological Review* 44 (June):367–391.

———1979b. "Public Opinion, Demonstrations and the Passage of Anti-Discrimination Legislation." *Public Opinion Quarterly* 43:157–172.

Campbell, Angus. 1971. *White Attitudes toward Black People.* Ann Arbor: Institute for Social Research.

Campbell, Angus, and Howard Schuman. 1968. "Racial Attitudes in Fifteen American Cities." In *Supplemental Studies for the National Advisory Commission on Civil Disorders.* Washington, D.C.: U.S. Government Printing Office.

Cantril, Hadley. 1951. *Public Opinion: 1935–1946.* Princeton, N.J.: Princeton University Press.

Caplan, Nathan S. 1970. "The New Ghetto Man: A Review of Recent Empirical Studies." *Journal of Social Issues* 26:59–73.

Caplan, Nathan S., and Jeffery M. Paige. 1968. "A Study of Ghetto Rioters." *Scientific American* 219:15–21.

Carmichael, Stokely, and Charles V. Hamilton. 1967. *Black Power.* New York: Vintage.

Clark, Joseph. 1984. "The American Blacks: A Passion for Politics." *Dissent* (Summer):261–264.

Condran, John G. 1979. "Changes in White Attitudes toward Blacks: 1963–1977." *Public Opinion Quarterly* 43 (Winter):463–476.

Congressional Quarterly. 1970. "Moynihan Memo." In *Civil Rights: Progress Report 1970,* pp. 23–24. Washington, D.C.: Congressional Quarterly, Inc.

———1972. "Presidential Messages and Statements: School Busing." In *Congressional Almanac* 28, pp. 50A–53A. Washington, D.C.: Congressional Quarterly, Inc.

Converse, Philip E., Jean D. Dotson, Wendy J. Hoag, and William H. McGee III. 1980. *American Social Attitudes Data Sourcebook 1947–1978.* Cambridge: Harvard University Press.

Crosby, Faye, Stephanie Bromley, and Leonard Saxe. 1980. "Recent Unobtrusive Studies of Black and White Discrimination and Prejudice: A Literature Review." *Psychological Bulletin* 87:546–563.

Dalfiume, Richard M. 1969. *Desegregation of the U.S. Armed Forces: Fighting on Two Fronts, 1939–1953.* Columbia: University of Missouri Press.

Davis, James A. 1975. "Communism, Conformity, Cohorts, and Categories: American Tolerance in 1954 and 1972–73." *American Journal of Sociology* 81:491–513.

———1976. "Analyzing Contingency Tables with Linear Flow Graphs." In *Sociological Methodology*. San Francisco: Jossey Bass.

———1980. "Conservative Weather in a Liberalizing Climate: Change in Selected NORC General Social Survey Items, 1972–78." *Social Forces* 58 (June):1129–1156.

DuBois, W. E. B. 1961. *The Souls of Black Folk.* Greenwich, Conn.: Fawcett.

Farley, Reynolds. 1968. "The Urbanization of Negroes in the United States." *Journal of Social History* 1:241–258.

———1980. "The Long Road: Blacks and Whites in America." *American Demographics* 2 (Feb.):11–17.

———1984. *Blacks and Whites: Narrowing the Gap?* Cambridge: Harvard University Press.

Farley, Reynolds, Shirley Hatchett, and Howard Schuman. 1979. "A Note on Changes in Black Racial Attitudes in Detroit: 1968–1976." *Social Indicators Research* 6:439–443.

Farley, Reynolds, Toni Richards, and Clarence Wurdock. 1980. "School Desegregation and White Flight: An Investigation of Competing Models and Their Discrepant Findings." *Sociology of Education* 53:123–139.

Farley, Reynolds, Howard Schuman, Suzanne Bianchi, Diane Colasanto, and Shirley Hatchett. 1978. "Chocolate City, Vanilla Suburbs: Will the Trend toward Racially Separate Communities Continue?" *Social Science Research* 7:319–344.

Fazio, Russell H., and Mark P. Zanna. 1981. "Direct Experience and Attitude Behavior Consistency." In Leonard Berkowitz, ed., *Advances in Experimental Social Psychology,* vol. 14. New York: Academic Press.

Fienberg, Stephen E. 1978. *The Analysis of Cross-Classified Categorical Data.* Cambridge: MIT Press.

Fishbein, M., and I. Ajzen. 1975. *Belief, Attitude, Intention and Behavior.* Reading, Mass.: Addison-Wesley.

Fredrickson, George M. 1971. *The Black Image in the White Mind: The Debate on Afro-Americans' Character and Destiny, 1817–1914.* New York: Harper and Row.

Gallup, George H. 1972. *The Gallup Poll: Public Opinion, 1935–1971.* 3 vols. New York: Random House.

Garrow, David J. 1978. *Protest at Selma: Martin Luther King, Jr., and the Voting Rights Act of 1965.* New Haven: Yale University Press.

Glazer, Nathan. 1975. *Affirmative Discrimination: Ethnic Inequality and Public Policy.* New York: Basic Books.

Glenn, Norval D. 1975. "Trend Studies with Available Survey Data: Opportunities and Pitfalls." In Jessie C. Southwick, ed., *Survey Data for Trend Analysis.* Williamstown, Mass.: The Roper Public Opinion

Research Center in cooperation with the Social Science Research Council.

———1977. *Cohort Analysis.* Beverly Hills, Calif.: Sage Publications.

Greeley, Andrew M., and Paul B. Sheatsley. 1971. "Attitudes toward Racial Integration." *Scientific American* 225:13–19.

———1974. "Attitudes toward Racial Integration." In Lee Rainwater, ed., *Inequality and Justice.* Chicago: Aldine.

Groves, Robert M., and Robert L. Kahn. 1979. *Surveys by Telephone: A National Comparison with Personal Interviews.* New York: Academic Press.

Haberman, Shelby J. 1978. *Analysis of Qualitative Data.* Vol. I: *Introductory Topics.* New York: Academic Press.

Hanushek, Eric A., and John E. Jackson. 1977. *Statistical Methods for Social Scientists.* New York: Academic Press.

Harris, Louis, and Associates, Inc. 1978. "A Study of Attitudes toward Racial and Religious Minorities and toward Women." Study no. S2829-B, prepared for the National Conference of Christians and Jews, November.

Harris, Robert J. 1960. *The Quest for Equality: The Constitution, Congress, and the Supreme Court.* Baton Rouge: Louisiana State University Press.

Hatchett, Shirley, and Howard Schuman. 1975–76. "White Respondents and Race-of-Interviewer Effects." *Public Opinion Quarterly* 39 (Winter):523–528.

Hastings, Philip K., and Jessie C. Southwick. 1975. *Survey Data for Trend Analysis.* The Roper Public Opinion Research Center.

Hill, Robert. 1978. "The Illusion of Black Progress." *Black Scholar* 10:18–24, 49–52.

Horowitz, Eugene L. 1944. " 'Race' Attitudes." In Otto Klineberg, ed., *Characteristics of the American Negro.* New York: Harper and Row.

House, James S., and William M. Mason. 1975. "Political Alienation in America." *American Sociological Review* 40:123–147.

Humphrey, Ronald, and Howard Schuman. 1984. "The Portrayal of Blacks in Magazine Advertisements: 1950–1982." *Public Opinion Quarterly* 48:551–563.

Hyman, Herbert H. 1969. "Social Psychology and Race Relations." In Irwin Katz and Patricia Gurin, eds., *Race and the Social Sciences*, pp. 3–48. New York: Basic Books.

———1972. "Dimensions of Social-Psychological Change in the Negro Population." In Angus Campbell and Philip E. Converse, eds., *The Human Meaning of Social Change.* New York: Russell Sage.

Hyman, Herbert H., and Paul B. Sheatsley. 1956. "Attitudes toward Desegregation." *Scientific American* 195 (Dec.):35–39.

———1964. "Attitudes toward Desegregation." *Scientific American* 211 (July):16–23.

Jackman, Mary R. 1978. "General and Applied Tolerance: Does Education Increase Commitment to Racial Integration?" *American Journal of Political Science* 22:302–324.

————1981a. "Education and Policy Commitment to Racial Integration." *American Journal of Political Science*, 25 (1981): 256–269.

————1981b. "Reply: Issues in the Measurement of Commitment to Racial Integration." *Political Methodology* 7:160–172.

Jackman, Mary R., and Michael J. Muha. 1984. "Education and Intergroup Attitudes: Moral Enlightenment, Superficial Democratic Commitment, or Ideological Refinement?" *American Sociological Review* 49:751–769.

Jefferson, Thomas. 1972. *Notes on the State of Virginia,* ed. William Peden. New York: W. W. Norton (orig. pub. 1785).

Jennings, M. Kent, and Richard G. Niemi. 1981. *Generations and Politics.* Princeton, N.J.: Princeton University Press.

Johnson, Lyndon B. 1965. "Forward." *Daedalus* 95:v.

Joint Center for Political Studies. 1982. *National Roster of Black Elected Officials.* Washington, D.C.

Jones, Faustine Childress. 1977. *The Changing Mood in America: Eroding Commitment?* Washington, D.C.: Howard University Press.

Jordan, Winthrop D. 1968. *White Over Black: American Attitudes toward the Negro, 1550–1812.* Baltimore: Penguin.

Katz, Irwin. 1981. *Stigma: A Social Psychological Analysis.* Hillsdale, N.J.: Erlbaum.

Kinder, D. R., and W. R. Mebane, Jr. 1983. "Politics and Economics in Everyday Life." In K. Monroe, ed., *Political Process and Economic Change.* New York: Agathon Press.

Kinder, Donald R., and Laurie A. Rhodebeck. 1982. "Continuities in Support for Racial Equality, 1972 to 1976." *Public Opinion Quarterly* 46:195–215.

Kinder, Donald R., and David O. Sears. 1981. "Prejudice and Politics: Symbolic Racism versus Racial Threats to the Good Life." *Journal of Personality and Social Psychology* 40:414–431.

King, Martin Luther. 1963. *Why We Can't Wait.* New York: Times Mirror.

————1967. *Where Do We Go from Here: Chaos or Community?* New York: Bantam.

Kluger, Richard. 1975. *Simple Justice: The History of Brown v. Board of Education and Black America's Struggle for Equality.* New York: Random House.

Kuklinski, James H., and Wayne Parent. 1981. "Race and Big Government: Contamination in Measuring Racial Attitudes." *Political Methodology* (Fall):131–159.

LaPiere, R. T. 1934. "Attitudes vs. Actions." *Social Forces* 13:230–237.

Lawson, Stephen F. 1976. *Black Ballots: Voting Rights in the South, 1944–1969.* New York: Columbia University Press.

Levine, Robert A. 1971. "The Silent Majority: Neither Simple nor Simple Minded." *Public Opinion Quarterly* 35:571–577.

Levitan, Sar A., and Robert Taggart. 1976. *The Promise of Greatness.* Cambridge: Harvard University Press.

Lipset, Seymour Martin, and William Schneider. 1978. "The Bakke Case: How Would It Be Decided at the Bar of Public Opinion?" *Public Opinion* (March/April):38–44.

Little, Roderick J. A. 1978. "Generalized Linear Models for Cross-Classified Data from the World Fertility Survey." Technical Bulletin no. 5/834. London: World Fertility Survey.

Litwack, Leon. 1961. *North of Slavery: The Negro in the Free States, 1790–1860.* Chicago: University of Chicago Press.

Margolis, Michael, and Khondaker E. Haque. 1981. "Applied Tolerance or Fear of Government? An Alternative Interpretation of Jackman's Findings." *American Journal of Political Science* 25:241–255.

Marx, Gary T. 1967. *Protest and Prejudice.* New York: Harper and Row.

McConahay, John B. 1982. "Self-Interest versus Racial Attitudes as Correlates of Anti-Busing Attitudes in Louisville: Is It the Buses or the Blacks?" *Journal of Politics* 44:692–720.

McConahay, John B., Betty B. Hardee, and Valerie Batts. 1981. "Has Racism Declined in America? It Depends on Who Is Asking and What Is Asked." *Journal of Conflict Resolution* 25:563–579.

McCrone, Donald J., and Richard J. Hardy. 1978. "Civil Rights Policies and the Achievement of Racial Economic Equality, 1948–1975." *American Journal of Political Science* 22:1–17.

Martin, Elizabeth, Diane McDuffee, and Stanley Presser. 1981. *Sourcebook of Harris National Surveys: Related Questions, 1963–1976.* Chapel Hill, N.C.: Institute for Research in Social Science.

Meier, August, and Elliott Rudwick. 1976. *From Plantation to Ghetto.* 3rd ed. New York: Hill and Wang.

Merton, Robert K. 1957. *Social Theory and Social Structure.* Glencoe, Ill.: Free Press.

Milgram, Stanley. 1974. *Obedience to Authority: An Experimental View.* New York: Harper and Row.

Miller, Warren E., Arthur H. Miller, and Edward J. Schneider. 1980. *American National Election Studies Data Sourcebook, 1952–1978.* Cambridge: Harvard University Press.

Morris, Aldon D. 1984. *The Origins of the Civil Rights Movement: Black Communities Organizing for Change.* New York: The Free Press.

Murphy, Raymond J., and James M. Watson. 1967. *The Structure of Discontent: The Relationship between Social Structure, Grievance, and Support for the Los Angeles Riot.* Los Angeles: Institute of Government and Public Affairs.

Myrdal, Gunnar. 1944. *An American Dilemma: The Negro Problem and Modern Democracy.* 2 vols. New York: Random House.

National Urban League. 1983. *The State of Black America, 1983*, ed. James D. Williams. New York: National Urban League.

Newman, Dorothy K., N. J. Amidei, B. L. Carter, D. Day, W. J. Kruvant, and J. S. Russell. 1978. *Protest, Politics, and Prosperity: Black Americans and White Institutions, 1940–75.* New York: Random House.

Oates, Stephen B. 1982. *Let the Trumpet Sound: The Life of Martin Luther King, Jr.* New York: Harper and Row.

Paige, Jeffery M. 1970. "Changing Patterns of Anti-White Attitudes among Blacks." *Journal of Social Issues* 26:69–86.

Pettigrew, Thomas F. 1979. "Racial Change and Social Policy." *Annals of the American Academy of Political and Social Science* 441 (Jan.):114–131.

Poskocil, Art. 1977. "Encounters between Blacks and White Liberals: The Collision of Stereotypes." *Social Forces* 55:715–727.

Prothro, James W., and Charles M. Grigg. 1960. "Fundamental Principles of Democracy: Bases of Agreement and Disagreement." *Journal of Politics* 22:276–294.

Rodgers, Harrell R. 1975. "On Integrating the Public Schools: An Empirical and Legal Assessment." In Harrell R. Rodgers, ed., *Racism and Inequality: The Policy Alternatives*, pp. 125–160. San Francisco: Freeman.

Rothbart, Myron. 1976. "Achieving Racial Equality: An Analysis of Resistance to Social Reform." In Phyllis A. Katz, ed., *Towards the Elimination of Racism.* New York: Pergamon Press.

Scammon, R. M., and B. J. Wattenberg. 1973. "Black Progress and Liberal Rhetoric." *Commentary* 10:35–44.

Schuman, Howard. 1966. "The Random Probe: A Technique for Evaluating the Validity of Closed Questions." *American Sociological Review* 31 (April):218–222.

———1969. "Free Will and Determinism in Public Beliefs about Race." *Trans-Action* 7 (Dec.):44–48.

———1972. "Attitudes vs. Actions *versus* Attitudes vs. Attitudes." *Public Opinion Quarterly* 36:347–354.

Schuman, Howard, and Jean M. Converse. 1971. "The Effects of Black and White Interviewers on Black Responses in 1968." *Public Opinion Quarterly* 35:46–68.

Schuman, Howard, and Shirley Hatchett. 1974. *Black Racial Attitudes: Trends and Complexities.* Ann Arbor: Institute for Social Research.

Schuman, Howard, and Michael P. Johnson. 1976. "Attitudes and Behavior." *Annual Review of Sociology* 2:161–207.

Schuman, Howard, and Graham Kalton. 1985. "Survey Methods." In Gardner Lindzey and Elliot Aronson, eds., *Handbook of Social Psychology*, 3rd ed. New York: Random House.

Schuman, Howard, Graham Kalton, and Jacob Ludwig. 1983. "Context and Contiguity in Survey Questionnaires." *Public Opinion Quarterly* 47:112–115.

Schuman, Howard, and Stanley Presser. 1981. *Questions and Answers in Attitude Surveys: Experiments on Question Form, Wording, and Context.* New York: Academic Press.

Schuman, Howard, Eleanor Singer, Rebecca Donovan, and Claire Selltiz. 1983. "Discriminatory Behavior in New York Restaurants: 1950 and 1981." *Social Indicators Research* 13:69–83

Schwartz, Mildred A. 1967. *Trends in White Attitudes toward Negroes.* Chicago: National Opinion Research Center.

Sears, David O., and Harris M. Allen, Jr. 1984. "The Trajectory of Local Desegregation Controversies and Whites' Opposition to Busing." In M. Brewer and N. Miller, eds., *Groups in Contact: The Psychology of Desegregation.* New York: Academic Press.

Sears, David O., Carl P. Hensler, and Leslie K. Speer. 1979. "Whites' Opposition to 'Busing': Self-Interest or Symbolic Politics?" *American Political Science Review* 73:369–384.

Sears, David O., and John B. McConahay. 1973. *The Politics of Violence.* Boston: Houghton Mifflin.

Sheatsley, Paul B. 1966. "White Attitudes toward the Negro." *Daedalus* 95:217–238.

Silverman, B. I. 1974. "Consequences, Racial Discrimination, and the Principle of Belief Congruence." *Journal of Personality and Social Psychology* 22:259–268.

Sitkoff, Harvard. 1971. "Harry Truman and the Election of 1948: The Coming of Age of Civil Rights in American Politics." *Journal of Southern History* 37:597–616.

———1978. *A New Deal for Blacks: The Emergence of Civil Rights as a National Issue.* Vol. 1: *Depression Decade.* New York: Oxford University Press.

———1981. *The Struggle for Black Equality, 1954–1980.* New York: Hill and Wang.

Smith, A. Wade. 1981. "Racial Tolerance as a Function of Group Position." *American Sociological Review* 46:558–573.

Smith, Tom W. 1980. "America's Most Important Problem: A Trend Analysis, 1946–1976." *Public Opinion Quarterly* 44:171.

———1984. "House Effects." In Charles Turner and Elizabeth Martin, eds., *Surveying Subjective Phenomena*, vol. 1. New York: Russell Sage Foundation.

Sowell, Thomas. 1984. *Civil Rights: Rhetoric or Reality?* New York: William Morrow.

Spilerman, Seymour. 1976. "Structural Characteristics of Cities and the Severity of Racial Disorders." *American Sociological Review* 41:771–793.

Steeh, Charlotte G. 1981. "Trends in Nonresponse Rates, 1952–1979." *Public Opinion Quarterly* 45:40–57.

Stember, Charles Herbert. 1961. *Education and Attitude Change.* New York: Institute of Human Relations Press.

Stephenson, C. Bruce. 1979. "Probability Sampling with Quotas: An Experiment." *Public Opinion Quarterly* 43:477–496.

Swafford, Michael. 1980. "Three Parametric Techniques for Contingency Table Analysis: A Nontechnical Commentary." *American Sociological Review* 45:664–690.

Swinton, David H. 1983. "The Economic Status of the Black Population." In James D. Williams, ed., *The State of Black America, 1983*, pp. 45–114. New York: National Urban League.

Taeuber, Karl E. 1983a. "Racial Residential Segregation, 28 Cities, 1970–1980." Center for Demography and Ecology Working Paper 83-12. Madison: University of Wisconsin.

————1983b. "Research Issues Concerning Trends in Residential Segregation." Center for Demography and Ecology Working Paper 83-13. Madison: University of Wisconsin.

Taeuber, Karl E., and Alma F. Taeuber. 1965. *Negroes in Cities: Residential Segregation and Neighborhood Change.* Chicago: Aldine.

Takaki, Ronald T. 1979. *Iron Cages: Race and Culture in Nineteenth-Century America.* Seattle: University of Washington Press.

Taylor, D. Garth. 1980. "Procedures for Evaluating Trends in Public Opinion." *Public Opinion Quarterly* 44:86–100.

Taylor, D. Garth, Paul B. Sheatsley, and Andrew M. Greeley. 1978. "Attitudes toward Racial Integration." *Scientific American* 238 (June):42–51.

Tocqueville, Alexis de. 1945. *Democracy in America*, vol. 1. New York: Vintage (orig. pub. 1835).

Tomlinson, T. M. 1968. "The Development of a Riot Ideology among Urban Negroes." *American Behavioral Scientist* 11:27–31.

U.S. Bureau of the Census. 1969. *Changing Characteristics of the Negro Population*, by Donald O. Price. A 1960 Census Monograph. Washington, D.C.: Government Printing Office.

————1979. *The Social and Economic Status of the Black Population in the United States: An Historical View, 1790–1978.* Current Population Reports, Special Studies Series, no. 80. Washington, D.C.: Government Printing Office.

————1980. *Social Indicators III.* Washington, D.C.: Government Printing Office.

U.S. National Advisory Commission on Civil Disorders. 1968. *Report.* Washington, D.C.: Government Printing Office.

U.S. President's Committee on Civil Rights. 1947. *To Secure These Rights.* New York: Simon and Schuster.

Useem, B. 1980. "Solidarity Breakdown Model and the Boston Anti-Busing Movement." *American Sociological Review* 45:357–369.

Weigel, Russell H., and Lee S. Newman. 1976. "Attitude-Behavior Correspondence by Broadening the Scope of the Behavioral Measure." *Journal of Personality and Social Psychology* 33:793–802.

Wilkins, Roy. 1982. *Standing Fast: The Autobiography of Roy Wilkins.* New York: Viking.

Wilkinson, J. Harve, III. 1979. *From Brown to Bakke: The Supreme Court and School Integration: 1954–1978.* New York: Oxford University Press.

Wilson, Barbara Foley. 1984. "Marriage's Melting Pot." *American Demographics* (July):34–45.

Wilson, William Julius. 1980. *The Declining Significance of Race.* 2nd ed. Chicago: University of Chicago Press.

Woodward, C. Vann. 1974. *The Strange Career of Jim Crow.* 3rd rev. ed. New York: Oxford University Press.

Zashin, Elliot. 1978. "The Progress of Black Americans in Civil Rights: The Past Two Decades Addressed." *Daedalus* 107:239–262.

Index of
Survey Questions

Index